SUMMER OF HOPE

SUMMER OF HOPE

THE POWER OF FRIENDSHIP AT A BOYS' SUMMER CAMP

IAN COTTON

SIMON & SCHUSTER

LONDON · SYDNEY · NEW YORK · TOKYO · SINGAPORE · TORONTO

First published in Great Britain by Simon & Schuster, 2002
A Viacom Company

1 3 5 7 9 10 8 6 4 2

Simon & Schuster UK Ltd
Africa House
64–78 Kingsway
London WC2B 6AH

www.simonsays.co.uk

Simon & Schuster Australia
Sydney

A CIP catalogue record for this book is available from the British Library

ISBN 0-684-86667-6

Typeset by Palimpsest Book Production Limited,
Polmont, Stirlingshire
Printed and bound in Great Britain by
Butler & Tanner Ltd, Frome and London

*The names of the boys, both the scouts and children with autism,
have been changed to protect their privacy.*

To Almudena
My wife and best friend

'There lives the dearest freshness deep down things'

(G. M. Hopkins, 'God's Grandeur')

INTRODUCTION

First of all, there is the forest. Straddling a cluster of hills, just thirty miles west of London, it is one of those rare places that the twenty-first century has left behind. Six centuries ago it engulfed the plain; today, it has retreated to the line of awkward, unfarmable hummocks that form the northern backdrop to the M4. Nevertheless, its ridges, half-glimpsed from the road, remain dreamily suggestive. Here, one senses, are secret valleys, summer meadows, hidden pools.

And in the forest's heart, near the small Berkshire town of Wargrave, lies Camp Mohawk. Camp Mohawk? It sounds like something out of the Wild West. In fact, the American name is a historical accident and few places could be more English. It is the country base of a troop of Explorer Scouts from Beckton in east London – themselves, like the forest, a kind of survival, for they are offshoots of a docklands' culture that has passed. It consists of a scattering of self-built huts and tents where the scouts go for their summer camp, and where, for thirty years now, successive generations of East Enders have looked after autistic and brain-damaged children of their own age, on average around twelve years old.

There is a fourteen-bed, on-site hospital, built by the scouts;

there is an Auditory Integration Training room, to help the autistic children's hearing; there is a 'white' or relaxation room, plus innumerable other technical aids that have evolved over the years. And there are, far more importantly, the scouts themselves, whose understanding of autistic children's minds is unmatched, arguably, by the most gifted adults. And yet, when the scouts, or anyone else from Mohawk, start talking about the place it is the forest, first of all, they talk about. And you can see why.

The camp, on the shoulder of a hill, sits in the middle of a grove of oaks that rise around it, tall and true, like pillars in a church. And these are no ordinary oaks. Forget that squat, broad, bulldog, Henry VIII shape that made the oak such a natural symbol of Britishness. Lopped and trimmed so they won't overshadow the camp buildings, these oaks have evolved into a veritable tree species of their own, light, lithe and greyhound-slender; some, indeed, so wiry they sway like firs. It is one of many things that makes the forest hereabouts seem special, a kind of woodland aristocracy. While further up the hill there is yet another, quite different grove, so different as to give the visitor a marvellous sense of variety. A cathedral, this time, not of oak, but of beech, its sheen, silky trunks soaring almost branchless up to a sudden bursting of limbs and leaves that have all the flutter – and even the sound – of water.

The forest's ridge is not high – it runs maybe a couple of hundred feet above the plain. And yet like all hills, it creates a world of its own, because its viewpoint works a curious alchemy. The city of Reading, for instance, not always the most poetic of English towns, seems suddenly – viewed from Mohawk's meadows – surrounded by woodland and green fields; add in its skyscrapers, three fingers of white that stand up like towers in the town centre and Reading is once again a medieval town. While local villages, mere scatterings of houses at ground level, are transformed, from above, into the compact little hamlets they once were. Not to mention the way the thick, close assembly of the forest ends suddenly at the camp perimeter, opening out – because of the hill's slope – into an infinity of fields and sky. This gives the camp a constant sense of adventure and possibility, like looking seaward from a port. From four o'clock onwards, throughout the year, the camp's activities – Mohawk faces west – are played out against the sunset.

Nevertheless, for all the beauty of the forest's parts, it is for moments, rather than places, that one remembers it. And such moments, surely, will include late summer afternoons when the sun has so insidiously soaked the forest, hour by hour, that every part of the air feels warm; when the forest paths have become so dry that the least puff of wind blows great coils and swirls of dust thirty feet high; when the leaves of the chestnut trees sag black against the sun, exhausted.

Then it is that the sense of relaxation can become so profound as to produce strange events. There was the time, for instance, years back, when an epileptic boy came to stay, with the warning that he suffered up to twenty fits a day. During his three-day visit, unprecedentedly, he suffered just two petit mals. The camp's director, Roy Howgate, put it down to Mohawk's 'stress-free environment'. The scouts themselves, perhaps surprisingly, put it down to the benign influence of 'the forest'; as if the forest itself had its own mysterious healing power.

But maybe they were talking about themselves as much as the autistic children. Certainly there are ex-scouts who have grown up and long ceased coming to Mohawk, men in their thirties who now make up Beckton's familiar London population – lorry drivers, firemen, security officers, chefs, mechanics, small builders – who still find they dream about the camp; it's symbolic, clearly, of their childhood happiness. Then there was the adult with autism, a few years back, who had his own way of remembering Camp Mohawk. He was on a day trip to the local agricultural college, it seems, three miles away, and while he was there he gave his carers the slip. It's worth noting that people with autism usually have great difficulty finding their way about. He started walking and finally turned up, six hours later, at Mohawk's gate. He had, it emerged, been on a one-day visit there two years previously and had not forgotten it. No one knows, incidentally, how he found his way along the lanes. Some sixth sense supposedly, like a homing cat.

ONE

One year, at Mohawk, there was a difficult scout. Eleven years old, he spent his days boasting, his nights arguing, and he was getting on the troop's nerves. So, finally, the camp's director, Roy Howgate, did what he often does with such children: he gave him a job.

He deputed the boy to look after one of the trickiest autistic children – a child who, like many children with autism, suffered from fits. The brief was to keep an eye on him at all times, especially at night, when the autistic child was especially vulnerable. But the outcome was unexpected.

Come the morning, Roy went to see how the two of them had got on. The autistic boy was sound asleep, but the scout was awake – hardly surprisingly, as he was poised precariously on a chair jammed at a 45 degree angle against the wall. He had, it turned out, spent the night like this. So why, demanded Roy. Precisely because, explained the boy, he wanted to stay awake to protect his child. Had he fallen asleep the chair would have tipped over and awakened him.

The history of Camp Mohawk is full of such stories; so many of them, in their different ways, strangely subversive of received ideas of both autism and childhood. As is this tale. All boys benefit from commitment – but that degree of commitment? At that age? Then there's the scout's almost feminine watchfulness and care. Do boys need tenderness as much as they need football or fights? Not to be forgotten are the physical demands of such relationships which go far further than mere loss of sleep. Children with autism regularly bite, kick, scratch and head-butt and, as often, they are incontinent – they fill their pants. So the scouts find themselves washing excrement off their charges' legs. Is this an 11-year-old's idea of a summer holiday?

It was questions of this kind – multiplied a thousandfold – that gradually made me interested in what seemed, when I first got to know Camp Mohawk, little more than a bunch of kids enjoying themselves on a Berkshire hill. And the central question, perhaps, was a summation of those above. You could see what there was in such relationships for the autistic children, but what was in it for the boys doing the care? Was there something about ordinary, everyday young boys' motivation that we simply did not understand? Come to that, what about the adults who also helped out at Mohawk, most of them without pay? After all, there was no wealth creation going on at Mohawk; if greed is good, then Mohawk was very bad indeed. If the sole true human satisfaction is self-interest, then why was everyone at Mohawk so self-evidently happy?

Indeed, as I got to know the place better, I realized Mohawk represented, in its own way, a modern heresy. Few choices in life are simple, but this one was clear enough. If the world at large and the values it has adopted these last thirty years were right, then Mohawk was clearly much misguided. But if Mohawk was in any important sense right, then what on earth did that tell us about the world?

In this little community there lay, ticking quietly and unobtrusively, some kind of ethical time bomb.

I first heard of Mohawk from a neighbour. He'd been fund-raising for it. His little boy had been killed in a car crash nearby; the au-pair had been driving and both my neighbour and I, independently, had come on the scene. He had set up a trust in memory of his son. The trust supported local projects. One day he suggested I go with him to Camp Mohawk, this 'autistic children's place' in the hills outside Henley, where he was presenting a cheque. It was a media event, really, aimed at the local press. He was photographed with one of those huge, six-foot long cheques made for photo opportunities. I didn't stay around, but I was intrigued by what I saw. I gathered the reason for my friend's support was that Mohawk needed no less than £250,000 to meet new EU-led safety regulations: a new medical block, new kitchens, camp security, that kind of thing. What a pity, I thought. It seemed a fascinating project but, clearly, they hadn't a prayer. The sum represented more than five times the annual running costs of the camp. My friend's trust, for instance, was putting in just £5,000. How sad.

So it was with amazement that I heard, some months later, that not only had they got the money, but they were opening, as usual, the coming summer. They had resilience, clearly, as well as idealism, not to mention a startling talent for fund-raising, and they were only just along the road. So one day I called up the camp's director, Roy Howgate, and asked if I could pay a visit. By all means, he said. Come for tea.

And so I paid the first of many visits to this curious community, just five minutes' drive from my home. At first I wasn't especially thinking of writing about it, I was just . . . curious. I was one of many locals, I realized later, who were intrigued by what the scouts were doing up there on the hill, and who were so readily welcomed by Roy Howgate and his troop.

Yet the longer I stayed around the more those initial questions multiplied. Autism is above all complex. Symptoms include communication problems, notably with speech; developmental problems, including toilet-training; an all-pervasive strange remoteness, as if the autistic children were somehow abstracted from the world (in past times such children were thought to have been taken over by fairies); and vast and ever-changing fears and obsessions, including certain sounds, smells, even the very sight of certain foods.

Nevertheless, a key symptom, accepted by all, is the obsessive desire of the autistic child for order. This is rooted, arguably, in the profoundest insecurity. Thus disorder will desperately disturb the child; and thus, in turn, a therapeutic programme – in the familiar view – must above all else be ordered: each day's events happening quietly, predictably and at set times.

Yet Camp Mohawk must be one of the most – charmingly – disordered places on earth. 'Spontaneous' is the word Roy Howgate prefers. Trips get cancelled – or arranged – at the last minute, coaches disappear en route to destinations, long-planned outings are suddenly switched because they 'just don't feel right'. I have seen a coachload of scouts, with six autistic children on board, wait forty minutes while a debate raged among the adults as to whether to proceed with the trip. Chaos! Surely the autistic children should have been clamouring to get out? Yet they sat there like lambs. How could this be? Are there subtler forms of security than mere schedule? Could the trust the autistic children felt for their young scout friends have rendered the abstract certainties of timetable irrelevant?

One day, at camp, I joined a group of scouts who were listening to a talk given by the mother of two autistic boys. She'd brought her sons along and, as she spoke, they wandered freely among the scouts. Neither son had speech; but the younger one kept running back and forth, making circling motions with his hands. Ahah, I thought, he's pretending to swim. I knew that both brothers, like most autistic children, adored water. Later on, however, one of the scouts, who'd been watching carefully, disagreed. The boy, he thought, had become bored and wanted to leave. So he'd started acting out the return drive home in mime; hence the running back and forth. The 'swimming' motions were his mime version of a driver turning a steering wheel. The mother later confirmed the likelihood of this, but, right or wrong, the clarity and originality of the scout's vision were beyond doubt. Are boys of twelve, who are less prone to preconceptions, better observers than grown-ups? If so, is this one reason why they and their charges get on?

Of course, there are also answers. That boy, for instance, who had spent the night propped up on the chair, became firm friends with his autistic child. They began a mutually reinforcing, virtuous circle of improvement. The boy with autism, who had been speechless, began to talk; the 11-year-old, who had been impossible, calmed down. By helping his boy, the young scout helped himself. By learning to love, he became himself more lovable. Indeed, the more those around the two observed them, the less it was clear who benefited from the relationship most. All you could say for sure was that it was profoundly good for both of them.

Nevertheless, even with Mohawk's successes, it was quite a question how such successes were achieved. There was, for instance, the whole matter of touch. The scouts, products of one of the last genuinely 'instinctive' cultures in England – the East End – are, to put it mildly, non-verbal. They're physical: they hug, punch, kick, kiss, roll around. And yet still another received wisdom about autistic children is that they hate touch. It is part of their broader shrinking from all human contact. At best, they may just about accept touch in strictly limited circumstances but always, crucially, on their own terms. They must have the say-so. Then it's all right.

Yet the scouts never waited for anybody's say-so. You must be joking. They plunged in merrily, where grown-ups fear to tread; and the autistic children showed every sign of not merely tolerating but adoring the warm, sudden bear-hugs of their friends. One memory, especially, seemed to symbolize this, as it does the whole flavour of the camp.

One afternoon, a whole bunch of children – both scouts and autistic boys – were flopped down inside a hut. They lay like resting lions, boys draped one on top of another, so it was impossible to tell who had autism, who had not. A video was playing, and suddenly the soundtrack started making these banging noises. Moments later an autistic boy called George – like many such children, George is hypersensitive to sound – put his hands over his ears and rushed, terrified, towards the door.

There followed a moment of pure ballet. Jon, one of the scouts, grabbed George as he rushed past. Lifting him bodily, he swung him over to a friend; the friend, in turn, swung him deftly over to the couch; there, a third scout, 14-year-old Mickey, caught George and enveloped him in his arms. He smacked a huge kiss on his forehead, and then, with a mother's smile, he bent over and asked him, 'Woshermatter?'

George's face lit up; grinning delightedly, he nestled close to Mickey's chest. He closed his eyes.

Given all of which, my first visit to the camp was a surprise.

Mohawk sits on the shoulder of a hill, at the top of a long, cratered drive. On the right, as I drove in, was the egg-shape of the all-weather swimming pool; on the left, a cluster of timber-clad huts; beyond, the large white tents in which the scouts slept with the autistic children. Outside the tents, on a grass terrace, was a group of white garden tables and chairs, complete with gaily striped sun-umbrellas; they gave the place a festive, Mediterranean feel. And, standing in the middle of it all was one of the largest men I have ever seen. With a profile somewhere between Yogi Bear and an all-in wrestler, he looked, from a distance, like a giant exclamation mark. He was having a furious row with some scouts.

'If you take it out, you put it back again!' he yelled. 'If you borrow it, you put it back!'

He stressed each point with downward sweeps of the arm, like blows from a hammer.

'IF! YOU! TAKE! IT! OUT! YOU! PUT! IT! BACK! . . . AY! . . . GAIN!'

He spoke in strange slow motion, each syllable articulated individually, like separate words.

'IF! YOU! BOR! ROW! IT! YOU! PUT! IT! . . . BACK!'

More arm-waving. He turned to me as if soliciting support. 'I mean!'

He turned back to the kids.

'So what do you do?'

'We take it out, we put it back again,' said a kid quickly.

He turned to another.

'We borrow it, we put it back,' said the second one. He looked terrified.

'All right! All right! Now get lost, for chrissake. 'Op it, the lotovyer!'

The kids vaporized. The man turned to me. 'I'm Roy Howgate,' he said, and stuck out his hand. And he smiled a wide, radiant smile, more of a cosmic chortle really, full of a wonderful sense of enjoyment and of Christmas.

It was extraordinary; his mood seemed utterly transformed. It was as if a thunderstorm had come and gone. Had he really been so cross, I wondered momentarily, or had he been just pretending? Whatever, he seemed quite happy now; so we moved over to one of the tables, while a scout rushed off to make tea.

I explained how interested I was in the camp; indeed, as a writer, it occurred to me it would surely make a fine magazine article, should he wish.

'That's fine,' he said. 'Well, quite fine.'

Things were not, he explained, too easy at the moment. There was a bit of a crisis. Well, quite a lot of one, actually. True, they'd got the £250,000, and it had enabled them to open. But this had meant, in turn, that they were short of money for the camp's day-to-day running and it was unclear whether they would have enough to carry on. Indeed they might – just might – have to close. (Such cliffhangers I came to understand, were part of the camp's emotional rhythm.) But then he supposed they could always put out another appeal. He always fund-raised for specific purposes, unlike some charities, who fund-raised all the time. 'That's immoral,' he said. 'In the end,' he reflected, gazing at me with penetrating, somewhat questioning eyes, 'it all came down – as things always do in life – to . . . faith.'

''Ere!' he yelled suddenly. He leapt to his feet. ''Ere! All of you! Come on! Come over 'ere! Caaaaaaaaaam on!' Though Roy had seemed fully concentrated on our conversation he had, evidently, been in a kind of dual consciousness. His antenna had been out there twitching all over the camp, and he had spotted something that had bothered him. Just as his mood had earlier suddenly sweetened, so now it abruptly turned sour. The scouts, who had discreetly scarpered after the last explosion, all came running back again.

'Who's looking after Jimmy?' Jimmy was one of the autistic children currently on site.

'I am.' This from a kid who looked exactly like a chipmunk.

'And who's the gofer?' (The 'gofer' is the carer's assistant, who fetches and carries – goes for – whatever is needed.)

'I am.' Thin and waif-like, this one.

'And where were you five minutes ago?'

'In the tent.'

'And where was your boy?'

Silence.

'Exactly. He was outside, wasn't he. He was on the TRACK! Cars drive up and down it, don't they! He could have been KNOCKED DOWN! If social services saw it we could be CLOSED!' (This is another cliffhanger, regularly deployed.) 'Look, get a grip, both of you, for Gawd's sake! Look after your boy. And as for you –' Startlingly, Roy spun 180 degrees to finger one of the boys he had been yelling at earlier. 'YOU HAVEN'T PUT IT BACK YET, HAVE YOU?'

'No.'

'Well, PUT IT BACK NOW!'

The scouts scampered off again; Roy turned back to me. 'Where were we? Ah yes – desperately seeking ten thousand quid.' He grinned. 'So what else is new?'And he leant back in his chair and laughed, his whole body heaving beneath that huge, delicious, chortling smile.

By now we had been joined by a tall, dark, Latin-looking young man, with deep-set, glowing eyes. This was John Lee, the Mohawk scoutmaster, twenty-four years old and himself an ex-Mohawk scout, who does the day-to-day running of the camp. Waiting his moment, he said, diffidently: 'Er. Skip?' (Skip, or Skipper, is the title by which Roy Howgate is known around the camp.)

'What?'

'It wasn't really their fault Skip because –'

'Eh?'

'It was me who sent them down the tent.'

'And they let the boy wander off? Come on John, you know the score. Safety comes first. Come ON John.' And another hammer blow of the arm.

John sat there for a bit, looking rueful. Eventually, with an 'All right Skip,' he wandered off. John often launched these mild rebellions; they always failed. He disappeared down to the swimming pool where a session was about to begin. Cheers greeted him; he was hugely popular with the boys.

Skip shrugged, winked, then looked reflective. 'John's very good,' he said. 'Been with me since he was a boy, you know. Started as a scout. He's very good.'

Not that you would have guessed it from the way Skip spoke to him. He seemed to dismiss what John said out of hand. Yet did he really? Later, I heard Skip had taken the two kids aside and praised them. And as I was to find, Camp Mohawk operated on many levels and the surface level was usually the least revealing of all.

One learned, for instance, never to be fooled by Skip's shouting.

It was just his way. He lived on his emotions. His faults, it's fair to say, do not include repression. (Much like the boys; no wonder they understand each other.) Added to which, half the time, for all his yelling, the kids ignored him. Beneath the authoritarian veneer (itself only spasmodic) Camp Mohawk was a kind of DIY anarchy, where boys ruled. As Skip himself put it, 'Adults should be seen and not heard.' A surprising view, on the surface, given the yelling, yet as I got to know the camp better, I could see its truth.

It was curious. Skip would sit there in his chair, the spider at the centre of the camp's web, and yet, for all his almost occult awareness of what was happening around him, the place went on its merry way. As usual, in the summer, there were around twenty scouts on site and six children with autism; each autistic child (who generally stayed three days) had a carer and gofer; thus at any moment there would be around twelve scouts caring, eight others in reserve.

That afternoon both scouts and autistic children were, as usual, dispersed around the camp. Some were playing in the adventure playground, superbly situated in an ash grove; some, with much shrieking, were in the ball pool, a ten by eight foot container full of plastic balls; some were in the 'white' or relaxation room, an audio/tactile room with white walls, New Age music and Californian light effects. There were a couple of other adult helpers on site, as well as John, but essentially the place was running itself. In each of the little isolated communities of four or five children, the boys were in charge.

The camp was in the second week of the summer session, when it runs for the six weeks of the school holidays. The scouts – there are around thirty in the troop, based at their East End headquarters in Beckton – had, as usual, been coming down in relays, though some stayed for weeks. The summer session, it emerged, was only the climax of a rolling programme that went on throughout the year: weekends in the winter (often used for working on the camp's buildings); weekends in the spring, when the first care sessions with the autistic children take place; trips abroad, come the summer months, that include visits to the French farmhouse the troop lately bought, at Bucquoy in the valley of the Somme.

Nevertheless, the six-week summer camp remains the main event, and the one which most easily develops a rhythm. In this second week, of course, the place was only just feeling its way; the awkward, clunky moments, so frequent with autistic children, came thick and fast. Shortly after John walked off, Skip, too, had to leave to take a phone call, and he deputed some boys to look after me. We joined a group hanging around the campfire circle. The weather was good, the moment felt right, and a walk was mooted – one of those spontaneous forest walks which are at the heart of the Mohawk tradition. Word went round, a group began to gather, but just as we were about to set off, there was a crisis. Omar, a 10-year-old, wide-eyed, dark-haired boy with autism, suddenly started wailing piteously, hands over his ears. 'It's his hearing,' said his carer, 14-year-old James Robinson, tall, pale and sombre, who was also my guide. 'He's hypersensitive, like a lot of autistic kids. If he hears someone walk across leaves, it sounds, to him, like a herd of elephants. And he's scared, too, of the bushes and trees – he thinks they're monsters.' Such perception problems are typical of autism; but what was typical of Mohawk, was that Omar's fears didn't stop the boys taking him out.

Gently encouraging him, they duly set off, walking single file because of the narrowness of the forest paths. Two scouts led the way, including a serious-looking James; next came Omar, bent over like a leaf; then two autistic kids including little George, small, blond and perky; then three more scouts bringing up the rear, notably a broad, fleshy-lipped boy called Ian Pool. The scouts scampered ahead. Every time we came to a bush, they pulled the leaves back so they wouldn't touch Omar; when a tree overhung the path, James shinned up a branch and pulled it back. And so we stumbled on, a most curious ensemble, full of stops and starts and sudden pauses. And slowly, the haunted look drained from Omar's face. Finally, very quietly, he started singing.

James smiled. 'Can you hear the song?' he said. 'Omar can't speak, but he loves music. So he sings songs to tell you how he feels. Some songs he sings are sad; but when he sings "Almost Heaven, West Virginia", that means he's happy.' James chuckled. 'Can you hear? That's what he's singing now.'

I was surprised. This kind of intense, demanding care was not what I thought boys of twelve wanted to do; surely they wanted to run down the path at their normal wild speed, not stumble haltingly? Why weren't they impatient? Nor was this how I expected them to feel; there was a delicacy, a high seriousness, almost, in the way they talked about their boys which I just didn't expect from 12-year-olds. And yet this caring work had never been imposed on them. In fact, starting all those years ago, it had come about by a series of accidents; and if the early, limited experiments hadn't worked, the process would never have developed as it did.

Originally there were only scouts at Camp Mohawk. It was back in the seventies that a Henley landowner, reading the *London Evening Standard*, realized Skip's scouts needed somewhere to camp and offered them Mohawk's present site. So the troop started coming down, and they stayed there every year. At this stage Mohawk was just a campsite for the boys.

Then one day, says Skip, a man wandered into the camp, walking his dogs, and it turned out he had a handicapped son in a local home. He liked what he saw, and wondered whether the scouts might have his son and some of the other handicapped children over as guests. So Skip thought about it and agreed. It might be good for his scouts, he felt, as well as the children from the home.

The children came, and their visit was a success, and so, over the years, such meetings became regular events. Today, as many as seventy children with autism may stay over the six weeks of the scouts' summer holidays, looked after by the Camp Mohawk boys. Nor, incidentally, do such relationships end with camp. John Lee, for instance, looked after the same autistic boy for years, visited him in his home, and even went on holiday with him.

Nevertheless, the starting point at Mohawk, stresses Skip, has always been the sense that such relationships are first of all good for the scouts themselves. So that befriending autistic boys has always been just part of the scouts overall, summer-camp enjoyment – and for the autistic children that is novel indeed. Because there are plenty of well-meaning people around – mostly adults – who will give autistic children care; what is unique about Mohawk is that the scouts are doing it for their own pleasure, as in normal friendships. 'I've never seen my son with boys who actually enjoyed his company before,' said one autistic child's mother. 'It's the thing, above all else, I know he needs.'

And, it is striking how often, when you see the Mohawk children together, you see them just as children, not carers and disabled.

Later that day I joined a group of children, boy scouts and boys with autism, at the swimming pool. It was a happy, excited time, because if there's one thing autistic children love (indeed, it can even become one of their obsessions) it's water. Both scouts and autistic boys leaped and cavorted like dolphins, indistinguishable in their play. With a roar big George, one of the older autistic boys, kept making these sudden rushes into the middle – for safety reasons the pool has two shallow ends – and out again. No one minded. Little George, the boy who had been on the walk, sat in the shallows and lapped up the water like a puppy, blowing it out again in long, arcing, joyful streams.

Of course, there were difficulties. Big George, for instance, periodically dashed right out of the pool and away into the camp, a scout hurtling after him in hot pursuit. Little George had tantrums.

Omar, who was also there, inadvertently wet himself. Yet what was striking was how these problems were dealt with. As often as not, you would scarcely have known they had happened. Omar, for instance, was taken away and changed so quietly I never noticed; indeed, within five minutes he was back in the pool.

And through it all the scouts themselves were splashing away as merrily as if they were on their own, managing simultaneously to protect their charges and play with them. It was as if they moved with ease between two separate emotional gears, playing and caring. Just one of many things, one suspects, they do a great deal better than grown-ups.

Throughout their reading of the autistic children's behaviour was constant and intuitive. Even on that first visit I was given an object lesson myself.

Twenty minutes into the session, little George took time out from his water blowing and moved vaguely, lurchingly, into what I felt was my space. George hardly talks. However, slowly I got this weird, indefinable feeling that he wanted to make contact. Shortly after, he moved away again, to do some more water blowing; then he was back again once more. I'd just decided, finally, I must be imagining the whole thing when he sucked one long last stream of water, rushed back to where I was sitting, smiled, and squirted the whole lot clean in my face.

The shock over, the incident made a kind of sense. Indeed, it felt quite flattering. For this, clearly, as the boys pointed out, was little George's way of trying to make friends.

Indeed, from the start, it was plain that however perceptive one might or might not be as an adult, the boys would always be much more so. So that it soon seemed ever more obvious that Camp Mohawk would make a memorable magazine article. I began researching and it was the psychology, and above all the motivation of the scouts, that swiftly took centre stage.

Where did they get their patience from? If, for instance,

they played football with the autistic boys, their charges would constantly fail to understand the rules. One could see how the scouts might tolerate this, but enjoy it? Not to mention the limited joys of being bitten, headbutted or punched; again, the scouts might put up with it, if they were feeling very kind, but how, precisely, was this fun?

Gradually, however, I began to understand.

There is, for a start, our gross underestimation of kids' need to do serious work. Not a mistake made by Maria Montessori. (Montessori, indeed, a touch excessively, even banned toys.) This need, fulfilled out of necessity by families in the Third World, is, arguably, quite as deep as play. This is especially so should a child's self-worth be unsure, when such commitment can transform it. This certainly applies at Mohawk.

But other, more maverick answers also emerged. The London scouts, quite plainly, actually preferred the more difficult boys with autism, as opposed to those whose symptoms were milder. Why? Quite simply, they found them more interesting. Adults get so used to their endless, adult worries that they spend a lot of their time, more or less consciously, looking for quietude. They forget that the dominant emotion of the young, by contrast, is boredom. The old crave peace; the young crave – need – drama. I remember the laughter in the eyes of one scout as he described how one of the autistic children would suddenly rush off from wherever he was sitting. This, too, is familiar autistic behaviour. 'You can see it in his face,' said the boy, with relish. 'You can see him planning it, working out where he's going to run to.' Mischief! Anarchy!

One characteristic of children with autism is that they act, in many ways, like 'normal' children do when still toddlers. Any child of twelve is still close enough to that earlier state to identify with a boy who acts so impulsively.

Yet there is a further dimension which is more intriguing still. It's the quality of the scouts' feeling for their boys, which you can sense, intuitively, in their very language. Or as James, struggling to express how he felt about Omar, his regular charge, put it: 'The thing is, you get so involved with your little boy, it becomes so hard to say goodbye when the camp ends.' Indeed, said James, such moments 'make me cry'. 'You see,' he said, struggling for the phrase, 'the thing about Omar is . . . he's such a . . . lovable little boy.' Lovable little boy. To my surprise, the word 'lovable' emerged almost as a leitmotif of the camp. Boy after boy described their charges as 'lovable' and more than one used precisely those same three words, 'Lovable little boy!' What is it about this phrase?

What it is, of course, is that this is less the language of a brother, more of a mother. These East End boys, so resolutely macho in every other department of their lives, are using the emotional language of women.

One thing became clear. People who read about Camp Mohawk, when the *Telegraph Magazine* finally published my article, were as struck by it as I was. Indeed, Mohawk's switchboard first jammed, and then temporarily collapsed, as literally hundreds of families countrywide tried to sign up their autistic children. Added to which, there was the response of people I knew personally. Journalism is a curious business in which articles read by millions are rarely mentioned by people you know. This one was different. Everyone seemed to have read it and been struck by it. Why? The sense I got was it was the way Mohawk embodied a particular idea of boyhood; an idea, perhaps, whose time had come.

Yet though the boys were central, there was also the wider ethos of the camp. Here, after all, were adults, too, behaving in ways which, if less than mysterious, were hardly fashionable. Clearly, at Mohawk it was the work itself – not what the work could get them, money or position – which had attracted them. When Freud said love and work were the grand cures for life's ills it was this kind of work he had in mind, clearly, not trading in futures. Also, the constant rallying round of Mohawk's supporters to solve its endemic financial crises made a mockery of the profit motive, since Mohawk's gains were only ever human – everything else ran at a loss.

There was another quite different reason, arguably, why people found the subject so compelling. This was to do with autism itself, which has, in recent years – as sometimes diseases are prone to – plainly become a symbol.

There is, after all, that most typically autistic quality of all: its curious remoteness, the cut-off, inward-looking quality that impresses everyone. Is not this exactly how we see ourselves, as a society, today? Community has collapsed, family has disintegrated, and above all, perhaps, abstract, market relationships have substituted for instinctive, subjective humanity in virtually every sphere of life. Isn't our very society, in a sense, increasingly autistic? There's nothing new about diseases taking on a symbolic role. In the sixties the slow, insidious assault of cancer, as opposed to, say, the overt, impetuous attack of a 'Third-World' disease like cholera, was widely thought to be emblematic of the denial-prone West. In the eighties Aids was perfectly suited, and enthusiastically recruited, to one of the main events of the period, Sexual Puritanism's Last Stand.

To each era its own. Autism is the disease for today. For along with its abstraction and remoteness autism is, equally, the control freak disease. Its sufferers are prone to intense, obsessive needs for predictability and order. How wonderfully appropriate to an age which increasingly expresses its disorientation by a manic, if carefully rationalized, desire to calculate and control everything in sight, usually by computer. And how appropriate that Microsoft's Bill Gates, of all people – one of the heroes of the age – should be said to suffer from Asperger's Syndrome, a related condition to autism! Gates is famous for his personal pedantry and remoteness. Typically, he is supposed to serve himself with drinks during meetings and ignore his guests. True or false? Less important perhaps than whether people believe it. Gates symbolizes far more than a technological new way; like autism, clearly, he suggests a whole new, abstracted way of being.

So, by a series of strange chances, the subject seemed to touch on some crucial aspects of modern life. And I wondered whether I should not try to explore some of these thoughts in a book. Clearly, the only way to do justice to such a theme was to carry out extensive research. There was the added advantage, rare with such projects, that much of the fieldwork would take place just down the road from our house. I would not have to spend months away from my own, young family. Whatever else, this was no seven years in Tibet.

My agent started looking for publishers, and it turned out to be quite easy to get a commission. The same qualities which impressed everyone impressed editors, and it was not long before Simon and Schuster suggested a deal.

So I offered myself as a volunteer, who would follow the story of Camp Mohawk, as a participant, through one representative year. Skip agreed. The tale began.

TWO

Most of the scouts' work with the autistic children happens in the spring and summer. But the troop operates throughout the year, and when they are not with the autistic children in Wargrave, they are at home at Beckton in the East End. So Beckton seemed the place to start. Because it was something about the way they lived back there, it seemed to me, and the philosophy it embodied, that the autistic children found so valuable.

So that winter I became London's most bizarre commuter, travelling regularly from thirty miles west of the city clean across to the east, as the scouts limbered up for a whole series of Christmas events.

The scouts' world is not that of their grandparents. The old, tight, dark East End has vanished: the long, soot-covered terraces have been replaced by vast new acres of pale green open spaces. Whole streets have simply vanished into thin air. Here and there an old Victorian church, or a huge, ornate, red-brick pub, survives in isolation, surrounded by the new emptiness like a beached whale. There are even rare leftovers of the old industrialism, notably the Pura edible oils plant, an acre of jam-packed industrial machinery rammed tight into a U-bend of the River Lea. Steaming ominously in the winter half-light, it looks more like a Second World War battleship than a factory.

But it is very much a survivor. For, since the sixties, the dock work which was the mainstay of the old economy has utterly collapsed. And with that collapse went the old, wild East End that used to be a little kingdom of its own.

Nevertheless, its new, more sober successor has its own characteristic atmosphere, even beauty. The high-rise tower blocks, which in the sixties replaced the low-rise terraces, have, in turn, been replaced by yet another low-rise generation. Snug little three-up two-downs, both private and council, in brickwork that has imported a whole new range of local colours: pale yellow, khaki, salmon pink. The docks, once so dense with cargo ships and liners, are now reduced to the simplicity of their original pure, rectangular lines. The Royal Victoria, in particular, has a quietness, an almost elegiac calm, that makes it feel more like a country house lake than the hub of a metropolis.

The calm can be misleading. The area's problems haven't gone away, they've been sanitized. Take employment. While the figures, on the face of it, look pretty good – claimant benefit in Beckton, for instance, 17.4 per cent in 1991, was down to 7.6 per cent by 2002 – such numbers games take no account of the reality that a statistical 'job' has for so many workers lately become: an ever-escalating regime of low pay and short-term contracts, bereft of respect, fulfilment or security, let alone pensions, holiday or sickness pay.

The work regime has been so transformed, in fact, that the relative stability of the post-war generation increasingly looks, even for those in jobs, like an ever-receding dream. This is not to mention the growing proportion of households in which there is no work at all. In London as a whole, in 1998, that figure was 20.8 per cent, up from 14.3 per cent in 1990 and 7.9 per cent in 1979. The figure for the percentage of children in poverty is more dramatic still. This is calculated on a still more geographically specific basis, thus highlighting local hotspots. In the London borough of Newham, in the late nineties, the child poverty rate was a remarkable 60 per cent, compared with a national average, itself high enough, of 33 per cent. In Beckton ward, a subdivision of Newham, it was 67.7 per cent.

And the scouts and their families are in the thick of it. Over at Ilford, for instance, on the eastern fringe of the scouts' catchment area, lies the council house home of the Smith family, where three of the five boys either have been, or are still, members of the scouts. The Smiths' dad, a lorry driver, had a blackout three years ago. It was largely induced, reckons his doctor, by overwork. Mr Smith was, apparently, putting in up to fifteen hours a day to make ends meet and since then he's been unable to work. Down at Canning Town, just north of the Victoria Dock, live the Cobbetts, with two brothers, 14-year-old Johnny and 12-year-old Tim, in the scouts. Their father, too, was working seven days a week, ended up in hospital, and has since cut his working hours. And yet, just as striking is the local resilience. Senior scout Dan Knapton's dad, for instance, beat over 200 other applicants to get his job on the Docklands Light Railway. While Mrs Smith – whom John Lee calls, quite simply, a 'heroine' – not only looks after her husband and five boys but works part-time at the local church, doing the flowers. She used to work in the crèche, but gave it up on health grounds. Yet you have only to see her look at her sons to grasp why they are among the very best carers in the troop.

Not that they are all that different from the others. At East Ham, overlooking a green, is the house where 15-year-old Bernard Naisbitt lives with his mum and sister. Bernard is the only boy in the Mohawk troop who is himself autistic. He's been working with the troop for five years, and has lately been made a fully-fledged scout. His mum reckons it's been his salvation. Far more helpful, she adds, than the local council, which have dragged their feet over Bernard for years. In 2000 it was so slow finding him a special school that the other scouts got wind of it and wrote a round-robin letter to the local paper, demanding they sort Bernard out.

Writing letters – writing anything much, come to that – isn't really the boys' style, but, says scout leader John Lee, they loved every minute of the evening they spent doing it.

One December day I found myself in a Beckton garage, in east London, trying very hard to put cotton wool ('snow') on to the wooden structure of the scouts' Christmas float. This float was a Santa Claus sledge, complete with mechanical reindeers, donated by Harrods. It had originally decorated the store's outside wall. The scouts towed it round the neighbourhood, on a trailer, to help their Christmas collecting. These collections, done every year, were the first step towards the working year to come. No money, no work, however worthy. So such fund-raising was crucial.

Meanwhile the tricky part was actually getting the 'snow', plus accompanying heavy-duty glue, on to the float rather than on to the floor, or round our legs, or round our throats. This was because we were working, not with cotton wool lumps, but cotton wool strips. This was the best way to do it, my co-worker, 17-year-old senior scout Dan Knapton, had explained. It was the only way to fit the cotton wool around the angles of the sledge.

It was simple enough in theory. You cut the strips off a carpet-like roll, with scissors. But in practice it was hard. The cotton wool was weirdly sticky, a kind of yuletide candyfloss, and you had to pull it off with one hand while unravelling the roll with the other, meanwhile cutting the roll with your third hand, not to mention simultaneously supporting the whole combination, at moments of crisis, by wrenching your knees up to your chest. This resulted in a series of sudden, waist-high jerks reminiscent of those dances Africans used to put on for the Queen.

It was exhausting, and quite dangerous. Not only was there the peril of simply falling off the float, or spearing yourself on a stray reindeer horn, but there was the threat we ourselves were posing to the structure. Above all, as Skip had briefed us, we were to avoid putting our feet through any of the float's lights while clambering about. They always somehow seemed to be under foot and it was, inevitably, so very easy to tread on them. The blue safety lights on the sides of the vehicle were particularly at risk.

Given all of which, and my own endemic clumsiness, it might be wondered why I had been chosen for this particular job. The reason, however, was pure Mohawk. For just as in the Mohawk community everyone is included, so everyone mucks in. As the huge daily raft of working tasks unfolds, whoever is immediately at hand gets recruited for whatever is most urgently needed. While the downside to such wide-eyed optimism is that it does indeed involve the odd debacle, the upside is that both kids and adults are constantly being bounced into doing things they never dreamed of. At best, they can emerge, hours later, with a whole new sense of who they are.

And there is great power in such expectation. Even I, after the predictable hiccups, got into gear. My, did we get those strips unrolling! I was helped, too, by my companion Dan. Like a lot of people around Mohawk he seemed not quite of this century and would have fitted in just as readily, say, as second mate on a battleship at Trafalgar. The kind of loyal, upstanding NCO who always sees the drummer boy gets his rum. Dan had a fine profile, a clear brow and rather noble, heavy-lidded eyes. He worked with calm efficiency and remarkably good humour as I asked him, for the third time, how to take the top off the glue. It was the first of many moments when I found myself being treated with exactly the same gentle condescension the senior scouts deployed when dealing with the younger boys.

The garage we were working in was just one of several buildings at Camp Mohawk's London headquarters, mostly built by the scouts themselves. In many ways it was the most intriguing of them all: a vast shed around eighty feet by fifty that housed a quite startling array of vehicles. All were there – supposedly – to act as props for the scouts' activities. There was the Santa Claus sledge, plus reindeer, that we were working on. It was fixed, in turn, on top of a trailer which could be towed by car when the sledge was taken out. There was a fire engine, brought back from a local scrapheap. There were two boats which could be driven on trailers down to Berkshire and used, à la sea scouts, on the river at Henley and Wargrave. There were also two garish fairground organs and the world's largest private collection of electric generators. But, above all, there was a gargantuan blue coach, with PEGASUS scrawled triumphantly along the side, together with the motif of a flying horse. This was the pride of the Mohawk fleet, the means whereby they voyaged around the country and even Europe. Donated by a coalition of supporters, from city firms to national newspapers, it boasted, in addition to normal coach seating of around thirty, a kitchen, a lavatory, and a whole, separate ambulance section at the back, with beds and bandages and a drugs cabinet for emergencies. These adjustments, mainly by adult volunteers – as ever at Mohawk – had been largely self-built. They meant the bus could take the autistic children anywhere and yet cope with any health crises en route.

The garage was just the kind of place that 11-year-olds find captivating. And there was more. Next door, up a staircase, was the store where the scouts kept their costumes, also crucial to their collecting. Here, in various crates, were to be found a vast selection of wrap-round, head-to-foot animal suits. The scouts wore these to charm the public. They included the full Disney range – Mickey Mouse, the Donald Duck twins, various chipmunks, the odd penguin – and also, of course, Santa Claus himself, who came as a full-blown outfit in startling, pillar-box red, complete with all-in-one moustache and beard.

It was curious. There was an overt rationale for every item in the sheds. And yet, as with almost everything at Mohawk, one sensed that a big reason for the presence of much of this stuff – there was a wild, even slightly grotesque exuberance about it all, especially the sledge – was that the scouts, and above all Skip himself, just liked having it around.

The garage was just one corner of the London HQ. Situated on the edge of the local business park, on ground formerly owned by British Gas, the Woodland Centre Trust – Camp Mohawk's London name – has about a dozen buildings arranged in a large semi-circle around a central terrace. They range from scout meeting rooms through storerooms and administrative offices to a large workshop next to the garage. Like Camp Mohawk, the whole place has a vaguely Wild West air, mainly thanks to the dark brown timber in which all the buildings are clad. Very Dodge City, 1878, is the Woodland Centre.

Paying for all this, unsurprisingly, has been hair-raising. Mohawk's history is littered with tales of financial debacle, followed by comebacks that put Lazarus to shame. Many such rescues are initiated by Mohawk's supporters. The fact that Mohawk's London HQ is just along the road from the City doesn't do any harm at all, and the Worshipful Company of Leathersellers, for instance, give Mohawk as much as £35,000 a year. However, the rescues are just as often initiated by the Mohawk staff, or even the scouts themselves.

There was, for instance, the time back in the seventies, when the troop operated in a prefab they had been given by the council. One day the scouts arrived to find the authorities had suddenly decided to close them down and they were locked out. So what to do? They took matters into their own hands. They had already noticed a nearby building site was vacant; now, with Skip's encouragement, they wrote down the estate agents' address from the sign outside and, without more ado, took off to the City to beard them in their offices. 'It is not often,' said Skip dryly, 'that City businesses get boys from Beckton dropping in unannounced.' They must have been persuasive: within a week Skip had been invited to Park Lane to meet the developer concerned, David Bloomfield, of County and Suburban Properties. He said the scouts could use the site for an HQ, on the absolute understanding they moved out the moment he needed it. They stayed seven years.

There was an even greater crisis, a few years later, down at Mohawk. Skip and the scouts were four weeks into the summer camp, there were twenty boys on site, and then, thanks to unforeseen problems, they ran out of money. As so often it was the scouts' reaction that was the surprise. 'The boys came to me, I didn't have to go to them,' said Skip. They told him that they reckoned they had enough food for two days – there were three tins of baked beans and some bread – so he should take the last £7 from petty cash, catch the next coach to London, and try one last-ditch local appeal.

'So I went home and wrote twenty-eight letters,' said Skip. 'And I kept it simple. I said: "All I need is £25 but I need it by Monday." Almost all responded. Then come the Monday, back at the camp, a little old man I'd never met drove up to the site. "You don't know me," he said, "but the chap you do know is away, so I read your letter." He'd been so touched, he said, that he'd got straight in his car and come round. He gave us £25.'

As Skip said: 'I always seem to find a man like that.'

Indeed, one senses there is something almost religious about the way Skip thinks about fund-raising. He describes, for instance, another crisis, also early in Mohawk's history, when he was working full time but without wages.

He was so worried that he couldn't sleep. 'I got up and went to sit for a while in the bathroom,' he said. 'I needed just £100, and everything would be OK.' Next day he went to the vicarage where he had an office. He opened the door and there, on the mat, was the day's post – most of it, as usual, addressed to the vicar. But there was one brown envelope addressed to Roy Howgate. 'I opened it and there was a note from someone I knew slightly. "I thought," it read, "you might find this useful. It's from the money my mum left me."' Inside was £100.

So it is less than astonishing, given the flavour of such tales, that Skip nearly joined the Church when he was young, although he gave up after his first, introductory course. This was, he said, because he found his fellow trainees so 'unchristian'. 'I've never met such a mean spirited mob in my life,' he said. Instead, he went into business – at one stage he was exhibitions rep. for Penguin Books – and his youth work, in the early years, was done in his spare time. But while he has left behind any early rigidities of belief, his faith, by contrast, has only grown. 'It's great when people help us,' he said, 'but I don't find it that surprising. It all depends on your view of human nature. I personally think it's quite natural for people to do nice things for others. People like being kind, it gives them joy.'

Where the scouts, too, take this view, they owe it quite as much to East End culture as metaphysics. There is a warmth, an instinctive comradeliness about the Beckton scouts, which is all about how kids feel when they have grown up feeling loved. For in Beckton the old, intense family loyalties still survive, and they apply even in settings that have untold other problems.

One scout lost both his parents but his grandparents took him in; their love for him is all the greater, arguably, for his loss. Another boy's father got sent to prison when his son was three; the dad's back with the family now, and they survived because their vast extended family rallied round. Then there was another family where the mother, this time, spent time in prison. Her elder son, reckons Skip, is simultaneously the most mischievous boy he's dealt with and the best carer he has ever known. There's the boy who still can't read at age fourteen. His very illiteracy, which makes his understanding of the world so very different from other children, arguably gives him his unique sensitivity to the signals the boys with autism send out.

There is certainly no simple cause and effect that can account for the scouts' capacities. Yet in all the complexities of their backgrounds, one quality stands out. They all come from a tradition, albeit under threat today, that puts people before things, and that can exert its influence even where the nuclear family has broken down. In part, of course, this is involuntary. Many families around Beckton don't exactly have the materialistic option. Nevertheless, it is this instinctive sense of priorities, this sense of what really matters in life, which makes the Mohawk community so magnetic, both to those they help and those, in turn, who so readily help them.

Come lunchtime, Dan and I went over to the Woodland Centre offices, and it was noticeable how the local family culture had been replicated there. You walked up an exterior staircase in the familiar Dodge City mode, then the moment you entered the offices this all-enveloping fug hit you: a soupy, bathroom warmth – the place was warmed by heaters – like the front room of a Beckton terrace. The lighting added to this effect. Though actually strip, it somehow felt like lamplight, golden against the window, the winter sky beyond.

There were desks against the walls, heaped with notebooks, files and computers. There was John Lee, in a baseball cap, looking preoccupied. There were two scouts, who turned out to be cousins, and there was Lisa, Skip's daughter-in-law, who works there. Stretched luxuriantly on the floor, as if in front of a fire, there was Skip's giant Alsatian, Tessa. It was Tessa, above all, who dominated the room. Like some spiritual mascot she embodied all its relaxed, wholehearted warmth and was the main reason why, though it was a workplace, it felt like home.

The other reason was 56-year-old Pat, mother of three, the office administrator. Pat is one of those small women who are so imposing you have to pinch yourself to remember she is short. Pat answers the phone and deals with the post and queens it up in best Beckton matriarchal manner, dispensing tea, sympathy and gossip with noisy elan.

There was a haroosh going on that day about the carols the scouts would be singing over Christmas. Phil Simpson, dark, swarthy, one of those 14-year-olds who look thirty, was trying to get the words printed out on a computer.

'Put it in big writing so the scouts can read it,' he said. 'Correction: make that very big. Some of 'em are a bit thick. Try sixteen point.'

'Hundred point,' said Dan.

'Shut up you; you can't read anyway, you're illiterate.'

'Thousand point.'

'Will you shut it? I'm trying to get a serious job done here, an' you're taking the piss. Tell 'im, Pat.'

'Million point.'

'Will you SHUT UP! Jesus!'

'That's sacrilege, that is!'

Phil aimed a blow; Dan ducked and Phil hit Tessa, who dived for cover. The doorbell rang and Tessa went crazy, barking frenetically until John silenced her with a bear hug.

'She's psychological, that dog is,' said Phil. 'Calm down, Tessa, for God's sake. Take one of your pills.'

Someone sent out for sandwiches and we ate lunch. The door opened and a bloke called Michael dropped in. People drop in a lot at Mohawk. Michael is one of the veteran scouts at Camp Mohawk, all of twenty-seven years old, who now runs a local carpentry business. He drives a neat little red van with a tree motif on it. For years he did the job John Lee does now, Mohawk scoutmaster. He started with the scouts back in the eighties. As late as the age of nineteen, he says, he could neither read nor write, but learned via Mohawk with Skip's encouragement. He'd come round to help with the Christmas preparations, and do a job in the workshop which he uses, with Skip's agreement, as he has no workshop of his own. He is a small man with a pale face, soft-spoken, and a shy, friendly manner; there are a lot of silences in his conversation.

All of a sudden he turned to Phil.

'Englishman, Irishman and a Scotsman,' he said. Michael had a serious, almost solemn air; he could have been announcing a death.

'Englishman gets on his motorbike, turns to the Irishman, an' says –'

'Hang about, hang about, there are ladies present!'

'Not *that* old joke, surely, that's a historical phenomenon that is!'

'It's not *that* old, blimey!' Pause. A little smile. 'Look, can I tell my joke if Pat goes out of the room?'

'If you tell that joke I'm going out the room.'

So gradually a little lunch-time party developed, full of gossip, sandwiches, tea, banter, and, increasingly, speculation (a Mohawk staple) as to where on earth Skip might possibly be at that particular moment. What with the different Mohawk sites and what with Skip's natural inclination to take off whenever he feels like it, he regularly vanishes. At such moments, indeed, phoning in sporadically on his mobile, he feels like some emanation from the ether, more divine than real.

There were those who thought he was en route to Wargrave; those who swore he was still in Beckton; those, the wild cards, who wondered if he hadn't made one of his shock dashes to the Mohawk base in France, as he every so often does. Michael, stirring his tea and looking thoughtful, said there were some who felt – not him, mind you – that Skip was spending too much time abroad, and would do better to concentrate on the UK. John, looking ever more preoccupied, wasn't too sure about this. John is Skip's great defender. He pointed out that there was always a lot of building work needed doing in France, and you couldn't do it, or even plan it, without going out to take a look. Pat, running her fingers through her hair, said that she didn't know, but she always said, that Mohawk was a charity and charity begins at home. She wondered, too, if I fancied another sandwich. The dog stirred luxuriantly. Michael chewed in silence. Dan sat there looking noble, and respectful of his elders. Grey clouds, glimpsed through the window, scudded past the cash and carry next door.

There was a cosy, front-room intimacy about it all but the really striking thing was that the office never actually stopped working, despite this seeming lunch break. Its times of formal activity faded seamlessly into theoretical time off and, through it all, phones rang, deliveries came, e-mails flickered, and Pat chatted extravagantly to various contacts down the line. Here, work and leisure, even work and pleasure, overlapped so much they finished up meaning pretty well the same thing.

In the afternoon, I joined Dan and Michael in the workshop, and that same relaxed, low-key working atmosphere continued there. The workshop is a large 70 by 50 ft room next door to the garage which both Dan and Michael use, Michael for business jobs (he does free work for Mohawk in exchange), Dan as a resource he's entitled to as a scout.

The workshop was lit by the same strip lighting as the office yet here, too, it felt as if lit by oil lamps. It smelled sweet with woodshavings and fresh-cut wood. There were shelves round the walls, full of carpentry equipment: lathes, screwdrivers, drills, saws, all neatly laid out. There were workbenches in the middle of the floor, piled with gleaming yellow planks. Work in progress included a new back being built by Dan for the Christmas sledge, replacing one damaged in a recent break-in. (Break-ins are a recurrent Mohawk problem. During the year I spent with them there were no less than three, including two in one month.) Across the room Michael was quietly working on some shelving for the office. Both he and Dan worked in near silence, with quick, adroit movements – Dan, especially, moving with a light elasticity of step, a perky optimism in his eye.

One reason Dan's movements were so sure was that he'd used the workroom for years. He and Michael had, in fact, largely shaped it to their needs, and they knew to the last inch where everything was. Dan spoke with pride about the systems they had put in. There was the cupboard they had built where, carefully arranged by size, they stored the screws. There was the machine they had rigged up to extract shavings from the machine saws. There was the fail-safe they'd invented so all the machines would switch off simultaneously in an accident. In a corner, Dan pointed to a battered-looking table. He'd found it in the street, he said, and was going to sand it down and varnish it. 'It's beautiful isn't it?' he said, running his hand over its surface, that sprightly look in his eyes. 'It's got drops, look, on either side. When I've finished it, I'm going to give it to me nan.'

Most striking was that Dan felt the workshop was his own place; what he did there was part of him, not something imposed from outside. And so, as the workshop had developed, so had he. The two were indistinguishable.

Eventually, across the room, Michael finished what he was doing, tidied up, swept the floor, and left. Dan suggested we go back to the sledge.

Dan had always worked effectively, but now I, too, was getting seduced by the local atmosphere. Not merely the difficulty, but the very nature of what we were doing seemed to change. The job no longer felt, as practical tasks usually do to me, like some huge imponderable, the embodiment of some larger, looming threat. It became a simple matter of cutting the materials up and sticking them down. Of course, it had only ever been that; the rest was personal. Even so, it occurred to me that my experience was a miniature version of what must have been Michael's, all those years ago, when he found there was no God-given reason why he shouldn't read. Confidence, like fear, is infectious. Mohawk therapy had worked for both of us.

But what is it they say about the need of our subconscious to bite back? At this moment I felt a terrible crack beneath my feet, followed by a crash and tinkling of glass.

I had stepped clean on one of those blue safety lights and smashed it to pieces. Rarely have I felt so foolish, or so guilty, not even the time I fell over Lee Trevino's golf ball during a championship match at Wentworth. But Dan's reaction was instructive. He merely shrugged. While John, later, said he'd often done the same thing himself. Of course he hadn't. But Skip's reaction was the most revealing of all. He above all found it funny; good for pleasure, in fact, good for a real, long, lingering, well-savoured laugh. That bloke from Henley? Now there's a cackle. It was just how the scouts used to react when the autistic children threw one of their wobblies. No problem, really. No, really, don't worry about it. Just part of the entertainment.

This was the troop, then, which was all set, by the middle of December, for a series of Christmas activities: parties, lunches, collecting sessions, visits to old people – the regular mix of carnival and good works. First of all was a visit to an old folks' home.

By 2.45 on a Friday afternoon the yard outside the London HQ looked like an assembly area for D-Day, as frenetic U-turns and backing culminated in the hooking up of the sledge behind a Land Rover, ready to set off. Around twenty of the scouts had got into their animal outfits: there were bears, a tiger, a penguin, even a snowman. They milled around the sledge in high excitement. John was in the Land Rover, Dan was herding the scouts, when suddenly, in all this movement, I became aware of a pair of eyes across the courtyard, fixing me, at thirty yards, with an intense gaze. This turned out to be Dave Hamblin, a countryman in his sixties from Reading who works as a volunteer all year. Even in winter, when the Berkshire camp is closed, he commutes to London, sometimes twice a week, to help out. Craggy, skinny, with darting, stumbling movements, he said hello in an old-time Berkshire accent as he clambered into the Santa suit and reached a precarious seat on top of the sledge. For Dave was Santa for the afternoon.

John jumped into the Land Rover; the scouts were herded into a minibus; and then, a moment of wild optimism, the sledge set off. As it started up, the lights came on all over it, a brilliant, translucent sight in the winter dusk, and, simultaneously, a shattering sound-system was activated, playing 'Rock and Roll Christmas'. Lights, sound, and then the *coup de grâce*, the reindeers' heads began to move. They moved very stiffly from side to side, with a kind of slow-burn jerk like the puppets in *Thunderbirds Are GO!* but the effect was dramatic. Then the engine stalled, to curses from Dave, and everything, lights, sound, reindeer, stopped. Then it fired again, and everything restarted. Ironic cheers. Finally, and to the palpable surprise of the security man next door, the uncertain procession began its progress down the street, Dave waving and bowing regally as we went.

But it was our arrival at the old people's home, ten minutes later, which was our finest hour. For, as so often with Mohawk, the whole thing had been cooked up at the last minute and most residents had no idea that we were coming. We swept down a short drive into a large forecourt and stopped there, pulsating with lights, belting out 'I'm Dreaming Of A White Christmas.' The scouts burst out like a task force from *The Jungle Book*; alarmed faces appeared at the windows. Soon the troop was swarming down the corridors, invading residents' rooms. Most looked pleased, in a dazed, 85-year-old-way, but one turned to Joe Beckford and told him to 'Buzz off!' 'How dare you!' yelled her companion, and dealt her a ringing smack, then sat back nodding and grinning, face round as a bun.

More of a problem, in fact, was the way the scouts felt about the old. Few had ever seen people quite so elderly, or ill, before. And it was, indeed, almost like a morality picture of time, the young in their animal suits, dancing and capering in the middle of the room, the old gazing fixedly from the side, poleaxed with age, rigid, some so weak they could hardly talk. Little Pete Pollard, cute and mischievous in his Paddington Bear suit, looked shocked as he came out of a bedroom where one old lady lay near-motionless, unable to speak. 'It's sad,' he said. 'It's out of order.' Were those tears? And he walked down the corridor muttering to himself, 'It's out of order, well out of order.'

Most surprising was the way some residents cheered us up. One blue-eyed Scottish lady, more paralysed, even, than the earlier one, but able to talk, was plainly delighted by this eruption of youth and colour into her room. 'You've made my day!' she cried, with glittering smiles, as Pete and Joe capered about. 'You've made my day!' And when the scouts were about to leave she called them back and insisted on planting a kiss on each of their foreheads, making them come up separately. You could not but wonder what magnificence of love, in her past life, meant she was still able to radiate such joy. She was old and ill and she made *us* feel the world was a fine and hopeful place. The scouts ran down the corridors back to the float.

Nevertheless, it was when we went collecting at the local Savacentre that we had the most festive trip of all. Festive? It sounds a strange way to describe a collecting session off the A13. Yet that was how it felt; not least because that was how it looked. Not only, as ever, was there the float, crazy and gay, but there was the setting. For one of modern life's secrets is just how superb the dullest townscape looks at night. Above us there was an almost melodramatic evening sky; while at ground level there was all the brilliance of modern electricity, the most intense scarlets, greens and yellows you ever did see, purples that you only find, elsewhere, in water twenty feet deep in a tropic bay, all glowing and twinkling like treasure. Indeed, it took quite an effort to police the mind, to remember that these were mere petrol stations, supermarkets, cash and carries, warehouses, and not the Aladdin's cave of dazzling beauty that they seemed.

But above all, there were the children. Not only were there the Mohawk scouts in their animal suits, but there were the kids constantly flooding in with the shoppers. The sledge was drawn up in the parking bay just in front of Savacentre's main doors. The scouts skipped and danced away to the music, and high on the sledge, like the star on a Christmas tree, sat Dave in his Santa suit. The music was 'Rock and Roll Christmas'.

Surprisingly, given his perilous position, Dave too was dancing; from the waist up, that is, sitting on the sledge. Mainly he used his arms. He either held them high above his head and waved them from side to side like a one-man Mexican wave, or he stretched them out parallel to his chest and then whirled them round and round in a corkscrew motion, like a soul singer from 1963. This was, Dave explained, necessary to draw attention to the float, and thus the collecting boxes. The effect was startling. Little children, decanting unknowingly with the rest of the family in the nearby car park, would start walking towards the Savacentre then suddenly catch sight of Dave and stop, rooted to the spot like frightened cats. Their parents, pointing and grinning, did their best to reassure them.

As did the scouts. Joe Beckford, a barrel-chested 12-year-old dressed up as a tiger, swore reflexively as a passing child trod on his tail, then ran after him, danced a pirouette, patted him on the head, and gave him a hug. Rob Ferndown, a 14-year-old black kid from East Ham, dressed up as a bear, danced a complex soul step which involved a series of slow, heavy paces as he simultaneously turned round. Local kids watched him, fascinated; he looked like a Red Indian doing a war dance. And meanwhile, as ever with children, a whole intense emotional life was going on between the scouts, quite separate from the adults they were with. One leant against a railing, sobbing inconsolably; an older boy, he said, had been acting 'horrible', but he never explained how. Then there was the row with the Christmas tree man. He was standing in front of the store, working one of those machines where you put a tree in one end and it comes out wrapped in plastic. For no clear reason he decided that three scouts, standing opposite, were laughing at him. Suddenly, incredibly, he abandoned his machine and tore after them like a rocket. They ran off, shrieking with delight.

But then it was all part of the Christmas excitement, which the kids felt so strongly that even the adults caught it. Nevertheless, after a couple of hours' arm-waving and capering almost everyone was beginning to wilt. Dave, in particular, was looking exhausted. So finally John came over to me and asked, with his usual diffidence, if I'd take over as Santa.

Santa! It was like taking over as God. We'd talked about it earlier, but it still came as a shock. In theory it was easy; in practice, you could spoil everything. Nevertheless, I said yes. You don't say no at Mohawk and I'd done very little that day.

And what is undeniable, for those who've never done it, is that being Santa is a revelation. You walk into the Savacentre gents a mere citizen: you walk out, costumed, a childhood fantasy. Just like that. I lumbered over to the sledge, hauled myself precariously on to my perch, and quickly realized the secret every Santa knows: that inside every last, hopeless, depressed-looking, cynical-looking human being, there lurks this spark of hope. For put that beard and cape on and each passer-by gives you the same smile they gave Santa when they were five, each wriggles with unashamed pleasure when you wave, and each feels delighted that the embodiment of Christmas spirit has finally, however briefly, paid attention to them.

Even so, after two hours heavy-duty arm-waving I, too, was

beginning to feel exhausted so I was relieved when Skip yelled that it was time to pack up. I began the climb down to go home.

Too soon. At the back of my mind I had suspected what now followed, for the sledge, clearly, had to go home too, and I'd wondered if I might not be expected to stay up there while Skip towed it. Surely not! It was dangerous enough stationary. Yet before I could squeak Skip was in the Land Rover and had the door slammed and we were under way, the freezing night air wonderfully cooling, the ride, very soon, a holy terror.

For if being Santa at Savacentre is fascinating, Santa on the A13 is something else. Cars swerved, headlights flashed, horns blared, people shot high fives and passing Essex carloads ranted and cheered. It was freezing and frightening, if strangely exhilarating, and while the near miss at the roundabout was memorable, the trickiest stage was when we turned off and began going over what felt like speed bumps on local side roads. Taken at anything more than five miles an hour these can produce an effect on a seated Santa much like going over a jump at Aintree and as you rise, involuntarily, you pray that when you come down again it will be at least somewhere near your seat, and won't involve the entire float spilling out all over the road, Santa, lights, reindeer and all.

It was like a white-knuckle ride at a fairground, but we made it. At HQ the scouts remained supportive. 'You done well,' said Rob, with the air of one who knows a thing or two about dancing. Like all good teachers, he singled out one particular point for praise. 'Your arm waving,' he said, 'was wicked.' I was grateful, but mainly glad to be alive. Then, as I got off, I noticed something I'd earlier missed. All that cotton wool I'd stuck on the sledge earlier with such effort, and such pride, had been totally redone.

The scouts' tact had been exquisite. No one had said a word.

THREE

I learned most not from those who taught me, but from those who talked with me. (St Augustine)

Crucial though the Christmas fund-raising had been, by the new year the troop was once again concentrating on its country base. Come the second week of January, regular parties were heading off to Berkshire. They hoped to do a little winter scouting, but mainly they needed to do the preparation which takes so much of the scouts' time. For although the first autistic children weren't coming down till February, everything had to be got ready meanwhile.

How different the camp looked from the Mohawk of the summer! It was locked in its winter sleep. The forest was leafless and silent; the tents, like the trees, seemed stripped bare by the season. Their canvas stored, only the steel skeletons remained. The landscape was transformed. The brilliant colours of summer had decayed into every variant of brown. The bracken lay stretched out as if it had been shot.

Most striking was the difference in the sounds. There was this utter, dead, hanging stillness everywhere. There was no rustle of leaves, no caress of the wind; above all, there was no bird song. Rather, there was a silence that itself felt loud, and the sounds you did hear seemed to stand out more, enhanced. A dog's bark. The crack of the campfire. The steady hum, strangely relaxing and almost rural, of a distant aircraft.

And in the camp, the shouts of the kids, a dozen of whom had come down with Skip and John for this first working weekend. Amazingly, many boys were barefoot, just as in summer. A stern rule that Skip tries to enforce year-long because, as he points out, no shoe or sock can ever be cleaned like skin. John Lee, as ever, leading from the front, was not only barefoot but wearing shorts. Five boys were sitting round the fire; others had vanished into the woods; some swept up leaves. The majority were clearing out the kitchen, in preparation for the main task of the day: the rebuild which had been demanded by the new safety regime. Yet another avalanche of stipulations – new EU-led hygiene rules – had descended on the camp. The kitchen had to be utterly reworked. And even doing most of the building themselves, Mohawk would still have to find at least £10,000. Nevertheless, the more they DIYed, the more they'd save.

But the troop is used to such challenges; indeed, it relishes them. The process started, as usual, with the most thunderous, stentorian yell from Skip, a roar of 'Caaaaaamooooon!' that re-echoed like a bugle call in the winter stillness and reached kids playing half a mile away up the hill. Moments later, as if by magic, boys you never even knew were on site came pouring down. First, as usual, was Ian Pool, the broad, fleshy-lipped boy who had been at Mohawk that time I visited two years earlier. At sixteen, he had turned into a huge, barrel-chested young man with jutting eyebrows and a dreadnought air. Dauntless and capable, he spoke little but was always at the heart of every job. There was young Fred Robinson, tall, pale and skinny, younger brother of James, the boy who'd looked after autistic Omar two years earlier. Like his brother, Fred's mature beyond his years. There was Phil Simpson, dark, swarthy, with ear-splitting, cat-like grins, the 14-year-old-going-on-30 I had met back in

London. And there were, too, boys who felt somehow different. Fourteen-year-old Christopher Hope, for instance, blond, gentle and with thoughtful eyes, and with a verbal intelligence utterly different from Ian Pool's. Not to mention the younger ones, like little Joe Beckford, who'd been a tiger back at Christmas, or 11-year-old Chris Smith, whose solemn, secret air masks a desire to 'teach disabled', as he puts it, when he grows up. So swift is emotional development at that age that the young ones lived, in effect, in another universe. They played separately.

This, then, was the horde that came flooding down to the canteen block, another of those low, dark buildings in Mohawk's Wild West mode. They lined up in front of the huts. Like all communities, Mohawk has evolved, over the years, its own unique way of doing things. At Mohawk it's like a military operation.

First a scout ran off to get Skip a chair. Skip's size makes it hard for him to stand for any length of time. Then another scout brought him a cup of tea; he placed it on the ground beside him. Then yet another brought his hat. Next, seated in the kitchen like Napoleon on the field of Austerlitz, the adult volunteers clustered round him like a staff, Skip dispatched his commands. The kitchen furniture – the cookers, stoves and hotplates – had already been moved into the next room out of the way. The floorboards, thereby, had been laid bare, and now, declared Skip, we had to rip them up, so the kitchen's wiring could be relaid. Of course, this could have been done professionally, but that isn't the Mohawk way. DIY's cheaper, naturally, and there's also the question of style. Why get someone else to solve problems you are perfectly capable of solving yourself?

At a roar from Skip the scouts descended on the floor like a horde of locusts and began wrenching, tearing and pulling at every point. After a bit, as the heavier planks momentarily slowed them down, the adults joined in, too. There developed an instant, unspoken division of labour. First the grown-ups would move in, using metal levers to pull up the planks; then the boys would swarm in and mop up the smaller bits that the adults had dislodged. First the heavy brigade, then the light. So each time the adults finished and backed off the kids rushed in, like water into a bath. Not a second was lost. For all Skip's yelling and shouting, he was hardly needed. The boys made an extraordinarily efficient workforce, swift, limber and energetic, while the elasticity of their bodies meant this job above all – which inevitably involves so much ducking, diving and rolling around – ideally suited them. When we started, we reckoned we were faced with a day's work; by lunchtime, incredibly, the job was done.

But then the kids were different. Their way of working was entirely their own. They completely lacked adult pessimism. They didn't prevaricate, nor did they grumble. They acted as if they believed any task at all was possible. After a while, intrigued, I found myself wondering whether such boys might not merely be the equal of an adult workforce (for this task, certainly) but even – hierarchical heresy! – superior. I put this to Skip.

'Absolutely,' he grinned. 'Kids are the very best workers of all. Until thirteen, that is – by adolescence they begin to lose it.' This was partly why, he explained, the troop has a cut-off age of fifteen. In all ways (notably, of course, in looking after autistic children) he finds young children better than old. 'I've had eleven-year-olds burst into tears when I've told them to stop working.' The key to it all, reckoned Skip, is that young kids are believers: they believe in the success of the outcome, in happy endings, in the competence of the boss. 'And because they believe, they don't worry; and because they don't worry, they don't tire.'

Of course we've all seen something similar. What adult has not asked 'Where *do* these kids get their energy from?' To which others answer: 'They've energy enough for play, just try them on homework!' But it's subtler than that. What counts, arguably, is not the children's task, but their relationship with the task; and what is unusual about kids is how readily they can transpose play relationships into areas adults would consider drudgery. Indeed,

Maria Montessori, source of so many fine perceptions about children, argued something more remarkable still: that happy children can come off a job not merely untired, but positively refreshed – with more energy, indeed, than when they began. Suffice to say this is not a quality most adults detect in themselves after, say, two hours mowing the lawn. But then Montessori, no doubt, would have said their relationship with their work was not what it should have been, and, no doubt, she would have been right.

All of which might make a day at Mohawk sound like a Rudolf Steiner seminar but this would be wrong. For Mohawk keeps its liberalism well hidden. On the surface, indeed, it can seem plain authoritarian. Not only is there Skip's routine yelling and shouting, or the constant, amiable punch-ups between the boys – little Pete Pollard, in particular, boasts a glancing side-kick, transposed from the football field, which can silence an opponent at three feet – but there is Mohawk's broader, all-pervasive culture of male machismo, which sometimes takes surprising forms. Later that morning, after the kids had gone away, I joined Skip as he walked into the kitchen to see how the electricians were getting on. Skip calls in outsiders now and then to help with the more technical jobs.

He poked around in silence; he looked at the gaps in the floorboards; he cast an eye over the wiring; an electrician followed him about.

Finally, after about ten minutes in which the two of them had walked around in total silence, Skip turned to the electrician and said:

'Irishman goes into a railway ticket office. "Give me a return ticket," he says. "Return ticket to where?" says the bloke. "Back here, of course!" says the Irishman. "Where the elljer think?"'

The electrician smiled. He turned to Skip and said:

'What'd the queen be if she had balls?'

'Dunno.'

'King.'

The two men said nothing else at all. Skip walked away.

But while intense building sessions like the kitchen regularly occur, more typical still is Mohawk's domestic routine – all those hours when the camp somehow coasts on without conscious direction, as if in neutral.

The main task of the day done, groups of boys went back to the campfire circle, a large, round area about thirty feet across, surrounded by grass banks. A bonfire burnt steadily in the middle. They chatted and chased each other; now and then there was a row. Elsewhere, metallic bangs and clatters showed other kids were preparing lunch, which the children make themselves. In the background, like some gargantuan Greek chorus, Skip trundled back and forth, his singing testifying, as it always does, to his good mood. He sung in true Old London style, that curious, quavering high-baroque which bears limited relation to the songs themselves but everything to a genre:

Arfur panda tu'any rice . . .

The choice, as often, was mysterious.

. . . Arfur panda tree – all . . .'
. . . That's the we-hey the maaaaaaaney goes . . .

The most stylized word of all was money, which Skip stretched to unthought of dimensions with a marvellous, vast, slow, elastic vibrato. When he wasn't singing, he maintained his customary high visibility by driving vehicles – the Land Rover, say, or the earth shifter – from one side of the camp to another, chortling as he went. The reasons for these journeys could be obscure.

Meanwhile, most of the boys, once again, had disappeared. By day, they ebb and flow like tides. Some, it turned out later, were in the lounge, some in the adventure playground, but the majority had gone back into the forest. For the woods remain Mohawk's prime attraction, not least because they are so big. Indeed Michael, the ex-scoutmaster, puts the area to which the scouts have access as high as 180 acres. The beauty of such vastness is it never gets mentally mapped; it retains the mystery of the unknown. Added to which, it provides a wonderful means of getting away from the grown-ups. Skip, in particular, has an effective range of around thirty yards.

But then you can tell how the scouts feel about the forest by the way they've given it their own, highly personalized, geography. Each area is named. There's High Top, for instance, the summit of Camp Mohawk's hill. This is the beech grove which is so exquisite in summer; even in winter, it's a favourite place to play games. Just down from High Top, the other side of the hill, is Kindling Heaven. So named because it's the best place locally to pick up twigs to light the fire. The area is also called Dark Forest from the pitch black fir trees that shed their branches there as they grow. Then there's Pear Field, so named, with faultless logic, because it's shaped like a pear; while half a mile the other way, a bit closer to the camp, is John's Tree, a chestnut which is covered with the names of scouts who've climbed it. Highest name of all is John Lee's, carved way up where the branches wave, at a perilous forty feet; you can see how he won his early status.

Yet even in this very home-grown geography you can see the strange split, half macho, half tenderness, of the scouts' minds. Walking back, halfway between Kindling Heaven and High Top, is The Grave. Here is a wooden cross, set in an oval of white stones. It marks the place where the scouts found, and buried, a dead bird.

And there are local legends. Up a steep escarpment, beyond High Top, lies Devil's Hill. This was, I was told, 'well haunted'. There are ghosts up there, apparently, demons, ghouls, 'the lot'.

Indeed, and it was Skip who told me this, in former years the local vicar got double stipend for dealing with all those extra spooks. One year the troop decided to go ghost-busting. Worst spook of all, the word went, was the Black Monk. So for a laugh a senior scout dressed up in a sheet and manifested from the bushes. Never in Mohawk's history, apparently, has the troop been known to run so fast. There's a scout who still won't go near Devil's Hill to this day.

In this landscape which the boys have made their own, they play games they have invented themselves. Most involve two teams, with one team disappearing and the other chasing them. The rules, as the boys explain them, seem hugely complex, although you gradually realize you can rely on one thing: however the game starts, come the finish the winners beat the losers up.

Most popular of all, however, was a game called 'Wide'. This is played on High Top, by the whole troop. The day I joined in one group defended a tree, while the other, broken up into small, attacking parties, tried to get at it. It was like a militarized version of 'he'. The fun, of course, lay in the way the attackers could use the vast area of the wood to camouflage their approach. Indeed, by judicious crawling, and standing behind trees, myself and Christopher Hope got within twenty yards of home before the defenders saw us. One sudden, lumbering rush and we were there, an achievement which brought sudden respect into Ian Pool's eyes: 'An old bloke like you!' he said.

Yet quite as interesting as how they played the game was how they didn't. They kept getting distracted. There was the moment, for instance, when the attackers set off down the hill to hide themselves. Halfway down they suddenly got fascinated by running furiously and throwing themselves, head first, into the winter leaves, which were up to three feet deep. And you could see why. The leaves made a wonderful haroosh sound as the kids disappeared in them and they were also excellent for ten-foot skids. Funnily enough, looking up the hill we could see that the defending team had got distracted, too. They'd started climbing around neighbouring trees. They seemed to have forgotten they were supposed to be playing the game. In short, 'Wide' completely ground to a halt for twenty minutes. Nobody cared. It was one of those times when you remember just how different is the boys' world. A place where things are only done just so long as they feel right, and where, the moment a better idea comes along, it's pounced on instantly.

What was happening, in fact, was play – quite different from any 'game'. A distinction most of us lose sight of at thirteen. Thereafter, the only idea most of us have of 'play' is something which involves rules, parameters, goals. The notion that it can be something, say, that reinvents itself every five minutes, that can finish up several removes from where it began, becomes unthinkable. And this need to improvise is one of many reasons why the boys are so keen to get off the campsite, away from the adults. Few grown-ups can get involved in activity of this kind without trying to change it, or give it a shape.

Then there's that other, constant grown-up concern, physical safety. Not only does it inhibit children's fun, it's quite a question, too, whether it doesn't actually make them more, rather than less, vulnerable. As we came down from the hill the inevitable, to an adult, happened. One of the eleven-year-olds lost it on one last, delicious slither through the leaves and finished up cannoning into the truck. He cut his knee. It wasn't much, but it hurt; and if the afternoon had been as controlled as some would wish, it almost certainly would never have happened.

Yet the accident had its good side. Without the freedom that led to it the boy would never have enjoyed all those other, accident-free slides earlier in the day. But there was a further point. Now, with the evidence throbbing on his knee, he was unlikely to make the same mistake again – a mistake which at other times, and in other places, might be more serious. Experience is a far better deterrent than the – often highly suspect – warnings of grown-ups. The boy's minor injury, in fact, could prevent major injury later. It was an inoculation.

But this is just one of the myriad ways in which Camp Mohawk operates as one huge learning zone. Although there are some formal lessons to teach the scouts about autism, these are rare. The crucial learning happens tangentially, almost by accident. But then this, of course, is the kind of learning that gets remembered.

During the kitchen session, for instance, there was a moment when we needed to sharpen a knife. There followed an instant speech by Skip on the three key things you need to know when using a whetstone. Other times I have seen Skip stop, in the middle of something else, and do a quick rundown of all the different trees around the camp, and as this will almost always start from a question by one of the scouts, their attention is absolute. Such sessions can take strange forms. One day a delivery man came to drop some timber off, and, in the course of unloading, it turned out he was left-handed. It then emerged that a couple of scouts were, too. There followed an instant, ten-minute lecture on left-handedness by the van driver: left-handedness and sport, left-handedness and music, even left-handedness and parking a van. The learning you remember . . . weeks later one of the scouts told me he'd gone home afterwards and looked up left-handedness in his encyclopaedia.

Indeed, such sessions, precisely because Mohawk is such an informal place, can end up being about absolutely anything in the world. One day, around a month after that January building-work in the kitchen, as the weather began its first hesitant, stumblings towards spring, I was standing in the campfire circle with Dave, the countryman who'd dressed up as Santa back at Christmas.

'Look at that!' he cried suddenly. 'Ain't that *beautiful*!' His grizzled, weather-beaten face, the colour and texture of well-varnished rosewood, was spread in a grin. His sharp blue eyes were staring at something thirty yards away – a large bird's nest, seemingly, on a tree, about four feet from the ground. 'That's the best I've seen,' he said, 'so low down, and so beautifully grown, too.' Grown? 'It's mistletoe,' he said, beckoning me to follow him. We went over. What I'd thought was a bird's nest turned out to be a plant: a dark green, ball-shaped bush around two feet in diameter. It was growing out of the tree the way most plants grow out of the earth, its suckers rooted in the bark. 'They do look like bird's nests,' said Dave. 'Especially when they're high in the trees, like that one.' He pointed over my shoulder to another 'bird's nest' thirty feet high in the oak behind me. 'Or that.' He indicated yet another, in the beech across the way. 'What a beauty it is,' he said, running his fingers through its tendrils as he might have stroked a horse. 'And there's money in them, too.'

How much? 'Oh, £20 or more for one like that,' said Dave. 'I used to go out collecting them when I was a boy. We'd climb up the trees, break them off and sell them for Christmas decorations. Gypsies do the same thing – and farmers, too, though they're more likely to shoot 'em down with twelve bores.'

By now a few scouts had drifted up to listen. Encouraged, Dave began to talk about plants in general and how hard it was for townies to understand them. 'No word of a lie,' he said, 'I've known kids who genuinely thought mushrooms grow on trees. And when you tell them how they really grow – and if you offer to take 'em mushrooming – they'll come like a shot.'

'I'd go,' said Pete Pollard. 'Go on, Dave, take us!'

'Can't!' said Dave. 'Wrong time of year! But I'll take you later. Ah, mushrooms,' he said, with that same rhapsodic, faraway manner with which he'd stroked the mistletoe. 'Now they're really something. They're such a delicate, tender pink colour. Unless you touch 'em, of course, and then they bruise, and go all dark. But the pink colour comes back again if you leave 'em.

Same thing happens – going dark – if you cover 'em, that's why they're sold uncovered, in baskets.

'Now I'll tell you this,' said Dave. 'No word of a lie –' Dave is much given to such sudden emphasis. He laid a hand on my arm. 'Who knows how long it takes for mushrooms to grow?'

'A month?' said Tom Pollard, Pete's elder brother, looking amused.

'Six months?' said Chris Smith.

'Ten years?' said Pete.

'I'll tell you,' said Dave. 'No word of a lie: three days. You wouldn't believe it, but I promise you, they grow so fast I've actually seen one getting bigger before my very eyes!'

'Come on, Dave!'

'No word of a lie!' said Dave. 'It's true! There's a field near here I go to sometimes, to watch 'em grow –'

'Do us a favour!'

'And I was squatting down there one day –'

'Took short, was you, Dave!'

'And I swear, they've got these buttons on the top. You know, like button mushrooms? And the button's a kind of helmet to thrust the plant through the earth's crust and, I swear, I saw this mushroom that had just broken through and it still had earth on it, and I saw the earth fall off just as I looked because it was moving!'

Catcalls, shrieks of laughter.

'No really, and that button's really hard at first, so it can break through, but when the job's done it goes all soft an' –'

At which Joe Beckford fell over, as if poleaxed, and lay on his back gasping, but there were others who were watching Dave acutely. And there was something else. Without anything being said, without perhaps even noticing it, the boys had sat themselves in a semicircle on the ground around Dave, knees pulled up to their chests. For all the world they looked like schoolchildren, sitting round a teacher.

Fred Robinson sniffed his knees, and gazed over to where the sun was struggling through the mist.

'You know,' he said, 'I swear I can sense the spring.'

And soon, we all began to sense it. By the end of February, when the scouts came down for their first full week of the year, there was this strange lightening in the air, as if a great weight were being lifted from the earth. The sky lost its hanging stillness, and turned pale violet; bluebell buds appeared in the woods, little yellow stalks peeping up through the ground like corn; the trees across the valley went pink, as the red of the new buds blurred with the black of the winter branches. And, as the troop spent longer and longer in each other's company, friendships were formed. And along with friendship came friendship's first cousin, rivalry. We began to get on each other's nerves.

This is true in any group but is especially true at Mohawk. Because Mohawk's consciousness is so dominated by the young, its ebbs and flows of mood are unconstrained. Nor is this confined to the boys. One day I was standing by the campfire circle. It functions like a market square; it is where you go to watch the world go by when you have nothing special else to do. Suddenly I heard the stentorian roar of Skip's voice, with that familiar, monosyllabic way of making his point.

'Don't! Use! A! Shovel! Use! A! Rake!' he roared. Nick Smith, elder brother of Chris and son of that same Mrs Smith who John Lee had called a 'heroine', was standing amid a pile of leaves, looking abashed. Skip had another go: 'Don't use a shovel, use a rake and pick the leaves up with your hands!'

Nick stood there, motionless, an invisible question mark over his head. Skip tried again, more succinctly still:

'DO IT!'

No one could accuse Skip of harbouring resentment. It comes straight out, like a shell from a howitzer. But young Nick still stood there motionless, looking simultaneously crestfallen and angry. He didn't move. Nor did Skip. Little and large, they stood there in cliff-hanging confrontation. After thirty seconds, Skip finally stumped off; Nick stood there still.

Beside me was Christopher Hope, the boy with the thoughtful eyes. It was Christopher who had interpreted for me when that autistic child had come on a visit, the one making steering-wheel movements who'd wanted to go home. Since I'd joined the camp Christopher had latched on to me a bit. It was almost as if he'd taken me under his wing, like a guide or mentor.

Christopher was smiling. 'You watch, they won't speak to each other for the next three hours,' he said. 'They'll both go off and sulk, and Skip will be the worst.'

Troy Northcote, another 14-year-old, agreed. Troy's dad is a graphic designer; Troy's clothes, even in the camp, look hip. He has a quick, clever face. 'It's weird,' said Troy. 'You never know how Skip's going to react. He gets in a real state about little things, like the leaves; then you get a big thing, like the earth mover breaking down, and it doesn't bother him at all.'

Now Dave joined in.

'He's not the same bloke as he was,' he said. 'Ever since his stroke.' For Skip had suffered a stroke the year before. Nothing too serious, fortunately, but a very definite warning light. It could well be affecting his behaviour – mood swings were the least of it.

'But there's something else,' said Dave. 'Skip's retiring this year and he just can't let the camp go. It's this that makes him find fault all the time; he can't bear the feeling of not being needed. He's got to feel indispensable.' And Dave was right there, too. Skip's impending retirement, partly through ill-health, partly because he'd just reached sixty-five, emerged as a leitmotif in Mohawk's story, in the months to come. Skip had to feel indispensable. Dave was a funny old bloke, and in many ways he was the camp clown, but he had these strange flashes of perception. Instinctive as an animal, infinitely sensitive to atmosphere, he was, in his own strange way – those piercing blue eyes! – almost a seer.

And Dave wasn't the only one proved right: Christopher was proved right, too. Within three hours Skip and Nick had indeed made up. After, that is, a sufficient sulk, on both sides, to satisfy honour.

There had been talk among the boys of a game of 'Wide' but suddenly word went out that Skip wanted help planting a tree. He'd bought one from a garden centre to commemorate one of the camp's long-time local supporters, Margaret.

No one seemed much bothered by this sudden change of plan. They rarely do, at Mohawk. It's as if the boys feel the adults are sufficiently on their side that most things they suggest should be OK. Six scouts trooped down the hill to the camp's memorial garden, near the front gate.

And there emerged yet another of those Mohawk educational moments, but with a further twist.

The site was indeed idyllic: a grassy paddock around thirty yards by forty, on the edge of the camp perimeter, overlooking the plain. There were several trees there already: a hawthorn, a cherry, a plum, each planted in memory of one of the camp's friends. Margaret's was an apple tree. She'd supported Mohawk for years, and had died recently of cancer, in her seventies.

The Mohawk machine duly rolled into life. Skip lurched down the hill; a boy followed with his seat; another brought his tea; and we began.

Under Skip's instructions the scouts plunged straight into the job, digging furiously into the earth. At the heart of the work, as ever, was Ian Pool, helped by Tom Pollard and a posse of 11-year-olds. And there ensued a strange dialogue, like an opera sextet, in which practical instruction – tree planting for absolute beginners – intertwined, as it so often does around kids, with surreal speculation.

'Now what you do,' said Skip, 'when you're digging this kind of clayey earth, is you take it out of the ground in lumps, then break it up with your fork –'

''Ere, Skip, what'd happen if you kept on digging, you know, if you didn't stop? Would you come out in Australia?'

'Now when you've dug your hole – that's it! – you make sure there's a good six inches round the tree on every side so there's plenty of fresh earth for the roots –'

'Naah, there's gravity down there, isn't there, you'd go fast enough down to the middle – you'd speed up – but by the time you got near Australia the gravity'd be working the other way round, it'd slow you down . . .'

'And when you put the pole in, to support it, make sure it's really firm so it doesn't move and damage the bark so it gets diseased – mind that spade, for chrissake, don't scrape the bark! –'

'This is it, you'd get twenty feet of short of Australia, and you'd just begin to see it, and then you'd start swinging back this way again, and then the gravity'd get you this end, too, and you'd go back where you was before. There's people been down there for centuries, swinging back and forth –'

'Will you shut it or shall I stick you in this hole?'

It was the weirdest mixture of practicality and pure fantasy, and it was quite different from Dave's nature notes. Because instead of being merely talk (poetic though Dave's chats are) it was a practical demonstration. The boys were being shown how to do something, by someone who knew every working trick in the trade. More, they were being taught by standing at their teacher's shoulder. At moments of crisis Skip would plunge in and do bits himself. They were learning by imitation, not just by command. Nor should we forget a further dimension, perhaps the most critical of all. They were learning a subtle but crucial kind of optimism. And they were learning it just by being around, by rubbing shoulders with someone who felt, intuitively, from thirty years' experience, that any problems the job threw up would always, finally, be solved.

In a word, they were experiencing apprenticeship, that most thorough and humane method of instruction that has all but died out. Not that it was unknown to Ian Pool. His dad's a mechanic, and he and Ian often while away long, silent hours working on cars. Neither father or son are talkers; but, says his mother, they are very close. Need one add that Skip reckons Ian is one of the best natural mechanics he has met. It's not so much that he works out problems logically, says Skip. It's more that he's got this mechanical sixth sense: he solves them by hunch.

'Dear old Margaret,' said Skip, as they patted down the earth around her tree.

Slowly the camp was beginning to make sense. But it was at the very end of February, just before the first autistic boys were due, that there occurred one of those emblematic moments that somehow sum a place up.

The kitchen was finished. We'd shifted the cookers back inside, lifting them bodily through the ten-foot-wide serving hatch – ourselves. Now all that remained was to move the biggest kitchen item of all, the fridge. But the fridge was different. It was heavy metal and twelve feet by four: it was a killer. Looming, implacable, it lurked in a far corner of the canteen, laughing at us. Not that I felt *that* bothered, on reflection, because, clearly, the cookers were one thing and the fridge was quite another. We'd leave it there, of course. It would stay in the canteen.

Not a bit of it. Skip was going to have his fridge back in the kitchen and that was the end of it. I felt a terrible sense of doom. This was madness, clearly. If we went ahead not only would we fail, there'd be a death. Nevertheless, with three adults and four boys, and Skip giving the orders, we managed the first part, which was to lay the brute on its side. Then with all seven of us pressing round wherever we could insert a finger, carefully timing ourselves so the pull was simultaneous, we tried to lift it . . . and nothing happened. We tried again. There wasn't a prayer. We tried again. The moment I felt that dead weight on my fingers I knew the truth. The fridge lived in another, quite separate universe of possibilities; it was beyond us.

But Skip didn't understand this. He rearranged our positions. He co-opted more adults. Above all, he sent out for more kids. This, especially, seemed absurd. What difference could 11-year-olds make to such a weight? However, we duly started. At every point, at every angle, there were kids hanging off the thing, like limpets on a rock. Then Skip cried 'Lift!' and we lifted. The fridge . . . levitated. All those tiny fingers, cumulatively, had made the difference.

They call it teamwork, but the real crisis was still to come. Moments later, lumbering and lurching, we got the thing up to the serving hatch and began thrusting it through. And then it happened. As it toppled out of the dining room into the kitchen, it went out of control. Four kids rushed round from the canteen side to rescue it, but it was too late. Suddenly it was only me and Phil Simpson, facing each other on opposite sides, who were supporting it.

It was too heavy. We couldn't hold it. I saw the wild surmise on Phil's face as he saw the terror on mine. What we both read, clear as a bell, was: this is death! Skip was up and out of his seat in a frenzy; the kids were rushing around in panic; but the crisis only lasted a moment. Seconds later, from nowhere, Dave Hamblin was underneath the fridge, skinny, wizened Dave, but he caught it. Then Ian Pool came rushing in from outside and plunged his vast, trunk-like chest under the most dangerous place of all and, holding it, like Samson under the temple, he steadied it. Then the little ones arrived and piled in too. We lowered the thing on to the ground. We'd survived.

'Thank you, thank you for saving us!' slobbered Phil and I to our two rescuers. But Dave, seemingly, thought nothing of it. He'd been a removal man in his time, he said, and it was surprising what you could lift when you put your mind to it. He'd shifted weights much heavier than that. Forget it.

After tea there was a further surprise. Dave mentioned, apropos of nothing much, that he'd had two hip replacements, and the last one hadn't even been a success. And yet he had plunged so readily into that crisis, and taken such risks. For all his skinny, bird-like arms, he was so strong – far stronger, seemingly, than me.

Or was he? When you thought about it, wasn't it all in the mind? And what about Skip? With his stroke he had no right to be standing there screaming. He was supposed to be 'avoiding stress'. Later on, with hindsight, it all seemed quite simple. The real problem Dave and Skip had, at bottom, was that they didn't fear death enough. Nor did Ian Pool, come to that. There was a valour in that little episode quite beyond the mere shifting of kitchen equipment. Not to mention, of course, the instant, instinctive comradeship that had erupted, the co-operative effort that had worked its curious magic. *Can* faith move mountains? Or lift fridges? At that moment, certainly, it felt like it could.

And it was this optimism, I came to realize, which was the most important thing the scouts would give, in the months to come, to the autistic children.

Because, despite all the equipment at the camp; despite all the scouts' helpfulness and patience; despite the hours they played with the children, the bites they put up with, the kicks, the flying head butts; despite all this, and all the infinite care it took, it was not, in the end, what the scouts did that mattered, it was what they were.

For, in all the cacophony of disagreement about autism, on one point there is consensus: that at the bottom of the autistic child's soul – whatever the reasons – lies a terrible pessimism. Whereas at the heart of Mohawk was an indefatigable hope.

FOUR

The first work with autistic children happened just a few days later: Mohawk's annual trip to the spring carnival in Heerlen, south Holland. Heerlen is Catholic; the carnival celebrates the start of Lent. Mohawk has been sending scouts and autistic children to this event since the seventies.

I'll admit I was surprised. A carnival, of all things? With autistic children? Aren't autistic children above all timid, inclined to hate almost everything one might associate with such a gathering: crowds, noise, chaos, unpredictability? And yet, the troop had been going to these events for a quarter of a century, and each trip has been more successful than the last.

By 8 a.m. on the Thursday of our departure – the carnival was over the following weekend – I joined the scouts at Beckton's Tesco, where they had met for breakfast. More than twenty of us were crowded around three tables in the café: twelve scouts, four adults and five autistic boys, three of whom had stayed overnight at the scouts' London HQ. Ian Pool was there, and Fred Robinson, looking responsible; Troy Northcote and little Pete Pollard; the Cobbett brothers, brown-eyed Johnny and young Tim, with the sticking-out ears; the Smith brothers, plus dazzling smiles. But where, I wondered, were the autistic children?

Slowly I realized that all five were already there. Threaded among the scouts like beads on a string, they were so calm, and had merged in so well, I had taken them for scouts.

Yet gradually, as I observed them more closely, little things stood out. Fourteen-year-old John Coats, for instance, a boy with autism who has been looked after by the troop since he was eleven, walked up to me and extended a crumpled hand, palm downwards. His carer, Troy, explained: 'He's trying to shake hands.' Then there was Peter Bell, dark, pale, snub-nosed. He, too, looked like any other mildly scruffy 11-year-old until you noticed that every so often his face would crumple and collapse, in utter devastation. Peter gets these terrible attacks of homesickness. Then there was 12-year-old David Knebworth, who was sitting between Fred Robinson and little Tim, his carer and gofer respectively. David, soon to be nicknamed 'Dreamy David' by the scouts, had a look, quite distinctive, that is shared by many boys with autism. His strangely beautiful, rather feminine face was pale, poetic, dreamy. Yet David, too, could be deceptive. He was one of those who'd stayed overnight at HQ and for some reason – it might have been nervousness, shyness, even over-excitement – he'd been sick three times during the night. He was only just beginning to settle down.

Added to which David was also, it emerged, 'a runner'. This meant he was one of the autistic kids who would suddenly get up, without warning, and start running blindly away from wherever they were. For this reason, with faultless logic, John had deputed Fred and Tim to look after him. They're the fastest runners in the troop.

Even so, it took an effort to distinguish this noisy, excited group from any other group of holiday-making boys. Which was why, perhaps, when we'd finished eating and begun to load the coach up for the trip, I was lost for a moment when Skip suddenly asked me what I thought of the way the scouts had 'dealt with' Bernard Naisbitt. 'Dealt with'? Who? I didn't even know who Bernard was. Skip pointed him out. No wonder I hadn't noticed him. Not only had I never met him, but he was the most ordinary-looking boy of them all. Fifteen years old, broad-shouldered, funky, with short-cropped hair, he was one of the ones I had been certain was a scout. But then he *was* a scout. For this was the self-same Bernard, the Beckton boy with autism, who had been the only autistic child to have been made a troop member – the one the scouts had written about to the local paper.

And then Skip explained what he had meant. Halfway through the meal, Bernard had had an accident, and filled his pants. The scouts had handled it pretty well, didn't I think? I had to admit I hadn't even noticed. The scouts had acted so quickly, and Bernard had been taken away so unobtrusively, that he had been out of the room within seconds. Later I found out hardly anyone else had noticed it either. Fred had whipped Bernard into the gents, changed his clothes, and brought him back into the café. The soiled clothes had been put into a carrier bag. Then Fred had returned to the café himself, and carried on with his breakfast.

It had been treated as if it were an utterly trivial event. But then, of course, so it was.

The scouts, in fact, had started as they meant to carry on. Shortly after, with much of that mildly irritating crashing about in which small boys specialize, and which adults can never quite pin down enough to do anything about, the scouts loaded themselves and the autistic children on to the coach. They reproduced the café seating plan inside there, too, each autistic child neatly sandwiched between carer and gofer. John Lee, like a sower going forth to sow the seed, walked up and down the central aisle scattering sweets and crisps to grasping hands. Our driver – Dan Knapton's dad, Harry, in his forties, with a grinning, toothy, nervous air – revved up the engine and we were away.

The troop swiftly settled into its travelling mode. A mode in which it feels comfortable, not least because autistic children, especially, love travelling by bus. They were happier still, of course, when we reached Dover and we got on the hovercraft, because there was the breathtaking expanse of the sea, and as we have seen, autistic children love water above all else. They pressed their noses to the hovercraft's windows, shrieked and laughed and pointed at seagulls and ships; their carers put their arms round them, and fed them sweets.

But it was when we landed at Calais that the journey got into its real stride, because we were then into the veritable, serious, 400-mile hike across Europe.

You could almost feel the group, like the coach, get into gear. Once again, emotionally, they recreated the Beckton front room. Some scouts fell asleep; a few adults got out books; the autistic boys dropped, as they so readily do, into their own, daydreaming world, lulled by the steady, reassuring drone of the coach engine. Dreamy David gazed on the passing landscape with the eyes of a seer. Christopher Hope and little Matt Polesden, a new scout, still unsure of himself, formed an alliance of the marginalized and disaffected; they snoozed quietly, heads on each other's shoulders.

Groups formed. Little clusters of four or five peeped over the seats, kneeling backwards, so they could talk to the boys behind. Others leant at grotesque, dangerous angles across the central file, like lizards stretching across a rock.

A group formed right in front of me. It was an alliance of the youngest, or at any rate the smallest, a group who were to become increasingly visible throughout the trip. There was 11-year-old Chris Smith, the boy who wants to teach the disabled. There was 13-year-old Fred Robinson, the one who cleared up after Bernard Naisbitt in the café. There was Chris's 14-year-old brother Nick, the boy with the brilliant grins. Nick is so small he could readily pass for eleven. He's got a growth problem, he says, which he's turning to his advantage – he's training to be a jockey. Little Pete Pollard was yet another boy who looked much younger than his age. Thirteen-years-old, he, too, could have passed for two years younger. With a cheeky-chappy, toothy grin, he was well aware that adults called him 'cute'.

Pete sat up, grinned at his friends, shot a glance at me.

'What made the sea?' he asked.

Good question! Cute, too.

His friends considered this.

'God,' said Nick eventually. 'On the Seventh Day.'

''E never,' said Chris, 'it was the fourteenth day.'

'You're wrong there,' said Pete, 'it was eleven days. The Ten Commandments plus a day of rest.'

'Eh?'

''E done a commandment a day, for ten days. Then he had a day of rest.'

'He never.'

'He *did.*'

Pause.

'Look at them poplars over there,' said Pete. 'Tall, aren't they?'

And then: 'Why do trees grow up?'

Another good question.

'To get to the sun.'

'So why do *we* grow up?'

'So we become adults,' said Chris.

Pete agreed with this. 'If we didn't grow up,' he pointed out, 'we'd grow down, an' that'd mean we'd grow smaller and smaller and, eventually, we'd entirely fade away.' Pete spread his hands: *c'est ça.*

The point settled, the kids fell back into silence. It's amazing how much time kids spend talking like this. Nor are such questions, though quaint, remotely stupid. As Einstein pointed out, all he did throughout his life was ask the same questions children ask. One of his favourites, aged six, was 'What would light look like if you were travelling faster than the speed of light?' The answer, later, gave him his theory of relativity. The only difference between him and anyone else, he said, was that he went on asking such questions throughout his career.

You need other ploys, too, to survive those long, desperate hours on the French motorways. So what to do? Well, what else? Games. These turned out to be a scaled-down version of the warfare games at Camp Mohawk. There's a limit, of course, to how much warfare you can conduct on a coach. Nevertheless arm wrestling went down well, not to mention 'Mercy' where you Chinese-burn each other's arms until one kid gives up. Then there was the most miniature warfare game of all, 'Thumb War'. ('One, two, three, four, we declare thumb war.') You end up, if you're lucky, pulverizing your opponent's thumb.

For the truly desperate, there's always the adults. The trick here is to sit, say, behind your adult and pinch him when he's not looking. When he turns round, you blame it on your mate. He blames it on you. You then blame it, in turn, on the kid the other side of you, who blames it back on your mate. Round and round and up and down, you can go on like this for hours. It's typical, incidentally, of the view kids take of adults: more like dolls than persons, really, to be toyed with or ignored according to whim.

Then, to go with the scaled-down games, there's a scaled-down version of that adult obsession: jokes.

'Two cows in a field,' said Pete. 'First cow turns to the second one. "Moo," she says. Second cow says: "I was just about to say that."'

And so our long journey continued on its bizarre way, until, that is, we got just past St-Omer. And then there arose a question: should we take the A26 south, towards Paris, or cut off earlier at the N42? Come to that, which *was* the N42? Should we turn north or south to get on it? Or were we on it already? Much arguing, arm-waving and looking at the map; much turning the map upside down to see if it didn't look better the other way up. Complete certainty, on Skip's part, that whatever it said on the map he *knew* this was the route, down here! He just *knew* it. In the end we went south. But what struck me, and what was confirmed as the trip unfolded, was that Skip just didn't like maps. They smacked too much of planning. Skip found them claustrophobic.

As it turned out, we needed such insouciance. Because the next thing that happened, around thirty miles further on, was that we broke down. We were off the motorway, trundling happily along the last few laps before our arrival, when suddenly, inexplicably, the bus drove to the side of the road and stopped. It had just started raining and there was, explained Harry the driver, a problem with the wipers.

This was one for the adults. So we got out, sensibly, like adults should; we clustered under the wipers and examined them; there was learned debate. Decisions were made, and tools sent for. Harry Knapton sat inside and pressed the buttons while Skip whacked away a spanner; then Skip sat inside and did some pressing, while Harry whacked away with a screwdriver. At this stage Phil Simpson, the 14-year-old-going-on-30, came wandering up.

Of course, not being an adult, he suggested something absurd. There were two wipers, he pointed out, we only had a few miles to go, so why not get some string, or even a shoelace, tie the wipers together and let the good wiper pull the bad? Ridiculous! said the adults, and tried the screwdriver again and then the spanner, and then a squirter, and then the screwdriver again, and it all failed, and we were still there, and it was raining.

'You really should try the shoelace?' repeated Phil, fluttering his eyelids, with his most appealing grin. So, finally, as much as anything to shut him up, the adults tried it – and lo! the wipers worked at once.

They worked all the way to Heerlen. It was a tricky moment

for the adults – it necessitated a lot of jokes – but the most striking thing was the response of Phil. Far from acting triumphalist, he behaved as if his success was the most natural thing in the world. Indeed, even before we restarted the coach he was down the other end, already interested in something else.

The next morning we awoke in Holland. We had arrived, late in the evening, at a scout hut on the fringe of Heerlen, a small town on the country's very southernmost tip. It's in a small peninsula of land, around 20 miles wide, neatly sandwiched between Belgium and Germany. It's one of those places most English people have never heard of, although it's been at the centre of European history for a century. It was first stop for the German invaders in both world wars.

It was dark when we arrived, so we had no more impression of the place than of a hut in the grounds of what looked like a school, with playing fields nearby. We bedded down on the floor all together in the one, main room, adults, scouts, autistic kids, the lot, the luckier ones with blow-up mattresses underneath their sleeping bags. It was a night of strange noises. This was partly us – the squawks of the autistic kids, the sleeptalk of the scouts, the farts and snores of the adults – but there was, too, this strange, insistent howling of the wind, very Hammer horror movie, very *Wuthering Heights*. The shutters rattled steadily, while a mysterious, slithering, bumping noise came from the roof, as if all-night snooker were being played up there by a gang of super-rats.

In the morning, all was explained. The gale had been a blizzard. The bumping had been the wind. The snow was a foot deep. The police college, improbably, had been transformed into a fairy-tale castle; the parish church, its gaunt, brick towers louring across the valley, looked almost festive. The sun lit up the whole scene like a postcard. The adults peered out of the window and were appalled: the kids took one look at it and were rhapsodic.

The troop prepared for the day. The scouts woke up the children. Ian Pool picked his way through the sleepers and delivered a swooping, plunging kiss on the cheek of John Coats, as he did every day thereafter. The scouts dressed their autistic children. Fred Robinson carefully unpacked David Knebworth's suitcase, raising each item of clothing in front of David and showing it to him before he put it on him. The scouts are trained to do this, so that the autistic children maintain a comforting sense of sequence and control. In the kitchen, a volley of song announced the advent of Skip, standing there in his vest, gold medallion round his neck, frying breakfast for the whole troop.

There were the usual problems. There was, it turned out, just one water tap. Luckily, there were several plastic bowls, and the congestion was solved by filling up the bowls and putting them in a row on a trestle table. A bigger difficulty was that it turned out the local scouts, whose hut we were borrowing, needed to use it that very same night for a meeting. So having turned the whole forty-by-thirty-foot floor into a bivouac, with inflatable beds, bedding, bags, books, board games, footballs and clothes strewn to a depth of two feet, we had to turn it back again. We managed it. Then there was the heating. We couldn't turn it on. The radiators were a mystery. Once again the adults set to. Harry the driver, with much muttering, tried to read the instructions on the radiator switches, which were in Dutch. Then – once again – Phil wandered over. Just a suggestion, he said, but have you considered . . . Predictably, he was turned down. Just as predictably, ten minutes later, Harry tried what Phil suggested, and it worked instantly. Not, incidentally, that adults like Harry are dumb; it's just that kids are better at figuring things out from scratch. They don't 'know' anything, and it helps. Whereas adults have this constant, confusing burden of preconceived ideas.

The kids were right about the snow, too. They knew it was a gift from God. If anything, the autistic kids were more delighted still. For snow is, of course, water, and what water, too: sparkling, glistening, magical. Eventually the adults, lumbering up in the rear, began to realize the joy of it as well, as the whole troop disappeared into the playing fields. The snow had transformed it into a kind of paradise. It was as if a dozen extra games had sprouted from the ground. First, naturally, there was building snowmen; the autistic kids got very keen on this. Then there was a range of skiing games, made possible as we were on a slope. Pete Pollard, plus three other tinies, found an old, wrecked push-bike and started skidding it down the police college drive. The bike was broken, the drive a glacier, but for Pete and his friends, it was wild delight. They made these long, lingering, slow-burn skids down the hill, thirty yards or more, finishing up with a delicious, curling swing to the right to stop. It was incredibly dangerous; it was fantastic fun.

But most of all, of course, there was the snow version of the basic, all-purpose scout game, fighting. The snowballs began whizzing in all directions, an arctic Agincourt. But at this stage the autistic children began to have difficulties. It wasn't the roughness so much as the uncertainty. After all, a snowball fight is not exactly structured. What you do, and when, and why, was a question you could see writ very large indeed on the faces of David Knebworth and John Coats. The very throwing movement, indeed, could create a problem. As so often with autistic kids, you could see them copying the others' actions and getting close, but somehow not managing the full 100 per cent. The movement came out uncertain, spasmodic, jerky, like a first cousin of the real thing. Bernard Naisbitt picked up a tiny bit of snow, tried to throw it, got the rhythm wrong, threw it up in the air, and it landed on his head. Then he stood stock still, alternately shooting little grins and nods and winks, in imitation of the others, and wincing visibly, and giving little starts of fear, every time a snowball came too close.

Eventually, it got too cold to stay outside, and the scouts

were called back in the hut. Now the indoor games began, performed at a cracking, hurtling pace, with the game switching suddenly, disorientatingly, to something else the moment it got dull. There was a kind of handball, which involved rolling a ball backwards through their legs. This involved a good deal of crashing around. There was a game called 'North, South, East, West', rules obscure. It also involved a good deal of crashing around. Ronny Silver, a blond, chirpy autistic boy, seemed mystified by the game itself but enjoyed sitting out once he'd lost. Phil played peekaboo with him and then tickled him on the ribs. Ronny chortled and shrieked and it was one of those moments when you thought to yourself, this child seems no different from any other happy, integrated youngster. But there was a difference. Ronny is eleven; but his behaviour was that of a perfectly happy, integrated child of three.

Little Ronny, like Dreamy David, is part of a distinct style of autism: there are a lot of boys like him, perky, noisy, inclined to tantrums, in many ways quite normal except that they seem to act younger than their age. Come to that, Peter Bell – pale, hypersensitive, inclined to tears – seemed so similar to a range of other boys at Mohawk that he, too, seemed part of a distinct autistic style, a mode of being. Nevertheless it was Dreamy David who attracted everyone's attention that morning. Not only was there his remote, seer-like manner, but his very body looked remarkable. Tall and willowy, he had the svelte, feline movements of a Russian ballet dancer. But in his own way he had as much difficulty as Little Ronny fitting in with the games. One of the stranger games the scouts liked to play was 'Pussy-cat'. In this game, as far as I could figure it, the object was to get down on your knees, pretend to be a cat, go up to another boy and say 'Poor pussy', or 'miaow' – more or less anything cat-like, really. But the challenge, the real point of the game, was not merely to say this but to avoid laughing while saying it. No easy thing to do.

The hard part for the scouts, understandably, was not to laugh. The hard part for the autistic children was to grasp the basic idea, just the kind of double entendre their literal minds find hardest of all. So when Fred started playing 'Pussy-cat' with David Knebworth, he explained that he would just try to get David to say something, anything, pussyish, and leave it at that.

The kneeling-down went fine; where David began to have difficulty was with the words. 'I'll tell you what, David,' said Fred, making it easier. 'Just say miaow.'

Silence.

'Go on mate,' said Fred, getting down on his knees himself, hands raised up like paws. 'Just like a little pussy-cat: miaow!'

Still silence.

'Look,' said Fred, patiently, 'why not try it very very softly, just a tiny, weenie sound like this . . .' He breathed 'miaoww . . .'

David eyed him thoughtfully. Fred leant over towards him encouragingly, hand cupping his ear. There was a further pause. A light flashed in David's eyes.

'MIAOOOOWWWWW!!!!!!!!!!!!!!!' he shrieked, at something over a hundred decibels. Fred tumbled backwards as if shot.

Perhaps it was natural that the first day should be frantic. The days that followed, certainly, were calmer, and Mohawk once again dropped into a rhythm.

Inevitably the weather meant we spent a lot of time inside, and the place gradually took on a low-key, Sunday afternoon feel: the adults, sitting about in a little room just off the main hall; the boys, once again, split up into groups, some chatting, some reading comics, some playing games. The autistic children seemed somehow semi-detached. Sometimes the scouts would involve them. Sometimes they would sit on the edge of a scouts' group, and go through the form of involvement – imitating the scouts' movements, gestures, odd phrases even – without the substance. Other times they would sit, quite openly, on their own.

At times like this the scouts seemed to respect their solitude and made no attempt to force them to join in.

One afternoon I came into the scouts' room to see Peter Bell sitting on his own, the other side of the room, facing the wall. He was drawing; he looked totally absorbed. In the opposite corner, on the floor, sat Rob Ferndown, Peter's carer. Rob is a plump, black kid of fourteen, deeply into music. Rob was the boy who did the Indian war dance at the Christmas fund-raiser. He was piecing together a railway set that Peter had brought with him. He was making no attempt, at this stage, to involve Peter.

Peter went on colouring on his own. Sitting at his table, facing away from the rest of the scouts, he had made himself a little nest. He had his tape player there, his crayon box, his books. He looked lonely. I walked over to him and peered over his shoulder.

He glanced up, expressionless. If anything, he looked slightly offended, like an old-fashioned chief clerk, say, disturbed at his work. He carried on drawing. Peter has a classic autistic obsession; he is passionately interested in railways, and this was what he was working on. But his 'drawing', it turned out, was actually writing. It was no ordinary writing; it looked more like a page from a medieval manuscript. Each line was written in beautiful calligraphy, each sentence in different colours: red, green, purple, blue. But the subject matter was not medieval. Peter had written:

Sir Nigel Gresley
Duchess of Hamilton
Iron Duke
Mallard

They were all names of famous, old-time steam locomotives.

It was remarkable, and, I thought, a bit of stuff on which I might build a conversation. For I had experienced something of Peter's enthusiasm myself, when I was nine. My father had given me a Hornby-dublo electric train for Christmas, and the engine, a dark rich metallic blue, had been Sir Nigel Gresley. I'd loved it; that train set had given me a truly deep, Christmas sense of luxury. I remember hugging the locomotive to my chest, even kissing it. Surely Peter and I had something in common.

I said: 'I used to have an engine called Sir Nigel Gresley. They're beautiful, aren't they?'

And again, Peter, very briefly, looked up; again, if anything, he looked slightly, almost superciliously pained. He went back to his work.

I watched a little longer, smiling foolishly, then tried again.

'The Mallard,' I said, 'didn't that look rather like the Sir Nigel Gresley?'

This time the chief clerk actually sighed; and very swiftly and efficiently, without saying anything, he picked up his book and his crayons and moved over to the opposite end of the room. I wasn't *certain* he was avoiding me, so I followed him. The moment I reached him, without saying anything, and with an almost balletic rhythm and sense of inevitability, he moved quietly and efficiently back to where he'd been before.

Now finally the message was clear. Even so I couldn't quite leave it alone. Next time I walked past Peter I didn't speak to him, but feeling I should at least be friendly, I simply shot him another rather wet, uncertain smile. And his time he did react: he grimaced back. He gave me a perfect parody, complete with affectation, of the smile I had given him. But then my smile had, of course, been essentially false. It was more what I thought I should have done than what I really felt. It was as if Peter, from some remote watchtower of his mind, had seen straight through me and was punishing my hypocrisy.

Meanwhile, Pete Pollard was watching this little pas de deux with amusement. 'I wouldn't worry, mate,' he said. 'He doesn't talk to anyone. Hang about, I tell a lie, he does speak to his mother. But no one else.'

And Rob carried on building the track the other side of the room, awaiting his moment.

Pete Pollard's remark had touched on something crucial, something I was to see a lot more of over the summer. And that was the strange fluidity, even subjectivity, of apparently clear and well-established autistic symptoms. Peter's talking was a fine example, because, it turned out later, it wasn't only with his mother that he lost his speechlessness. It had happened at the camp, too. Of course, predictably enough, it had happened with Rob. Peter didn't talk much, said Rob – mainly about trains – but he wasn't dumb. More surprisingly, it had happened with a student volunteer called Diana, who'd worked at Mohawk the previous summer. With her, at first, Peter had once again been speechless; and then, one evening, he had one of his recurrent, devastating attacks of homesickness, and was in floods of tears. Naturally, Diana had been sympathetic; more surprisingly, perhaps, she seems to have got through to him, for he had seemed touched. And he had started talking to her there and then. And then he went on talking with her throughout the camp. So one thing was plain: there was nothing 'physical' or hard-wired about this autistic symptom of Peter's. Rather, at the deepest possible level, it seemed a matter of trust.

Not that trust seemed much of a problem for the other 11-year-olds on the trip, the scouts. Like most kids they were naturally friendly, once they felt reassured by some small, if sometimes esoteric, event. In my case, the breakthrough came when I dropped something on my foot and started swearing. At that moment, Fred told me, the scouts reckoned I was all right. Indeed, their giving or withholding of trust seemed almost a question of taste, of whether or not they felt it was the right environment for self-revelation to occur. Some times and places suited, others didn't.

What were not suitable, curiously, were moments when adults

and children were alone together. When, say, you had gone off site together to go shopping. Sometimes they would talk frankly at such moments, but just as likely they would close down. It was as if they felt the situation too loaded, too highly charged – as they did, indeed, if I ever committed the outrage of sitting down with a notebook and trying to do the thing formally. What they liked were moments when we might find ourselves alone by accident, or even where our privacy was somehow disguised – typically, for instance, on the bus. For here, to all outward appearance, we were part of a group. And yet, if you ended up sitting next to each other on one of the coach seats, you were, in practice, sitting in private. At that moment they would start talking with surprising freedom about their hopes and worries; about how their dad nearly died of an illness, or their mum might be going to prison, or how the thing they especially liked about working with autistic children (a 13-year-old, this) was how it prepared you for fatherhood.

Such conversations could be happy, or sad, or funny, or all three. One day I was sitting on my own in the adults' room when Joe Beckford came in. Joe is a cheery, moon-faced 12-year old, shaped like a barrel. It was around three in the afternoon and there was nothing much on. Joe was plainly bored, so bored in fact he was prepared to resort to desperate measures, i.e. talking with an adult. So even though we hardly knew each other he sat down opposite and began to chat. When he started he probably thought he'd stay two minutes; in the end, he stayed three-quarters of an hour.

'This is the first time I've ever been away from me mum for a length of time,' he said. 'She'll miss me. There's five of us in the family, the oldest is sixteen but she's a gel an' I'm the oldest boy and I think me mum finds me special.

'The first time I was away I done a weekend camp at Mohawk and when I got home she'd bought me all these gifts, she got me a new video recorder and a pair of trainers and a tracksuit and a coat, they cost £150. She'd even redecorated my room, she missed me that much.

'She done it all West Ham, see, that's my team. She done me a West Ham lampshade, and a West Ham lamp, and a West Ham bed and West Ham flags on the wall. She done it all in West Ham colours, blue and white and mauve, and she done me a West Ham carpet, too. Well, I say a carpet, more of a rug really, it's got this big West Ham badge on it, it's lovely. Well, it *was* lovely – until our dog bit the corner out of it, that is. He's a Staff, see, that's what they're like, and what made it worse was he got lockjaw, his jaw locked on to the rug and we couldn't get him off it. We had to send for the vet to give him an injection, before he'd let go.

'Me mum's smashing, but me dad's great, too. E's a lorry driver. 'Is dad was a lorry driver and *'is* dad too, *and* 'is dad, going right back into the mists of time. You could say I come from a long line of lorry drivers, and guess what I'm going to do when I grow up? You guessed it: lorry driver. It's a family tradition, isn't it? But, as I say, I get on really well with me dad. When my birthday comes e's going to give me this gold bracelet with me name on it an' this set of golf clubs an' we're goin' to play a round of golf together, part of the gift. And when he dies he's going to leave me his car, and his jewels – his bracelet, and his necklace, and his ring. He's going to leave me his golf clubs, too, but I won't use 'em, I'll keep 'em, look after 'em like, keep 'em clean, in his memory.

'We're a very close-knit family. We're always seeing me aunts and uncles and me mum says whatever you do Joe, when you grow up, you keep seeing your family, you have 'em round every weekend, just like we do, and I say to her, I will, mum, I will, I promise you, and I can tell you, I really will. Because I'm really fond of my family. As I say, there's five of us, three gels an' one other boy apart from me, that's me brother Freddie, he's two.

'He's a weird baby, to be honest. He's advanced for his age. He walked before he crawled, he ran before he walked – he even walked up the stairs. I look after him a lot and, to be honest wiv yer, I've learned a lot of things that have come in really useful with the autistic kids – how to do nappies and play with him and wash him and put him on the potty and all that.

'Because this is it, it all stands you in such good stead with the autistic kids. It prepares you. And I really like working with the kids. I'm gofering for Peter Bell right now. He's a lovely kid, Peter is. Misses 'is mum, though, something chronic. So I cuddle him and that cheers him up.

'He's a lovely little boy. He's really bright. He can spell these really big words, like responsibility, words I couldn't spell for me life. And trains? He loves trains. We took him to the beach once and, even there, he made this sand castle in the shape of a train. His mum sent these presents out with him, a present a day for all the days we're out here, just to cheer 'im up and most of them were train things, Thomas the Tank Engine an' all that. No, I don't think that's spoiling him. If it makes him happy, so what?

'I think you should give kids what they want. I'm going to have – now let me see – four kids when I grow up and my opinion is, whatever they want I'll give them. If they want it, and I've got it, they can have it. It's as simple as that.

'The only thing I haven't got right now is a motorbike. All right, you think I'm a bit young for that, twelve years old an' all? I tell you mate, my friends have got 'em. Their dads buy 'em these little bantam motorbikes, real engines, mind, and they ride 'em down the street. Drives the police potty. They chase 'em, but the kids drive down these alleyways where the bikes can go but the squad cars can't. They're too wide, aren't they, and whammo, one flick of the bike's accelerator and the kids are gone.'

Eventually Joe got bored and wandered off. Need one add that Joe is regarded as one of the very best carers on the camp?

By the weekend, however, boys like Joe had proper entertainment, for the carnivals had started. The Heerlen neighbourhood is full of carnivals at this time of year, its Lent celebrations are spectacular. We went to three: two processions and a party at a school for the disabled. They all involved the most elaborate dressing up. Indeed, the Dutch revealed a wholehearted enthusiasm for doing things right, down to the most remote, esoteric detail, that reminds you that this part of Holland is quite as much German as Dutch.

The party in the school, for instance, was themed to the tropics, and each protagonist had given it their all. There were khaki jackets and shorts naturally, and sun helmets carefully intertwined with tropical greenery. In addition there were the most elaborate battery of props: rifles, pistols, binoculars, maps, you name it. You could just imagine the rigour with which they'd hunted it all down. And as the guests linked arms and sang, big, lusty, reverberating folk songs, this complicated kit swayed and jangled on some of the largest human beings I have ever seen. For the Dutch are as big physically as they are big-hearted. Everything about Holland, indeed, is *big*: their food, their furniture, their arms, their legs. This compulsive gigantism, this thunder-thighed spirit of place somehow permeates the land.

Nevertheless, it was Heerlen's main carnival for which we'd come, and throughout the Sunday morning, we made, in the authentic Heerlen spirit, elaborate preparations of our own. Predictably, the animal suits from Christmas had been brought over, but a whole, other range of clown costumes had been magicked forth as well. We spent the morning getting into them and, then, to the delight, especially, of the autistic boys, putting make-up on our faces. First was a white powder as a base, then face paintings, at which several of the scouts turned out to be strangely adept.

It was curious how naturally the boys seemed to drop into their carnival characters. Pete Pollard, mischievous as ever, found himself a jester's hat and bells. Troy Northcote, dressed as a clown, still managed to maintain his streetwise élan. His cone-shaped hat sat at just the perfect angle on his head, neither too upright nor too jaunty, while his trousers fitted as if he had been poured into them. More remarkable still were the autistic boys. Dreamy David, also dressed as a clown, looked more like a Russian ballet dancer than ever. Then there was Bernard Naisbitt, the autistic boy who was also a scout. With his uncertain, hovering manner, his smile that seemed to cover such depths of sadness, he appeared – he was dressed as Harlequin – straight out of Picasso.

And yet, as ever, the autistic boys had only half-grasped what was going on. For all the strange appropriateness of his outfit, Bernard Naisbitt looked bemused. As so often with autistic boys he seemed to parrot what the other boys were doing, as if he could only ever do the right thing, socially, by imitation. So Bernard was nodding, grinning and even laughing out loud because, one sensed, this was what he thought the situation demanded. Yet it was all strangely abstract, unrelated to anything in particular. One time I saw Bernard doing a little shuffle-shoe dance, and for a moment he looked genuinely self-sufficient. Then I realized he was imitating Troy Northcote, on the other side of the room.

It was strangely reminiscent of the phenomenon called 'echolalia' in which autistic children repeat back the words others have said. That is, parroting, without understanding. Although one phenomenon involves movement, the other speech. Then there's a similar parallel between movement and speech in the syndrome of the autistic 'near miss'. Back at the first Mohawk camp I ever attended, little Omar would say it was 'snowing' when he meant it was 'raining', or would point out 'twigs' in a tree, when what he meant to say was 'leaves'. Many of us have experienced something similar in ourselves, when stressed.

It was as if he'd got his mind into the right general ballpark, but had failed with the final fine-tuning.

Well, here in Heerlen, you could see something similar in the way the autistic children moved. I was walking across the room when David Knebworth suddenly leapt at me, with a high pitched shriek, and aimed a blow. For a moment I had no idea what he was doing, and then I grasped it. Dressed up as a clown, he was, he felt, doing the appropriate, clownish things; but they hadn't come out quite right. Nearly, but not quite. The jump was more like an assault, the cry, like a scream. So very nearly right. A near miss.

Not that the autistic kids seemed too bothered. But then, as I began to realize, they could drink in atmosphere even when mystified by social mechanics, and they seemed to pick up easily on the scouts' characteristic, infectious jollity. Because the scouts, it's fair to say, are carnival naturals. We took the bus into town, parked, and as we walked in through the side streets we quickly fused with the partying Dutch. The streets were empty but this was, it soon became clear, because they were all in the bars, which were overflowing with gargantuan men dressed up as animals, thunder-thighed women dressed up as milkmaids, lions, tigers, bears, fairies, crocodiles, devils and angels, all drinking breathtaking quantities of beer, all guzzling huge sausages laced with the sweetest, sickliest cream I have ever tasted. It instantly became hugely popular with the scouts. Each bar erupted with banging, re-echoing, Germanic oompah drinking songs of the 'Ein, zwei, und . . . boomsadaisy!' persuasion. The locals seemed very fond of English tunes, too: 'Roll out ze barrel!/Let's 'ave ze barrel of fun!' was very popular.

Battered by the din I bailed out, momentarily, on to the pavement, where I was buttonholed by a large, brown-furred bear, paralytic with drink, who'd spotted I was English. He was feeling evangelical.

'Carnival,' explained the bear, 'is about identity, about finding out who you are.' A surprising view, on the face of it, for a bear, though he went on to explain that carnival lets you explore aspects of yourself you might otherwise avoid. However, he continued, carnival was changing these days, and not always for the best. 'Zere are zose,' he said darkly, 'who zink all is about food and drink, and chasink ze pretty girls.' He lurched out of my eyeline for a moment; he lurched back. 'But these are people from the north, from Amsterdam, who are coming down here with their city ways and their swingink lives and no, they do not understand the true spirit of carnival. Because ze true spirit of carnival is . . .' I never did find out, because one final lurch took him back into the bar and out of my life for ever.

But then it seemed plain enough what carnival was about: the most tremendous, exuberant, wholehearted binge imaginable. It involved everyone in town. There were, it turned out, special seats kept for us, on a large stand that overlooked where the carnival procession would end. Opposite, on the other side of the road, was the grandstand for the local elite. And they had no intention of being left out. Even those wearing suits wore bright red festival hats, which looked, to an English eye, like the hat worn by Punch. Others, unabashed, were in full costume: There was a pirate, a Pluto, a Puss, complete with Boots, and they greeted each other with smacking, resounding kisses. One tried hard to imagine English councillors doing the same thing, but one just couldn't conjure up the moment. With their huge, fleshy, heavy-lidded faces they fell somewhere between Falstaff and the Laughing Cavalier. Many of their children were dressed up, too. One exquisite little girl of about eight, bubbling with excitement, looked a poem in a jerkin and Sheikh of Araby pantaloons. She was aware of it, too; she strutted and preened.

Come to that, several of the burghers looked remarkably like Skip and it was then that I noticed yet another English song striking up nearby, a song that was to reoccur throughout the day.

What?! Were my ears deceiving me? Wasn't that 'Yes! We Have No Bananas!' in Dutch? And so it turned out, the oldest, most raucous cockney song of all. And from thereon we heard it everywhere, in bars, from bands, in the parade throughout the day. The Dutch, it turned out, loved it better even than the English.

At that moment I realized that, whatever the surface rationale, the troop had yet another of their subliminal motivations for being there. True, they'd got to know the Dutch scouts at a conference in the mid-seventies; the carnivals had sounded fun; these were great holidays. So far, so rational. But there was a deeper, more instinctive reason why they came, in deepest winter, to this remote and unheard of corner of southern Holland. It was because here was possibly the last place in Europe where there were people as raucous as themselves, as fun-loving, larger-than-life or, as Skip would put it: 'wholehearted'. They liked the Dutch, in fact, in the original sense of the word. They were like them.

So we settled into our seats, and opposite us, with much kissing, laughing and back slapping, the Dutch burghers settled in theirs, and round the corner came the first of what turned out to be a massive parade. Boomf! Boomf! Boomf! Boomf! Hey! Hey! Hey! Hey! Float after float after float after float, with kids dressed up as mice, cats, dogs, rabbits and sheep, adults dressed up as Vikings, women done up in baggy Eastern trousers. These last were very popular, presumably because they had a nice, lascivious carnival feel. The most spectacular float of all, one that looked even more suggestive than the rest, involved a mass of devils in tights and tails, and in their middle, the head devil and an angel on a huge mechanical see-saw. They were going up and down in a way that looked, without your being able to exactly put your finger on it, extraordinarily sexual. The burghers laughed and cheered and shouted, arms round each other's shoulders; the beer glasses swayed, from left to right, many feet back and forth; while, to the delight of both kids and adults, each float that came round showered sweets on the spectators. Kids rushed around furiously picking them up; more surprisingly, in a sudden childhood reversion, so did the adults. They ruthlessly elbowed each other out of the way. One little old man, who'd clearly seen a carnival or two, stood there with his umbrella inverted, like a giant cup, netting sweets by the score.

Boomf! Boomf! Boomf! Boomf! Hey! Hey! Hey! Hey! The scouts, diving furiously around to catch the sweets, loved every minute of it while Skip, a stirring sight that day in red nose and orange wig, looked in his element. But you couldn't help wondering about the poor autistic kids, notably John Coats, who was said to dislike sudden noises. I eyed them carefully. John Coats, as it turned out, looked perfectly OK. Little Ronny, chuckling and gurgling like a three-year-old, looked delighted. Only Peter Bell looked distressed. After a bit, he froze, with his hands over his ears; then his face crumpled once again into utter devastation, and at this moment Skip and a couple of scouts took him off to a McDonald's across the road.

The scouts, meanwhile, were getting on better than ever. They'd twigged that while many of the sweets thrown were indeed caught, still more were missed, and tended to drop down under the stand we were sitting on, between the planks. The best pickings of all were down there. You could see them – the younger ones that is, Pete Pollard, the Smith brothers, the usual suspects – six feet below, scurrying about like chickens, until suddenly, mysteriously, they disappeared.

Where had they gone? The parade came to an end. With much last-minute swaying and backslapping, the burghers packed up and started to go home. With the other adults I slowly jostled my way back down the street, carried along by a roaring, surging, delighted Dutch crowd. Suddenly, the little ones reappeared, all staggering under vast hoards of sweets. Moments later Nick Smith was walking beside me, and one of those strange, accidental intimacies occurred.

He was rhapsodic and, gazing upward, with his brilliant grin, he told his story.

The reason the kids had vanished, he said, was that while the pickings underneath our stand had indeed been excellent, the eagle-eyed Pete Pollard had noticed an even better source of sweets across the way, beneath the stand of the elite. So they'd decamped across the street. The explanation was simple: the people in the procession were local citizens and they wanted to keep in with the burghers. So they threw more sweets at them than at anyone else.

Nor was this all. (Another brilliant grin.) Nick had done especially well. He'd used his carnival hat as a giant bag, and filled it up. And then, just as he was about to scarper with his loot, he'd seen Heerlen's Lady Mayoress heading towards him. Panic! Maybe they weren't supposed to be under the stands at all! So with no more ado he stuck his hat, sweets and all, on his head; when the Lady Mayoress passed by, he was empty handed.

'Poor little English boy!' the Mayoress had said. 'All those sweets, and you have nothing!'

And she made him stretch out his jacket to make a basket and she fished out every last sweet she had about her person, a golden shower of treasure into his lap. 'Thank you, thank you, ma'am, for being so kind to a poor little English boy!' cried Nick, and scampered off.

A brilliant grin.

It was no surprise that the scouts loved the carnival. As we have seen, it was right in their psychological territory. More surprising was the response of the autistic children. For they, too, looked vaguely, if a touch uncomprehendingly, happy. Even Peter, the only one who had actually fled the scene, achieved something that day. Because his visit to McDonald's, it emerged, was a first.

Like a lot of autistic children he was a desperately pernickety eater and would normally refuse to go near any such place. Yet he'd sat there with Skip and the scouts quite happily chomping away.

Nevertheless, there was little doubt who, out of all our party, had got the least out of the procession. So we began wondering, more or less consciously, how we could cheer young Peter up.

That evening, Rob, who had been setting up Peter's railway set, finally finished it – and realized the engine needed batteries. He hadn't got any. He told me and I mentioned it to Skip. Skip, who'd hired a car locally for the duration, said he'd go into town later and buy some.

And nothing happened. I thought Skip had forgotten it, but I'd reckoned without his unusual sense of time. It was a bit like ordering something from a Portuguese waiter. It comes eventually, but only when you're finally *sure* he's forgotten it. It must have been an hour later when Skip suddenly said why didn't I come into Heerlen with him, to get the batteries. And off we went, to a shop on the outskirts. We took the toy engine, to make sure the batteries would fit.

We bought them, and for twenty minutes at least Skip sat in his car, fiddling away, trying to fit them. 'I give up,' he said finally. 'Rob will do it.' Rob? 'Yeah, Rob. You'd be surprised. Kids are very good like that.' There was no urgency, no irritation in his voice; he seemed quite certain all would be well. Then he pointed out we were right near the German border. So, on the spur of the moment, he took me up there to have a look. It was less than thrilling, just a hut and a roadblock in a flat landscape. Nevertheless, we stayed half an hour and drove slowly back, and once again I was struck by Skip's relaxation. He'd been in no hurry to make the trip, yet had always meant to. He wasn't bothered when we wasted twenty minutes trying to fit the batteries. He'd found all the time in the world for our further jaunt. What was it the philosopher said? 'Time is anxiety.'

Skip was, incidentally, quite right about Rob. Later on, without much hope, I gave Rob the batteries. I explained the problem. If an adult couldn't do it, I thought, why should Rob, bright though he was, succeed? I sat ten yards away and watched him. And now Rob, too, began fiddling around, to little avail. Then he paused, and then he had another go. Suddenly, the engine slipped out of his hand, and fell with a crash on to the floor. He picked it up. The batteries were in place.

Skip, coincidentally, had been watching. He chuckled. 'See what I mean?'

To cap it all, when Rob finally presented the finished railway train, complete with batteries, to Peter he wasn't interested. But Rob reacted with the same equanimity as Skip, and by then it was nearly bedtime anyway, and the scouts began to close down for the day.

As every evening, out came the wash bowls, the sleeping bags and the rugs, and we lay down, like bivouacking soldiers, all around the room. I ended up, as I did every night, lying next to Troy Northcote, the neat-looking streetwise boy with the flair for clothes. And lying like this alongside a kid in a room full of nineteen others was, of course, yet another of those disguised moments of intimacy when the scouts would talk.

He was a curious kid, Troy; quick, witty, intelligent. Yet, as so often, he'd been a handful at the carnival that day, always on the very verge of an incident. One memorable day later in the summer, I was in charge of Troy's group on a visit to Beale Park, a wildlife park just outside Reading. He picked up rabbits by their ears, chased geese around their pen, and jumped on and off the miniature railway so often that the conductor stopped the train. Yet now, in a change of character as marked as if I was talking to a different boy, he described to me how he was writing a year-long diary of the troop for his school, and wondered if I'd help him edit it, you know, sort out any problems with grammar, punctuation, that sort of thing?

I'd be delighted, naturally. And then, as if encouraged, Troy said: 'Ian, do your kids miss you when you're here?' I have two girls, aged seven and four.

'Yes, they do,' I said, 'and I miss them, too.'

Troy considered this. 'I miss my mum,' he said suddenly. 'I miss her terribly. And I know she misses me.'

That was all he said, and yet the boy who was talking to me at that moment was a different child from the one who had been creating mayhem earlier. But was it really so surprising? And weren't the two things connected? Troy's original dad had 'left me', as he put it – one noted the 'me' – when he was a year old and he has become hugely dependent on his mother. It's hardly surprising that he sometimes feels disturbed. More interestingly, Troy turns out to be yet another scout who's somehow turned such sadness to advantage. For it seems to have given him a special empathy with autistic children. He is one of the camp's star carers. He needs, and thrives on, such depth, and seriousness, of relationship. In London, too, he regularly visits the disabled. And that's quite separate from his work with Mohawk.

The weekend finished. Monday was the 6th of March. The skies cleared, and as the sun appeared, the snow vanished and the first distant breath of spring came to Heerlen, as it had a week earlier in the UK. Suddenly you could see crocuses, yellow, gold and blue, along the edge of the police college drive. The playing fields were tufted with new spring grass. There were daffodils in the woods below the church. Perhaps it was something in the air, some wild, seasonal exuberance, but now Skip had another of his inspirations. 'I know what we'll do,' he said. 'We'll go to France.'

France! This seemed wild indeed. We were currently in Holland, we had to cross Belgium to get to France, and we were due back in England the very next day, Tuesday. Even so, there wasn't much doing in Heerlen. The carnivals, the local ones anyway, were already finished and in France there was, of course, the troop's new base, at Bucquoy in the valley of the Somme, where we would be headed. The truth was, as ever, that there was an emotional reason behind it. And in this case, surely, it was that Skip was in love with Bucquoy, not to mention the local French villagers, who reminded him, he said, of Londoners forty years ago.

Skip had bought the Bucquoy farmhouse two years previously. True, it was still in the process of being converted. Weren't all the scouts' buildings? But it was sufficiently finished that the scouts had dormitories to sleep in. And the adults had their own rooms – and even beds! After five days of sleeping on bare boards in the snow the adults, notably one Cotton, began showing sudden enthusiasm for this France lark, once they'd twigged about the beds.

So the decision, instinctive as ever, was duly made. The Mohawk machine started on its brisk and efficient process of packing up. By late afternoon the scout hut was clear. The coach was loaded with our baggage, including, notably, several crates of beer and great cartons of that fatal, sickly local 'cream' which turned out, in fact, to be curry sauce. Then we were off.

And after the customary, eccentric processes of a Mohawk journey – the rows, the games, the kids sleeping one on top of another, the jokes ('two fish in a tank: one says to the other, who's driving this fing?') – we finally made it into France. Late Monday evening, Pegasus started threading its way, in pitch darkness, along the last of the lanes leading into Bucquoy.

The joy of that bedroom in the farmhouse! I shared it with Harry the driver. Even the thunderous snores with which the two of us shook the rafters couldn't prevent us sleeping blissfully till morning. We woke to find ourselves in a large, redbrick building, shaped as a quadrangle and fronting on the high street. You entered through two vast, Babylonian gates, twelve feet by ten of solid wood each, which led into the courtyard. On the far side was the farmhouse, which had been turned into living quarters for the adults. On the right hand were the barns, which now, converted, housed the scouts. On the left hand were the outhouses, still unconverted, but for which Skip, as usual, had elaborate plans. The upper floors of the barn block had been turned into dormitories which, with the single rooms, could accommodate up to eighty visitors. There was a large green field at the back, for games.

No sooner had we breakfasted than we were on the move again, because there was no other real reason for our visit than the mere joy of a night in France. Skip takes any excuse to go to Bucquoy; he often flees over there for weekends. However, there was one final event before we left. Skip had arranged for us all to have lunch in a local restaurant, Le Poppy in Pozieres, eight miles to the south.

Pozieres was the scene of some of the most desperate fighting during the Battle of the Somme, and this was, of course, why the restaurant, with an eye on English visitors, was called Le Poppy. But the really striking thing about our lunch, the last meal of the trip, was how it mirrored the very first. For once again, as the scouts and the autistic children sat down together, it was nearly impossible to tell them apart. We were ending the trip as we had begun, a group of boys on holiday, friends, first of all, rather than carers and disabled. And you could sense the richness of the event for everyone, scouts, autistic children and grown-ups, especially for the many boys in the troop who hadn't spent that much time abroad.

The fresh white tablecloths, the adults with their red wine, the uniquely French spruceness of the waiters, all combined to create that familiar Mohawk atmosphere of opulence and good fun. And, as ever, spontaneity was at the heart of it. It had been the right idea at the right moment. Even though we were supposed to be hurrying home, we had somehow found time.

But then, of course, we did have time; the fantasy would have been to think we didn't. We were only sixty miles short of Calais, and it wasn't much of a run up to the coast, as long as we got our ferry time right. So it was with a comfortable, end-of-holiday expansiveness that we got on to the coach and headed north. A feeling that was compounded, for me, when Rob dropped into the next seat on the coach and started chatting.

I asked him about Peter Bell, who Rob had been looking after. Had Peter ever been really happy, throughout the trip? I'd noticed how uninterested he'd been in the train set when Rob finally got it going. After all that preparation! It must have been depressing.

'Not really,' said Rob.

After a moment he said: 'Why do you say Peter's always unhappy?'

'Well,' I said, 'I've never seen him smile.'

'He often smiles,' said Rob. 'He's often happy.' Peter was happy, said Rob, when he was doing his drawings, when he was eating breakfast. He was really happy when he was looking at his Thomas the Tank Engine books. Indeed, said Rob, his enthusiasm growing as he spoke, Peter was a great kid, really clever. Did I realize how well he could read? He'd been reading to Rob, he was that good. Oh, and some people thought Peter never talked, or only talked to his mother. Well, all Rob could say was that Peter talked to him all right. Rob sat there with a fond, appreciative look, searching for the phrase to sum it all up. 'He's such a . . . lovely little boy,' he said at last, and there was that phrase again, the eternally reoccurring leitmotif of the scouts.

It was a reminder, as well, of that other reality in which the boys lived, so different from my strictly adult perception. And by implication, too, of the alternative character Peter, too, lived out when he was spending time with someone of his own age he could trust. No wonder, as I was to discover later, that his parents found him transformed after every Mohawk visit.

They only wished, they said, he could spend several weeks with Mohawk every year, but there just wasn't room on the Mohawk courses.

As ever, it had been a pleasure to hear a scout talking about his boy. As we sped towards Calais, I found myself feeling one of those surges of optimism that came so frequently at Mohawk. Outside, the late afternoon sun lay across the Pas de Calais landscape, while we all dropped into a late afternoon doze. Two seats ahead Ian Pool was sitting beside Little Ronny, dropping kisses periodically on Ronny's head. Opposite sat Christopher Hope and Matt Polesden, leaning against each other's shoulders, asleep. Round came John every now and again, with his smile, his drinks and his sweets.

On and on we rolled, and the flat, hypnotic landscape slid past, the lines of pylons, the long, straight, placid canals, all touched and gilded by the evening sun. We reached the outskirts of Calais. You could see the coast in the distance, we were just a mile or two from the docks. Then, mysteriously, without any apparent reason, the coach suddenly slowed, pulled in to the side, coughed and chugged, and stopped.

There was silence, a hubbub of voices, and then the news. Just a mile from Calais, after driving halfway across Europe, we'd broken down. The driver revved up the engine: lots of noise, but no movement. He revved it again: same result. The clutch had gone. Skip, who had been in the coach loo when we broke down, appeared at the door. We told him what had happened. 'Friginell,' said Skip.

Off he went to the front of the coach and started ringing up everyone in northern France: the French police, the French equivalent of the AA, the highway police, the French equivalent of the RAC. The minutes ticked by, and the cars whizzed past. The lorries thundered up behind and pulled out to overtake us at the last minute because, although we had pulled on to the hard shoulder, we were on a motorway. We were trickily placed on a slope and a right-hand bend, by no means where one would have pulled in by choice, especially in a coach.

Yet try as Skip might, he couldn't get anyone to rescue us. Clearly the police, at least, would have to come out eventually. Meanwhile, with twelve scouts and five autistic children on board, our position was perilous.

And then occurred one of those Mohawk moments that make some people think the troop's watched over by God. Yet another lorry passed us, but this one wasn't a lorry, it was a bus. It drew up in front of us and stopped. It had UK number plates. Out got the driver and walked back. He poked his head through Harry's window. He was short and broad, built like a refrigerator. He'd stopped to help.

The briefest of exchanges, and coach driver Dave Green, from Ratby in Leicestershire, offered to put all the kids on his coach and take them to the ferry. There was no time to lose. The kids, led by John and the adults, moved out in groups, swift and controlled, down on to the kerbside and into the new bus. Soon, only Skip was left in Pegasus, with the eternally loyal Ian Pool sitting up in front beside him; the rest of us, on Skip's strict orders, were on our way back to the UK.

Within an hour we were on the ship. At Dover we were met by a new, hired coach, and were in London within two hours, as if the breakdown had never happened. On the ship Dave Green had pointed out that we were even luckier than we knew. He'd broken down himself a few hours earlier – a problem with the gear pedal he had fixed himself – and if that hadn't happened he'd never have come along when he did. We could have been stuck there on that hard shoulder for hours.

Like Skip says: 'I always seem to find a man like that.'

The other striking thing about the episode was the way Skip

coped. He was always dauntless, whatever the crisis, but there were many times when he'd get het up. Yet in this case, outwardly at least, he hardly seemed fraught. But perhaps that was not so mysterious. It was Troy who'd noticed, back at the camp, that Skip could get furious at little things, and react calmly to the big. But that was because it was not the event itself that dictated his reaction, but how he felt about it. And the arch-question, always, was did it make him feel dispensable. And in this particular cliffhanger one thing, certainly, was plain: for half an hour we were all truly dependent, for very life and limb, on Skip. He was indispensable. And so, despite all difficulties, he was at peace.

However, even Skip got stretched over the next few days. Though the troop got home easily, it was harder for him and Ian. By the time they'd been towed off the motorway, arranged for the repair and crossed the Channel, it was two o'clock in the morning. And when the final bill came in – for the rescue, the coach hire, and the odds and ends – it was over £3,000.

The troop simply didn't have that kind of money. However, by coincidence, a few days later Skip went to see a City firm, which had been a long-time Mohawk supporter, about a possible gift of furniture. While there, he got talking with some staff members about the latest financial crisis. And, as sometimes happens with Skip, he finished up in tears.

The word, clearly, got round the office. A little later, one of the firm's senior staff came down to say hello. 'I hear you've had some tough luck,' he said. 'Maybe this will come in useful.'

He gave Skip a cheque for £3,000.

Yet another man like that.

FIVE

With every passing week, I was understanding more about the troop. But what of that other world which made up our life that year, that of the autistic children? At first, I only knew them at the camp, but gradually, over the summer, I got to know their home lives too. They were as different as could be imagined from the scouts.

There was, for instance, the home life of Peter Bell. He lives with his parents and younger brother in a large detached house just outside Guildford. Two semis had been jammed together into one. The work was done by his father, Chris, a builder. Indeed the very fabric of the place speaks volumes about the Bell family's life.

There is the very size of the building, for a start. Chris and his wife, Jo, fear for Peter's future and want to find some way in which he can continue living with them when he grows up. So the extra rooms, they hope, will gradually evolve into Peter's own, self-contained living space. Thus, he will be able to live as independently as possible and yet remain close enough for them to come to his help in emergencies.

The style of the interior, also, is eloquent. Jo says, as the parents of children with autism often do, that in some ways Peter's autism is an exaggeration of her and Chris's own character traits. That is, a mild social uncertainty and reserve and, possibly linked, emotionally, a notable desire for order. In part, this seems to express itself in a certain spartanness about their home's interior. The large sitting room is sparsely furnished somehow, impersonal, almost like the lobby of a hotel, with huge, brown leather armchairs, bare wooden floor softened with just a small piece of carpet, an absence of ornaments, odds and ends, domestic mess.

And yet there is a practical reason for this simplicity. The solidity of the furniture, the absence of clutter, the shiny, washable surfaces, especially that vast expanse of bare floor, all go very well with a child who is always capable, at any moment, of causing accidents. Just before Peter went to Holland, for instance, he got hold of the family toothpaste. Like everything else, it's usually locked away, but he somehow found it and, squeezing it out like paint from a tube, drew pictures with it all over the bathroom. The Bells wiped it off, but it's an indication of why all their household surfaces are as shiny and wipeable as the bathroom's. Such incidents are routine.

For theirs is a life which is very hard indeed to imagine without living it. As someone once put it, kids don't get autism, families do. Not that their lives have always been like this. Like so many children who later develop autism, as a young baby Peter was absolutely fine. Till the age of twenty months indeed, Jo says, he was a 'textbook child'. He could drink out of a cup, he would point to a 'girl' or a 'dog' in a picture book, he was affectionate, giggly, he loved cuddles. He said words: mummy, daddy, drink. He ate everything that was offered him.

Then one day he caught an ear infection, it got worse, and in the end it carried on for a year.

'During that time,' says Jo, 'he forgot everything he had learned. He lost his language. His spontaneity disappeared. He became remote, withdrawn, as if he lived alone in his own little world. He developed obsessions. He would only eat three things: strawberry milkshake, Weetabix and oats cereal.' But worst of all, says Jo, he developed this 'devil inside'. He would have these terrible, violent rages. She and her husband would have to pin him down, sometimes for as long as an hour while he screamed and shouted. If he broke free, he would try to break everything within sight.

He was given antibiotics. When he was two his ears were operated on; it made him worse. At two and a half they took him to a clinical psychologist who specialized in autism and he diagnosed him 'in fifteen minutes'.

They had lost their beautiful, affectionate child. They had gained an egregious and uniquely difficult life. They began a complex sequence of therapies, 'running into hundreds,' says Jo, to deal with specific disabilities. Some were to help Peter's speech, some were for his fears. Peter was terrified, for instance, of entering supermarkets. Others were for obsessions. Peter still won't drink a glass of orange unless it's filled to the top; if it is so filled, and he drinks half of it, it must be refilled to the top again before he'll drink another half.

Some therapies worked. He overcame his terror of supermarkets, and was able to join his mother, albeit with much difficulty, when she went shopping. His terror of entering his grandparents' house, a source of much anguish to them, was gradually, in a series of escalating behavioural steps, reduced. But for every obsession that has been conquered another remains, or a new one has been born.

There is, for instance, Peter's ongoing food problem.The eating obsessions continue. Worse, he refuses to eat in company with his parents. When they are eating he has to eat in another room, because he says seeing the food they eat makes him feel sick. When the scouts took him to McDonalds, in fact, it was a double achievement: not only did they get him to eat a burger, which he has continued to do ever since, but they got him to eat in company.

Then there is his typical autistic fear of change, which takes innumerable forms. As we have seen, he can find it far more difficult than other boys to move away from the familiar environment of home. Peter's homesickness, on Mohawk trips, is legendary. Then there is his dislike of meeting strangers, even in his own house. When the Bells have visitors, Peter will routinely retire to another room. If somebody knocks at the front door and asks if his parents are in, he will, unusually, manage one clearly articulated word: 'No.'

Even so, these are, in a sense, merely exaggerated versions of tendencies one might see, to a lesser degree, in any kid. But with Peter this extreme emotional conservatism can take more curious forms. Christmas and birthdays, for instance, throw him completely. He abhors the idea that one day can be so different from the rest, so that Chris and Jo have been known to leave their Christmas presents unopened until Peter was temporarily out of the way to avoid underscoring the day's difference. Then there are more esoteric fears, like the terror Peter feels when he sees the quirky BBC2 station identity signs on TV. Here is a Number Two behaving, by definition, as unpredictably, even surrealistically, as possible. Peter can't watch it. And Peter's insecurities, shading into obsessions, can take stranger forms still. Around the age of four, just when Peter's clinical psychologist had finally got him into supermarkets, he developed an obsessive fear, of all things, of the family car turning left out of the drive. The result was that for months the Bells had to turn right when setting off on any trip, with obvious route-planning implications.

But what can make Peter's concerns even harder to cope with is their unpredictability. Two years ago, given Peter's obsession with trains, his father dreamed up an ideal Christmas present: the most elaborate electric railway layout imaginable. Using his building talents, he put it all together himself. It took him four months, a veritable labour of paternal love. There were yards of track, engines, goods wagons, stations, sidings. It monopolized a whole room of their house. More, aware of Peter's intense concern for detail, he made absolutely sure that everything about the trains was right, the names correct, the colours appropriate, the station furniture just so, as would please the most pernickety curator of the most authentic railway museum.

Then came Christmas, and the surprise was sprung. The Bells took Peter up to the room where all this work had been secretly prepared.

He wasn't interested. Why? Because it was supposed to be a Christmas present and it wasn't wrapped. This from the boy who, in another mode, was disturbed by the unwrapping of his parents' presents. Months later the layout still sat there unused. Jo wondered desperately what else they could have done. Would Peter have reacted differently if they had, so to speak, 'wrapped' the room – put a ribbon or a garland on the door, perhaps? But such speculations are impossible. Peter can be just as unpredictable about the things he *does* like. Another time Jo was at a car boot sale and saw an old, wooden train she thought Peter might fancy. She brought it home, painted it up and put a face on it, like Peter's beloved Thomas the Tank Engine. He adored it from the start. Even after all these years, his likes and dislikes can remain impenetrable to his parents.

Unpredictability, in fact, is one of the hardest things about living with an autistic child and every parent highlights it. It applies just as much, for instance, to David Knebworth as ever it does to Peter. But then that poetical, dreamy manner of David's is strangely misleading. David, it turns out, is above all a prankster. And yet, come to think of it, that is how he was always read by the boys. For it was David the scout had been thinking of, back in 1997, when he described, as an authentic, drama-loving 12-year-old, the joy of looking after a real 'runner', a boy you could actually *see* working out the itinerary of his dashes. But then perhaps David the Russian ballet dancer, the autist artist, is essentially a figment of adult imagination. The kids, less romantically inclined, are better placed, maybe, to observe his real behaviour.

Indeed, when you visit the Knebworth family, the surprises start at their front door. So what kind of family is a Russian ballet dancer supposed to have? Probably not the Knebworths, for they are big and jolly, solid. His dad's a heating engineer, his mum works in a care home, and they live in a bright, neat little red-brick detached house on the outskirts of Canterbury. They are informal, friendly, practical.

They need to be: David doesn't, in fact, spend his time dreaming up autistic-savant art; he dreams up scams. Some seem pure whim. There was the time, for instance, one Christmas, when David's dad was finally settling down for a nice wind-you-down Christmas drink when he saw water coming through the sitting-room ceiling. He rushed upstairs: David had suddenly, inexplicably, decided to give himself a shower, a thing he'd never done before, and had further twigged that if he stuck his foot in the plughole he could make a pond.

Other ploys have at least some logic. There is, for instance, David's obsession with throwing things out of windows, notably clocks. David has a classic autistic obsession with clocks. It takes a love-hate form. In his benign mode, he will sit and watch them, fascinated, for hours; but if he comes home from school, say, in a bad mood, out of the window they go. Nor is it just clocks. One day his parents took a much-needed evening off, and David's grandparents came round to look after him. They put David to bed. After a while, there was a knock at the front door. It was David. A passer-by was with him; he'd just seen David jump out of his first-floor bedroom window, and had delivered him home.

Another of David's obsessions is loos. Many autistic children have a toilet obsession, but usually this is part of a wider love affair with water. Typically, they love to flush. But with David, it's different. His fascination is with lifting and banging down the seats; he loves the 'plock' sound they make. He has been known to do a runner, dash into a public loo and rush from cubicle to cubicle, raising and banging the seats, till finally captured. Clearly, there is some symbolism here, though nobody has yet quite cracked it. Even so, some background knowledge can make at least a little sense of incidents that might otherwise seem inexplicable. One day a couple were standing out in their front garden when David walked past with his sister. They'd left their front door open. David wasn't going to let an opportunity like that slip! He was in the door and up the stairs and in their loo in a flash, banging away like crazy. On the face of it, it's fair to say, this must have struck the couple as pretty strange, but some context would certainly have helped.

Indeed, some of David's most bizarre behaviours are the easiest to understand once you know the background. All autistic kids, when they join the troop, come with some kind of fame. The big story among the scouts the year I volunteered was that David Knebworth had started doing these runners into motorbike shops, the kind of places where they might have, say, a dozen motorbikes lined up for display purposes in a row. He would make one of his rushes at them and cerclish cerclash cerclishcerclash kerzunk crash! knock the whole lot over like dominoes. Johnny Cobbett, in particular, told this story with relish. Well, actually, it seemed unlikely that he knocked whole rows over. That turned out to be more in the telling, more what the scouts might have wished he did than what he actually did, one suspects. But what he had been doing, unquestionably, was knocking over individual bikes, as he walked down the street.

Simultaneously, another of his 'inexplicable' behaviours, performed at quite different times and places, was to rush headlong into, say, his parents' sitting room, throw himself on the floor, and roll around.

In fact, these two behaviours are connected, and make more sense than might at first seem. But who, without being told, would see the connection?

His parents explained that it all went back to David watching motorcross on TV. He loves every part of it, but what he especially adores are the moments when the riders lose control, part company with their bikes, and, as the bike goes one way, the riders go the other and roll around in the dirt. True, David's version divides the original phenomenon into two discreet parts, each acted out on separate occasions. But the explanation makes sense of behaviour that would otherwise seem utterly mysterious.

Even so, it would be easier living with David, say his family, if there were only more consistency in his inconsistencies. When you enter the world of autism you enter an utterly elastic universe; a kind of Alice in Wonderland dream world, shot full of paradox. The moment you have pinned down one behaviour, however bizarre, the child will come up with the opposite.

Like Peter, like almost all autistic children, indeed, David has moments of frenetic, uncontrollable rage, in which he can scream, shout, kick and roll around. Or, at least, that has been the experience of his parents, notably, in early years, during certain car journeys across town. Yet, making the same journeys in the school bus, he acted differently. (David has been at a special school since he was four and will stay there till he is nineteen.) Indeed, his teachers simply wouldn't believe what David's parents were telling them until the Knebworths made a ten-minute video of David in the car, complete with eruptions, and sent it to the school. The video speaks for itself. Nevertheless, the Knebworths are perfectly prepared to accept that at school David does act differently. Like Peter Bell, eating his hamburgers with the scouts, David can behave in utterly different ways in different circumstances and when travelling the same route in the school bus will behave impeccably.

Which leads one naturally to think of his behaviour being conditioned by those around him. (In the hamburger incident, certainly, Peter's would seem to have been.) And in this particular part of David's life, perhaps it is so. Yet in other areas of his life it's more confusing.

There is, for example, the whole question of his deafness. Again, like Peter Bell – like so many autistic children, indeed – one of his first problems, when very young, had been apparent deafness. He'd progressed excellently during his first year until around sixteen months old, says Mrs Knebworth. He'd started talking: he was saying simple things, mummy, daddy and so on. Like Peter again, this suddenly stopped; but unlike Peter with his ear infection, there was not even the semblance of an organic cause.

The Knebworths first suspected his hearing because he no longer responded to his name; but, of course, this *could* have been an example of what Clara Claiborne Park, in her famous account of being the mother of a child with autism, *The Siege*, called 'willed deafness' – a refusal to listen which was, in some strange way, some kind of profound psychic choice. And yet, surely not! For, points out David's father, you could burst a balloon behind his head and, far from jumping, David wouldn't even flinch. He really did act as if there was something organically wrong. And yet, surely so! Because although he didn't even blink at the balloon, he was perfectly able to hear *Postman Pat* when it came on the telly. But then he loved *Postman Pat*. What was happening to the nervous system, or the psyche, of this boy?

The moment the Knebworths decided his symptoms were 'organic', something would happen to suggest they were in the mind; the moment they decided they were psychological, something else would suggest that they were 'organic'.

There was the matter, for instance, of food. By the age of three David had stopped eating regular foods. His diet had contracted to Bernard Matthews' Golden Drummers, no vegetables, fruit, yogurt, nothing like that, just Bernard Matthews' Golden Drummers – and they had to be grilled. Come Christmas, for instance, while everyone else in the family was eating their

Christmas dinner, David's only concession to the festivities was that his Bernard Matthews' Golden Drummers were at least made out of turkey.

Along comes the school again, when they heard what was happening at home. Eating obsessions? Absolutely not! At school, they said, David ate everything that was thrown at him. So now it was the parents who were unbelieving, and the school who sent a video to them. There was David, centre screen and in full colour, chomping away at his roast lunch with the best. So then the school sent a teacher to David's home, and in her company David duly ate as if nothing had ever been untoward. He has eaten perfectly well ever since. Back to psychological . . .

As the contradictions multiply, as the videos hurtle back and forth, David's family could be forgiven for thinking they have strayed into a painting by Salvador Dali, a world in which conventional reality no longer applies. Yet the worst sufferer of all, clearly, remains poor David. Lost in this surrealist universe to which he has somehow gained entry but now cannot leave, he remains, for all his, sometimes, seeming game-playing, as mystified by what is happening to him as everyone else.

For above all, however David experiences the world, the one thing you can say for sure is that he is in his own, unique, psychological place. There is a terrible loneliness about David. Which is why it is so important that the scouts have their own ways, however unconventional, of getting through to him. They give him the one thing he needs above all else: the friendship of other boys.

Of all the autistic children at Camp Mohawk none can have gained quite as much from the relationship as Bernard Naisbitt. For Bernard, of course, is the boy with autism, local to Beckton, who is, himself, a member of the scouts.

Bernard lives with his single-parent mum and his younger sister in a little house overlooking a green. It's ten years since Mrs

Naisbitt's husband left, in part, at least, thanks to the pressures of living with a child with autism. Nowadays she is thin and wiry and tired, she bears the marks of that ten-year struggle. Yet the moment she starts talking about Bernard's time with the scouts, she comes to life. It's as if she hooks into a drip-feed of enthusiasm; within a quarter of an hour she looks physically transformed.

She first heard about the scouts, she says, from the local paper. It was six years ago, when Bernard was nine, and she'd been at her wits' end to know what to do with him. The social services had been 'a dead loss'. But as soon as she contacted the scouts, she says, John Lee came straight round on an initial visit, plus two scouts, and from the start she knew he understood her life. 'He didn't ask me things, like the social services do, which display their ignorance. Things like "Is it okay to leave him with a video for half an hour?"'

However, the first time Bernard joined one of the scouts' evening sessions, it didn't work. He was going through a wild stage at the time – swearing, being spiteful – and he scared some of the younger scouts. But what struck Mrs Naisbitt was that they didn't give up. They simply suggested they gave it a rest for a bit; then a few weeks later, they tried again. Round they came once more and took Bernard off for another evening. This time it took them a month of patience and persistence, she says, but gradually Bernard began to change. First he stopped swearing at the scouts; then he stopped swearing at home, too. He seemed to poke his head outside the autistic bubble, and, says Mrs Naisbitt, as the information began to trickle in, he realized there were behaviours people wouldn't put up with.

It had been a different story at Bernard's schools. True, at primary it had not been too bad. Bernard even had friends. There was one boy in particular, little Joseph, who 'adored' Bernard. The children seemed readier, at that age, to accept a child who was different. But at secondary school the real problems began. The school was supposed to give him help. But he got little, least of all in the area which bothered him most, his relationships with other kids. By this age, with the onset of adolescence, other children had become less tolerant. Nor was this just kids who were new to Bernard. It included some of his old friends who had joined him at the new school. Once there, they dropped him. Worse, he began to be bullied. Kids would tease him, hit him, make a fool of him, tell him to walk down the corridor with his trousers down. Bernard, whose speech was very limited, especially at school, developed his own language of protest: he soon started refusing to eat anything at school, only at home.

It got to the stage, says Mrs Naisbitt, where Bernard was like two children: fine with the scouts, whom he loved, miserable at school, which he hated. And meanwhile she was having to struggle with the customary pressures of life with an autistic child. Things like his food fads, which he shares with Peter and David, were a particular problem for Mrs Naisbitt because money was so tight. 'He'd suddenly demand chicken, and I'd give him sausage and beans. It would go smash against the wall.' Or the evening when Bernard's speech problem meant he spent three hours trying to get Mrs Naisbitt to understand one word. He wouldn't give up, even though he got wildly frustrated, breaking things, kicking his mother, biting her. In desperation Mrs Naisbitt phoned his teacher at eleven o'clock at night and together they sorted it out. Or the time he got a piece of glass stuck in his foot. This one took six hours, from seven in the evening till one in the morning. Bernard was in agony, and Mrs Naisbitt simply couldn't shift it. Eventually she had to wait till Bernard fell asleep and then, she says, she put her mouth over his foot and sucked it out through her teeth.

Yet in the right environment, as she says, he can be another child. Which is why Mrs Naisbitt was so sad that later this year, now that he was fifteen, he'd have to leave Camp Mohawk. For this is the cut-off age. She's heartbroken, she says; she'd always believed that only she could look after Bernard, but she felt differently about the scouts.

There are other places that Bernard has fitted in. He loves animals, and recently did work experience at the local zoo. He fed the animals, he cleaned them out, he was happy and came back with excellent reports.

There do seem to be ways forward, but he still desperately needs help. Fortunately, even though he has officially left, his friends in the scouts have stayed in touch. It was the scouts, as we saw earlier, who wrote that letter to the local paper demanding a special school for Bernard. And Joe Beckford and Matt Polesden were round looking for him, said Mrs Naisbitt, only the other day.

If all this seems confusing, this is unsurprising; autism has confused everyone from the start.

Although it's really only been in the last ten years that autism has entered public consciousness, and even become fashionable, it was first named by Leo Kanner, the American psychiatrist, in 1943. Its prevalence, of course, depends on how you define it (itself a matter of dispute), but a typical estimate is one in every 2,500 births. No one knows why, but there are up to five times as many boys being diagnosed as girls. Lately these figures have been challenged, and some put the figure as high as one in a thousand, even a remarkable one in a hundred. However, awareness alone could be enlarging the figure, let alone different criteria for diagnosis. The widening of the autistic spectrum, to include cases that would not have been so diagnosed previously, has been a phenomenon of recent years.

But then there are few of us who have encountered officially diagnosed autism who won't have had the maverick thought: 'Aren't there people I know personally – people whom no one has ever considered labelling autistic – who nevertheless exhibit distinct autistic traits?' People, say, who are exceptionally, almost psychopathically remote; people who maintain, in adult life, the kind of obsessions typical of autistic children, extreme trainspotters, perhaps.

Indeed, as I personally began to research autism one classic instance struck me from my own past. Years ago, I had worked with someone I shall call Jim. For years Jim had held down, with some difficulty, admittedly, a conventional job; and he had never been diagnosed with any serious illness, mental or physical. Yet, in retrospect, he surely exhibited several typically autistic symptoms. First of all was his extraordinary social remoteness. He had no partner, no friends, no relatives with whom he stayed in touch. But more than this, there was his utter inability to empathize, even, seemingly, to conceive of empathizing, with other people at all.

Two incidents were typical. At one stage, uncharacteristically, he did lurch, however briefly, towards something approaching friendship with another man I knew. One day this man received a birthday present, but it was only later that he found out it had come from Jim. Because what he got, through the post, was just a book: no card, no greetings, no indication, even, of who had sent it: just a book. Then there was the time when the same friend met Jim for a day's drive in the country. When they met, it turned out that Jim had planned every detail of where they would go, without even thinking of consultation. He had even written the itinerary down. And another suggestive detail: Jim, who lived on his own, decorated his entire house with maps. And maps, with their overtones of planning and control, are, as we shall see, yet another classic autistic obsession.

Yet nobody had ever thought of diagnosing this man as 'autistic'. But then neither has such a formal diagnosis ever been made of the long list of celebrities who have also been claimed, often by other 'mild' autistics, as one of theirs. This includes, for instance, Albert Einstein, Peter Sellers and Winston Churchill. And yet, in each case, one can see the qualities which have led to the claim being made. Take Winston Churchill. He famously lived in his own emotional world. His secretaries, notably, complained of his seeming incapacity even to conceive that they might have lives, and needs, of their own. He also exhibited certain more obviously bizarre behaviours, his habit, for instance, of wandering around Chartwell naked. Nor did he lack the more positive qualities which can also go with autism, especially very mild autism. When all around him declared doom and defeat in 1940, he persisted in his perverse, idiosyncratic view that England would win. His friend Violet Bonham-Carter pointed out that he managed with remarkable success to bring others into his world, even if he showed little interest, in this as other things, in entering theirs.

Yet Churchill, too, is not exactly in line for formal diagnosis.

So how do you diagnose autism? Suffice to say, given such complexity, diagnosis is a phenomenon in itself. Nevertheless, a typical diagnostic tool, which most would broadly accept, is the so-called triad of impairments. The first of these is 'social interaction': difficulty with relationships, seeming aloof and indifferent to others. Then there is 'social communication', both verbal and non-verbal: failing to understand gestures, facial expressions, tones of voice. Then there are problems with 'imagination', including play: having a limited range of imaginative activities, possibly copied, and pursued rigidly and repetitively.

Even this highly minimalist diagnosis, an attempt to pare down to a working tool the world's most complex, contradictory condition, immediately resonates with the stories of the autistic children above, as well as other children in contact with Camp Mohawk. 'Social interaction'? One thinks of the intense withdrawal of Peter Bell, the abstraction of David Knebworth. Social communication? One thinks of all three boys' difficulties with speech, most memorably David Knebworth's crisis with the 'Pussy-cat' game, assuming that wasn't just David Knebworth being devilish. Rigidity, repetitiveness? David Knebworth's loo seat obsession, Peter's railway fixation, complete with remorseless listing of train names.

To which one might add, of course, a thousand other 'bizarre' behaviours, as we have also seen. David Knebworth's passionate vendetta against bikes; Bernard Naisbitt's compulsive swearing at the scouts; Peter Bell's capacity, described by his mother, for noticing the tiniest changes in the layout of the camping ground where they take their annual holiday. One year the proprietors moved a four by two foot notice. Peter spotted it immediately, and was distraught. Little wonder, in all this behavioural morass, that professionals quickly reach the stage where they diagnose by a sort of internal computer, a sense of autism's overall feel, its flavour. Typical would be intangibles like that faerie king manner of David Knebworth's. The style, if not the detail, can be seen in a flash.

Nevertheless, noting characteristics is one thing; interpreting them, vital for any sort of real help, is something else again, and leads straight into yet another minefield. Effectively it is an expression of the oldest debate of all, the nature/nurture argument. The question, broadly, is this: is autism something physical, a brain defect or glitch in the nervous system, internally engendered, or is it brought about from the outside, from the environment? Above all, could this environment include the emotional environment, notably parenting? And here, over the years, is where the politics of autism have got very passionate indeed.

Much of this passion goes back to the sixties, when the American developmental psychologist Bruno Bettelheim published his *The Empty Fortress* (1967), an account of his experiences looking after autistic children at the school he ran in Chicago. Bettelheim argued that autism was caused by a fault in the child's emotional development, notably bonding with the mother. He had developed his theory in a remarkable way. He had grown up in pre-war Austria and had been sent to a concentration camp. There he saw that one way prisoners coped with this unthinkable situation was to withdraw into a death-in-life, zombie-like existence. So extreme, indeed, that other prisoners nicknamed them 'Moslems'. Bettelheim felt autistic behaviour was a similar withdrawal, practised by children in response to intolerable emotional pain. Maternal deprivation was just one possible cause of this pain – indeed Bettelheim said 'autism has essentially to do with everything that happens from birth on' but it was maternal deprivation that gained him his notoriety.

His work enjoyed a considerable vogue. It was arguably part of a broader sixties/seventies tendency to see emotions as a cause of illness. There was a comparable theory of schizophrenia, not to mention cancer. But by the eighties it had become anathema to the autistic studies mainstream, and remains so today. For a start, runs the argument, no serious research has ever proved this emotional causality. Second, even to suggest such a thing is an outrage anyway. It's bad enough to have an autistic child, should the parents' pain be compounded by being blamed?

Later research has tended to stress two aspects. The first is the notion that something physical is adrift in the brain, genetic perhaps, or the result of physical trauma or disease. One thinks of Peter Bell's ear infection. The second is that there is some malfunction in the process of development, some strange incapacity (not emotionally grounded) for otherwise intact brain machinery to move forward in the normal way.

More recently, however, the thinking seems to have swung towards a kind of multi-causality, with renewed emphasis, especially in treatment, on relationships. Where everyone does agree, however, is on the extraordinary nature of the condition and the immense pain it causes, both to sufferers and their families. However, there are also certain intriguing positive aspects, as we will see.

Surprisingly, it is possible, these days, to get some idea of how autism feels from the inside, because at least some recovery, undoubtedly, is possible. More than one 'recovered' autistic adult has written a book. Donna Williams, for instance, a woman with autism who is now in her late thirties, highlights her utter inability, as a child, to project herself into the minds of other children, something the rest of us do all the time, usually without even realizing it. This incapacity sounds unspectacular but it can, in fact, create havoc. Put simply, she never knew, as a child, if the friend she was playing with was unhappy, angry or bored; worse, she could scarcely conceive of the friend having any kind of separate emotional existence. This is one reason, she says, why kids like Peter, and she herself when young, are so keen on stories about 'mechanical' playmates like Thomas the Tank Engine. Their machine-like qualities make them predictable while their emotions are so unmistakably, exaggeratedly explicit they can be grasped. Donna can just about read other people's emotional states if they are vivid enough; her great problem is with nuance, irony. Indeed, in one of the great backhanded compliments of all time, she says she's always loved TV soaps precisely *because* their characters are so extreme, so cartoon, so irredeemably black and white.

Better still 'I got a lot of my life rules and responses from things like TV sitcoms and TV commercials where certain responses and phrases were repeated again and again in a highly predictable way.' Thus Donna, lacking home-grown emotional intelligence, could use the soaps, effectively, as a form of rote learning. She especially recommends the old sitcom *Gilligan's Island* for this.

Shading into this 'autistic aloneness', as it has been called, is that other most marked quality of autistic children, their obsessive love of order and control, especially sequence. Thus Peter listing his train names was typical; as was the period in David Knebworth's life when he had to touch the neighbouring telephone poles, in a particular sequence, every time he left the house. Travel, in particular, anxiety-provoking for all of us, can lead to very curious behaviour in those with autism. Maps, of course, with their implication, not always fulfilled, of planning and control are one antidote. Unsurprisingly, a favourite autistic obsession is maps. Donna Williams describes how, as a partially recovered autistic adult, she can now drive to the local supermarket, but only along one, regular route which she has learned sequentially. The smallest break in the sequence is fatal, even if she is right on top of her destination. Should she find herself, for example, approaching the store from the opposite way – through a diversion or whatever – she can't make the correct turn even if she is passing right in front of it, because it becomes a right turn rather than a left, which is how she knows the sequence. To arrive, then, she has to drive past and come back again, so that the turning is once again on the familiar side. Only then, she says, can she truly 'see' it – and take it.

There seems, indeed, to be a direct relationship between such rigidities and a profound sense of underlying confusion. In part, at least, this must be due to the sensory malfunctions we have already encountered, notably hearing. When Peter Bell, at the carnival, put his hands over his ears; when Omar, at the 1997 camp, showed his terror of leaves, when other children have described being overwhelmed by the roar of their own blood rushing through their heads – all were experiencing sound in utterly different ways from the rest of us.

Least of all is it a question of simple loudness. Annabel Stehli, in her book *The Sound of a Miracle*, described the hearing of her daughter, Georgie. Georgie developed speech as she got older, so she could describe her earlier experiences. Like Omar, she hated the sound of leaves; like James Robinson paraphrasing Omar, too, she used the phrase 'like monsters' to describe a hated sound, although in her case it was the blowing out of a candle. But worse, there seemed a strange dysfunction in her whole process of selecting sound, as if her filtering system worked differently from ours.

One day her mother was driving with Georgie through New

York when suddenly her daughter threw her hands over her ears in a frenzy of pain. Eventually, and with much difficulty, her mother worked out what was bothering her. Out of all the multitudinous and complex sounds of New York it was a ventilation hatch in a nearby hotel wall which was emitting a spasmodic puffing sound. Not traffic sounds, not buses, sirens or jets, no, a puffing sound, one which was way off from the road and to one side of the car and lost, one would have assumed, amidst all the other competing Gotham din.

'It made no sense,' said her mother. But then neither do so many other sensory problems of autistics. The sense of smell can be affected. Annabel Stehli's daughter described how strong smells, in particular, could be intolerable, especially deodorant and aftershave, while she could smell hand lotion, she said, from the other room. The sense of shape, size and even position may be affected. Objects may seem smaller or larger than they are, or even move about. One child sat on a radiator thinking there was room to sit on it; there wasn't, so he fell off on to the floor. Donna Williams described a day when all the buildings in her town seemed to change place. The sense of pain, even, may be affected. David Knebworth once burnt his hand on the kitchen grill: despite a nasty injury, says his mother, he not only failed to cry out, he didn't react at all.

It is as if the whole process of selection, editing and volume control has gone awry. And yet there can be positive aspects, too. Annabel Stehli described an incident that happened when her daughter was a teenager, recovered sufficiently to be able to speak, but still with many experiential idiosyncrasies. She was looking through a microscope at a speck of dandruff, of all things, and exclaimed at the beauty of the colours she could see in it. Her mother dutifully looked, and saw nothing, except the predictable pale grey; yet gradually, as she kept on looking, over many minutes, she began to see the colours her daughter had seen immediately.

Suggestion? Perhaps, and yet you can't help wondering, too, whether 'normal' seeing is not quite as much about filtering out as it is about perception. Both Van Gogh and Gauguin recorded colours in nature that many contemporaries felt simply were not there. Our communal editing system, arguably, has gradually shifted. Today, many of us would feel that yes, indeed, the colours were present all along. In this connection it's interesting to note a remark of J. B. Priestley's, who began as a Gauguin sceptic: 'It was after I had spent some weeks in Tahiti and Moorea, early in 1931, that I realized that the charge against Gauguin of being an impudently wilful colourist was unfounded; his decorative forms and pattern-making might be his own, but the strange lights and shadows were there in the islands.'

This chapter has concentrated, so far, on the defects associated with autism, but there is also the fascinating, and much trumpeted, area of autistic talents, or savantry. An area made much of by films like Dustin Hoffman's *Rain Man*. Estimates of such capacities among autistic children vary from 5 to 10 per cent – not huge, but well above the societal norm. While if you reverse the question and look at the proportion of savants who are autistic you come up with a far more dramatic figure: up to 50 per cent! Typically these will be 'calendar' or memory talents. In *Rain Man*, Dustin Hoffman's character becomes a blackjack card counter, a form of gambling that depends above all else on memory. However, exceptional mathematical abilities are also evident, as are precocious drawing talents. Notable is the architectural drawing of Stephen Wiltshire, who some will have seen on TV. We will pursue this fascinating area later on – at least one gifted child ended up with Mohawk – but it's worth perhaps noting, at this stage, that the obvious weaknesses and subtler strengths of autistic children seem curiously linked.

Take those confusions of place, position and identity, for example. Some autistic children can go even further than David Knebworth with his 'near misses' and actually confuse a duck, say, with a dog, or even a tree with a devil, especially if the tree is sufficiently frightening looking. Here, surely we are getting very close to what in a poet we would call metaphor. A skylark, Shelley tells us, is 'like a glow-worm golden', or 'like a high born maiden'. Well, it isn't, not in any everyday sense, that is. But it does feel like one, inasmuch as it somehow lives in the same emotional landscape. A relationship comparable in quality, though not in flavour, to that of scary trees and devils.

All of us have strange memories from early years, the reliability of which, with very good reason, we should doubt. Even so, when I first heard of the above, I recalled one of my own, very earliest memories.

The way I recall it, I was around two years old – or even younger – and I was in my parents' car. We passed an amateur airfield, bright green in the afternoon sun, on which were parked a crowd of dazzlingly painted little monoplanes, red, yellow, royal blue. I was entranced and also confused, because just days earlier I had seen my first parrots and at that moment, as we passed the airfield, I didn't know whether I was looking at parrots or planes. It wasn't the name that I was confusing – I don't think I knew the word for either parrot or plane – it was the identity of the objects before my eyes. Parrots or planes? They occupied a similar emotional territory, labelled, to my groping sensibilities, that which is dazzling, gaudy, tricked out in primary colours. I don't even remember if I realized both parrots and planes could fly.

Of course, I grew up and grew out of it, and learnt to make the sharp-edged conceptual distinctions which give us our customary sense of order in the world. Could it be that autistic children – and poets – never manage this?

Indeed, it is an extraordinary world, this world of autism, full of illogic, illusion and what sometimes feels like the miraculous. It is a world reminiscent in many ways, of post-Cezanne art, with its infinitely flexible sense of time and perspective, its heightened, surreal sense of colour, its unions of opposites.

We have already seen how some of the more everyday curiosities of a boy like David Knebworth – his sudden dashes into strangers' loos, his knocking over of motorbikes – make a certain limited sense, once one grasps the behavioural context. Yet there are deeper understandings of such phenomena than that. Because, in many ways, autistic kids live out in daily life the kind of symbolism – Freudian, Daliesque – which most of us keep safely locked up in our dreams.

Take that familiar tendency of autistic children to fill their pants. You could blame their lack of social understanding, their difficulty, even, exercising basic motor control over their bodies. But Donna Williams, writing as ever from the inside, sees it as self-assertion.

She describes how, to her parents' despair, she used to pee on the carpet of her bedroom. But this was no accident. Rather, she says, for a child with a diaphanous sense of identity, 'symbolically this was my world with a "me" in it. The more I covered that carpet, the more of a "me" in the world there was.' Her incontinence was intentional, an attempt to establish who she was.

In the same way another 'recovered' autistic, Temple Grandin, explained her childhood obsession with every kind of door. They represented change, possibility, the passage from one emotional state to another – alarming, of course, to all of us, but above all to the infinitely insecure autistic. But would her local supermarket manager have understood that, as he saw this kooky-looking kid rush in and out of his sliding door ten times in a row? Likewise, Donna Williams tells us, her obsessive tearing of paper was about 'symbolically disintegrating the threat of closeness . . . I often did this when I had to say goodbye to anyone as though I had first to symbolically destroy the closeness in order not to feel any sense of desertion or loss.'

Perhaps the most omnipresent autistic obsession of all must

be spinning: spinning coins, spinning in a swing, or quite simply, spinning around on the spot. Innumerable Camp Mohawk autistic children did this; and of all autistic obsessions it must be said that it is one of the strangest to see. And with the interpretation of *this*, both recovered autistics and psychologists have had a field day.

Donna Williams describes her 'repetitive spinning', and feels this may have been an instinctive attempt to stimulate a malfunctioning vestibular system. Temple Grandin describes how obsessive spinning 'made me feel powerful, and in control of things', and cites studies that show how spinning hyperactive children in an office chair twice weekly(!), by stimulating the vestibular system, reduces hyperactivity. Swings, also, calm both autistic and 'normal' children. Other theories suggest spinning lessens any imbalance between the left and right hemispheres of the brain, thus restoring equilibrium.

Yet another theory, one of the most remarkable, focuses, like Temple Grandin earlier, on the symbolism of thresholds, both physical and emotional. It should be remembered that autistic children hate any change of state, a key reason for their obsessive need to keep everything around them, food, clothes, travelling rituals, the same. The idea is that the person with autism is terrified by novelty, especially the emotional novelty of meeting new people, and can get into a symbolic dance, at such moments, of approach and retreat. Two steps forward, turn, then two steps back, turn, two steps forward, turn, then two steps back, turn . . . advance/retreat, advance/retreat, ad infinitum. And a way of simplifying the process is to run both movements together, in fact – to spin! (A notable advocate of this theory was the Nobel Prize-winning ethologist Nikolaas Tinbergen, who wrote a book about autism. In his ethological fieldwork in the jungle, he said, he had seen 'an exact analogue' of autistic spinning in 'the pendulum movements of animals in an ambivalent state'.) And if this all sounds somewhat far-fetched, then consider the following. A noted historical spinner (one is tempted to say the first spin-doctor) was, of all people, Dr Johnson, the eighteenth-century author and (obsessive?) compiler of one of the first English dictionaries, of whom his friend Miss Reynolds said: 'On entering Sir Joshua's house with poor Mrs Williams, a blind lady who lived with him, he would quit her hand, or else whirl her about on the steps as he whirled and twisted about to perform his gesticulations; and as soon as he had finished, he would give a sudden spring and make an extensive stride over the threshold, as if he were trying to wager how far he could stride.' This ritual was repeated at every doorway.

It is not known whether Dr Johnson suffered from autism. Some argue he suffered from Tourette's syndrome, a related condition. He certainly suffered from depression, and had great difficulty with new acquaintances. What is known is his famously patrician manner, not to mention his very considerable weight. The whole notion of a rotating, let alone leaping, Dr Johnson is heroic indeed.

All this talk of symbolism, of course, takes us straight back into the heated question of the role, if any, of emotion in all this. For the received view today, as we have seen, is that the causes of autism are 'organic', they are not emotional. Yet if it is true that certain so-called 'bizarre behaviours', like spinning, have this emotional basis then we have found one aspect of autism, at least, which *is* connected with a child's deep fears.

But though there is indeed a broad church which says that *all* emotional causes of autism have been discredited, one can sense that the key antipathy to this line of thought is that such a thesis blames parents. And yet hardly anyone, not even Bettelheim, argued that parental deprivation was the only relevant trauma. Tinbergen, for instance, felt a range of life events – early, severe illness, like Peter Bell's, the birth of a sibling, even moving house – could, above all in combination, have just as devastating effects.

Even parents of autistic children have argued the importance of emotional factors. Typical is a famous book in the autistic studies canon, *The Siege*, published in 1967 by Clara Claiborne Park, the American mother of an autistic child. The chapter headings alone are suggestive. Chapter four, 'Willed Weakness', is followed by chapter five, 'Willed Blindness', which is followed, in turn, by 'Willed Deafness' and 'Willed Isolation'.

In these chapters Clara Park argues that her child had a variety of faculties – hearing, speech, sight, the ability to walk – which she used or withheld according to her (albeit profoundly deep-seated, presumably unconscious) choice. Park describes how at one time she herself had thought her child organically incapable of walking; yet by the age of three she realized she was performing all the appropriate motor movements in different ways. Bending her knees when sitting down, for instance, 'in an exhibition of controlled grace unusual in any child at that age'. One day Clara Park had a revelation: 'Why Elly, you're a fraud! This the child who couldn't walk? Obviously she could walk. She would walk as soon as she wanted to put one foot in front of another.' And something comparable, relating in turn to Elly's sight, hearing and emotional isolation, was explored in the following chapters. It was as if, comments Clara Park – and she herself stresses the 'as if' – her daughter had decided that 'anything is preferable, even total withdrawal, to the risks of activity and growth'.

Suffice to say that in all manner of quantifiable ways, it would have been possible – at the right times and places – to show that Elly was deficient in a whole range of skills: perception, hearing, touch. And yet at other times and places, her mother suggests (rather like the infinitely variable David Knebworth) Elly might not have been. Of course, Clara Park was observing behaviour, not recording, say, the neuroscience of her daughter's brain. Nevertheless she mentions at least two occasions when her daughter's apparently mechanical incapacities seemed to change.

One was when she found 'an unusually active and imaginative baby-sitter', who transformed Elly's ability to draw. Elly had previously drawn geometric shapes, but she never copied directly; anything she saw, and decided to reproduce, appeared days later. Such delayed-action copying seemed symptomatic of her 'strange remoteness, the denial of interpersonal contact. The child would draw a circle, but it must not be an imitation of someone else's circle; it must come out of nowhere.'

But with the new babysitter, Jill, things changed. Hearing that Elly recognized shapes, Jill drew a sheet of triangles. After she had drawn thirty, Elly began making faint, wavering triangles of her own. These triangles, said Clara Park, were 'doubly remarkable . . . they acknowledged not only hidden capabilities of eye and hand and brain, but a personal contact as well. The intensity and interest of this young girl had got through to Elly, who usually looked right through a stranger.'

The other event was one of those sudden, intense flashes which pass like a storm in the night and yet, by happening at all, throw everything into question. She described how more than once, 'some big loud, friendly daddy of a man', passing through town, would visit them, take a look at their baby and having no preconceptions about the child to make him act otherwise, would lift her off the floor, 'hug and tickle and toss her while she squealed and chuckled with the most ordinary baby delight. During one such visit I watched, incredulously, as Elly – impervious Elly – got up off the floor, went over to the stranger, and crawled on his lap.'

More curious still: 'A year and a half later, at the time of her second hospital examination, we remembered [this man's] magic and took Elly to visit. But he had lost it. He now knew something was wrong with her and he treated her as any intelligent and sensitive person would – tentatively, cautiously. Elly never even saw him.'

Elly's symptoms, in fact, seemed curiously dependent on how she was being treated. Suffice to say that the literature affords several examples of this kind, instances in which apparently 'hard-wired' brain defects have been reversed by circumstances, however temporarily. The point being, of course, if they are genuinely 'hard-wired', it should be impossible to reverse them at all.

Essentially we plunge into the eternal merry-go-round: does matter rule spirit, or spirit matter? Epilepsy is a measurable state, and up to a third of children with autism have epilepsy. Yet epilepsy is notoriously responsive to stress; how do we rule out 'emotional' factors here? Equally, the latest brain research shows that we effectively construct our own, individual brains by a process of redundancy. We all start with capacities which we lose, or keep, according to stimulation. These include our capacity for affection, for empathy. Where does 'organic' start and 'emotional' finish here? Equally, as Tinbergen points out, '"neurological" evidence is often – and we submit, rashly – interpreted as proof of structural damage. It should not be forgotten that the vast majority of "neurological" tests carried out on such children (and on others) demonstrate no more than malfunctioning, and that the conclusion that such malfunctioning is due to structural damage (either to the brain or in the sensory or motor periphery) is no more than an inference.'

I came across a striking, and curious, example of something similar a few years ago when researching a book about religious experience. The neuropsychiatrist Peter Fenwick, of the Maudsley Hospital in London, wanted to study the 'hemisphericity' of mystical experience – the extent to which its conduit is the left or right hemisphere of the brain. He managed to persuade a visiting Indian guru (no mean achievement in itself) to subject his brain to neurological testing. Fenwick had already found that many mystical experiences were associated with activity in the right hemisphere. To what extent, in everyday life, did his guru employ his left hemisphere (linear, logical) or his right hemisphere (intuitive, instinctual)?

He found, remarkably, that the man's left hemisphere, while perfectly undamaged, wasn't functioning – not during Fenwick's tests, anyway. He used his right hemisphere throughout. At some deep level, seemingly, he was choosing to employ only part of his brain. Or as Fenwick puts it: 'it was as if he had had a left-hemisphere lobotomy'. But he hadn't. Nevertheless, tests could easily have suggested that he had such a 'hard-wired' problem. They would have been wrong.

Then there is the further, constant conundrum of chicken-and-egg. Studies show that children with autism have neurochemical abnormalities; but do the abnormalities cause the autism or does the autism cause the abnormalities? Gary Kraemer of the University of Wisconsin has shown that if young monkeys are brought up alone, they will develop neurochemical abnormalities and will show autistic symptoms; equally, and encouragingly, if they are reintroduced to other monkeys their neurochemical levels will return to normal. Rat studies at the Center for Neurodevelopmental Studies in Phoenix, Arizona, found that rats with climbing gear and other stimulating equipment had better neuronal growth in the brain than rats in regular cages.

It is surely interesting that Donna Williams and Temple Grandin are more than ready to go the emotional route. As Donna Williams puts it in her *Nobody Nowhere* (1992):

> The perceptual problems [among sufferers from autism] of deafness, dumbness and blindness are experienced as very real. They are nevertheless caused by shutdown caused by extreme stress, brought on by an inability to cope with incoming information – often to do with emotions.
>
> Perhaps, as in cases of shock, this very real perception and the behaviours it leads to are caused by over-sensitivity triggering protective chemical or hormonal responses in the brain experienced as extreme emotional hypersensitivity. Perhaps as something of a vicious circle the shutdown and withdrawal resulting from this emotional hypersensitivity in turn leads to developmental problems which arise from the

> inconsistency of changes in consciousness and leaves such children functioning on a far more sensory and subconscious level most of their waking lives as well as their sleeping ones. My tendency to night terrors pointed to this. My constantly changing sense of time and space also indicates that some of this emotional insecurity arises from drifting in and out of a dream state.

While Temple Grandin has this to say:

> Children have to be taught to be gentle. Since I missed out on this, I have to learn it now. The squeeze chute [a tactile stimulant she invented and employs on herself] gives the feeling of being held cuddled and gently cradled in Mother's arms . . .
>
> Research with baby monkeys has indicated that if they do not receive enough contact comfort, they have a weakened capacity for future affection. It is likely that in order to have feelings of caring, one has to have experienced the feeling of comfort. Animal experiments reveal that comforting tactile stimulation causes distinct biochemical changes in the central nervous system. I speculate that regular use of the squeeze machine may help change some of the abnormal biochemistry which was caused by lack of comforting tactile stimulation during my early childhood. Maybe the lack of empathy in many autistic adults is caused by their avoidance of hugging and affection when they were children.

The real difficulty in this most anguished debate is, of course, the intense emotions raised by autism, especially when the arguments involve children, and, above all, when they introduce parental 'responsibility'. And yet there is surely a calmer wisdom available, one that fits in with common sense.

As so often we hear it from Oliver Sacks, the neurologist from

New York whose case studies have received so much attention in recent years, notably through the film *Awakenings*. He is surely one of the most humane and sane voices in this most passionately debated area.

Summing up similar disputes when writing about Tourette's syndrome, he says: 'Neither a biological nor a psychological nor a moral-social view point is adequate; we must see Tourette's not only simultaneously from all three perspectives, but from an inner perspective, an existential perspective, that of the affected person himself. Inner and outer narratives here, as everywhere, must fuse.'

We live, in fact, in a multi-causal world.

What are the implications of all this for Camp Mohawk? For these questions plainly bear on the care of autistic children. If autism is anything other than exclusively organic then relationship-based work like that at Mohawk gains significance. We know that Mohawk offers autistic children a delightful holiday; we know it offers vital respite care for the parents; in addition, as we have seen already, we know it can have remarkable effects on the caring boys themselves.

But can it offer more? Can such care help autistic children in deeper ways? In fact, there have been a whole series of therapies, quite unconnected with Mohawk, which have argued that relationships, especially nurturant relationships, can make profound differences to the autistic condition. The legitimacy of these claims, and how far they bear on what the scouts are doing, will be looked at in a later chapter.

Meanwhile, the only real difference between an outsider like myself and what has been called 'the autistic establishment' is that I find I am still asking questions they feel were answered long ago. Francesca Happé, for instance, of the Medical Research Council, in her *Autism – an Introduction to Psychological Theory* (1994) writes 'evidence for an organic cause is overwhelming'. It's not perversity that makes me raise such ghosts, merely what I have seen, and heard, and read, myself, throughout one memorable year.

Any answers this story may stumble on, inevitably, will be at best half-truths. And as for certainties, in autism, above all, they are in short supply.

SIX

Our meddling intellect
Misshapes the beauteous forms of things:
We murder to dissect.
William Wordsworth, 'The Tables Turned'

It was early summer, and I was sitting just outside the hut which the leaders use as an office. The door was open and there were five people inside.

On the right was Clare Higginson, Camp Mohawk's 25-year-old administrator. We had seen little of her during the winter months but, as the year advanced, and we spent more time at Wargrave, she was more and more in evidence. In previous years she had worked as a volunteer and was so successful, especially at administration, that Skip offered her a permanent job. She is tall, blonde and imposing and has an organized, logical mind. She was sitting at a computer, buried deep in an analysis which involved an array of charts and diagrams and more arrows than the Battle of Agincourt. So absorbed was she that she was temporarily oblivious to what was around her.

Yet at the other end of the little room, just ten feet away, were four of the scouts. There were no machines around them. Tom Pollard was there, and Ian Pool and a couple of tinies. As ever, they looked quite as much like animals as boys. Strewn around on chairs, and the floor, with Ian Pool stretched horizontally across a desk top, they were full of lazy, dozy, late-afternoon sweetness. The banter flew between them; they were tight as a jazz quartet. Yet simultaneously their antennae were stretched out all around the camp. Now and then they'd see something, out there through the open door, and chat about it and joke. On the left the boys, on the right Clare Higginson. It felt like two worlds.

It was two worlds. One was the old Mohawk world of laid-back, rough-and-ready instinctiveness; the other was the urgent, abstract world of modern health care, crisp, organized, efficient. In one all the focus was on the present, on what was being experienced right there at the moment; in the other on the future, on the avoidance, above all, of anything hurtful or untoward occurring through lack of planning.

In the one the world felt friendly, a place where, somehow, everything would work itself out in the end; in the other the world felt threatening, full of a constant, nagging sense that without the appropriate precautions – usually 'expert'-imposed – things would go wrong. One world used words like 'concept', 'focus' and 'model'; in the other, the only model anyone was interested in worked for *Vogue*. In a word, one world was amateur, the other professional.

Both amateurism and professionalism are virtues. The instinctive ways of Mohawk, as we have seen, produced their own unique and very human successes; yet its confusions, equally, sometimes even dangerously, wasted great swathes of time, energy and resources. More organization, clearly, could produce more consistency, and might not consistency be fairer on the autistic boys? Not to mention the virtues, self-evident to any professional, of proper training. How were young kids from Beckton supposed to grasp a condition as complex as autism? And then there were those strange philosophical hinterlands, where one world-view virtually took on the other's clothes. Professionalism unquestionably flattened the Mohawk day, making it less individual. Nevertheless, that most classic piece of professionalism, the individual care plan – whereby each autistic child was first assessed, then allotted an individually tailored set of targets – was above all predicated on making each autistic child's care more individual. As in all wars, cultural or otherwise, there were arguments on both sides. Unfortunately, as in all wars, this only made things worse.

Take Clare's viewpoint. When she'd first worked at the camp, a couple of years earlier, her time, she said, had been 'idyllic'. But then that had been at a particular stage in the camp's history. Mohawk's financial crisis had been momentarily solved, there had been plenty of volunteers, while the moment had not yet arrived when Skip announced his retirement, with all the uncertainty and disorientation that involved.

This year, however, Skip's retirement was official, and he was meant to be – indeed, was – dropping into the background. Clare was no longer the beginner, the blameless ingenue. Whether she wanted to or not, she was being forced to take control. Moreover, her natural bias towards organization was being reinforced by yet further demands, as still more flood tides of legislation washed up on the camp. Notable, this year, were rules about the kitchens, the rebuilding of which, in conformity with new EU regulations, had been the cause of so much of the heavy work we had done back in the spring. There was now a further requirement that everyone who worked in the kitchen had the appropriate diploma. Then there were all the other, ever increasing, demands of measurement of care. The result, certainly, was that Clare was increasingly forced into acting as the embodiment of the new ways, and in a place as tradition-bound as Mohawk, that was always going to be hard.

Quite soon, predictably, things got difficult between Clare and

Dave. You could see it from both their points of view. Here was Clare trying to introduce some semblance of order into the creative chaos that was the camp. Here was Dave, used to the rough and ready way things had been for years, unable to understand why Clare was so pernickety. I remember him being especially struck when Clare asked him for receipts after buying ice creams for the boys. 'Receipts?' said Dave, a look of wonder on his face. 'I mean have you ever queued at an ice-cream van, with people yelling and shouting and getting in a state behind you, and asked the ice-cream man for a receipt?!'

Perhaps the best example was Clare's Customized Shopping List, star innovation of the summer 2000 camp. The idea was superb. Instead of writing out an ad hoc, seat-of-the-pants list based on an uncertain combination of what we thought we needed with what, we hoped, we usually bought, Clare produced a series of photocopied sheets. Down one side of a sheet of A4 were printed, in a list, all the items the camp regularly used: bread, butter, baked beans, toilet rolls, you name it. Down the other side was a matching column in which you put a series of ticks. First you checked the whole list, which jogged your memory, then you ticked off everything required. Result, one customized yet all-embracing list, in which what was needed immediately was always measured against what might be needed shortly, based on the past.

It was, without doubt, an excellent idea, and could have saved a lot of mess-ups. It begged, however, one fundamental question, the kind that only applies, really, in an educational institution: what, in the end, was the reason why we were all there? Was it to run a crisp and efficient organization? Or was it to help the boys to learn and to grow? If it was the second, and it surely was, then the problem was that the idea had come from the adults. Had it come from the boys, it would have been perfect; but as it was, it had inadvertently blundered into the boys' educational space. The whole meaning of Mohawk was surely the extent to which the boys organized their own lives (which included the shopping) and this inevitably involved them making mistakes. The point was they learnt from their mistakes. It was rather like those first wrong shots at a dartboard which lead to the better shots later. Pre-empt the mistakes and you pre-empted their self-education.

Not that anyone should have worried. Within weeks the lists had foundered, seemingly, on the rocks of the scouts' inertia, or conservatism, or instinctive desire to self-educate. Whatever the cause, they mysteriously vanished, and we were back to instant, seat-of-the-pants purchase.

And there were other ways, too, in which the onrush of professionalism got bogged down. There was the time, for instance, when my American neighbour wanted to help fund-raise. He was, in fact, the very same neighbour who had first introduced me to Mohawk, the one who had given Mohawk some money from his trust. Being an energetic and amiable fellow, and a businessman to boot, he was appalled by Mohawk's chronic financial crisis, and resolved to fix it. So, with Skip's agreement, he circulated Mohawk's supporters and asked them to replace the previous ad hoc fund-raising, so often desperate and crisis-related, with some sort of regular commitment.

It made perfect sense, but Skip's supporters hated it. It just wasn't what they expected of Camp Mohawk. 'I had people ringing me up in a dreadful state,' said Skip. 'They'd always been addressed by me personally, yet here was Mohawk approaching them in this impersonal, abstract way; they wouldn't have it.' The scheme had to be dropped. Skip went back to his old, cliffhanger ways. And the stream of money, manic-depressive, as ever, full of stops, starts and sudden spurtings, resumed its flow.

Meanwhile, no concept, spreadsheet or marketing model could affect the onrush of spring, which was now, as we moved towards the end of April, gathering pace. The trees, which had been tentatively budding, now burst into leaf; the hedge below the memorial garden, where we had planted Margaret's tree, spawned clouds of hawthorn blossom, gay and brilliant against the brightening sky.

Meanwhile the camp, whose winter had been so notably defined by sound, was now transformed by smell. No longer were these the rancid smells of mud; now they were the warm, sleepy smells of summer, mainly wood. The timbered huts, cooked by the sunshine, smelt like incense. Sweetest of all were the wood chippings, put down as a walking surface. As you smelt them every instinct said, relax. Other senses were involved, too, notably the sense of touch. Not only did the wind, now, feel like a caress, but the new-spread chippings felt quite different under foot. Where the mud used to claw you and hold you back the wood chippings seemed to give the earth springs, so that each step seemed to be helped on by the earth itself, rather than held back.

It was as if the landscape had changed sides and was in our favour. The chippings-induced bounce could be so strong, at times, that a stroll across camp could feel, and look, like a Michael Jackson moonwalk. More chippings arrived every day, on lorries that skulked uncertainly up the drive. Dave Hamblin supervised the spreading of them, anxious it should be done fast. Leave them in mounds, he explained, and the chippings could quickly heat up inside, even set on fire. It happened in haystacks, sometimes, with dire results.

Even so, despite the new-found benevolence of the season, there was a strange tension and lack of direction in the air. In part, as we have seen, this was caused by the uncertainties of Skip's retirement. With Clare and John Lee taking over, it was quite a question who exactly would end up boss. Then there was the eternal, hovering threat of twenty-first-century bureaucracy. Mohawk had passed all social services inspections so far, but who knew what further tests – including the one, finally, we couldn't pass – might wait in the wings? Then there was a further unsettling question, typical of Mohawk's last-minute ways. Even though five autistic children had been booked in for a Mohawk trip to France that very coming weekend, it was still not entirely clear (at least, Skip said it wasn't) whether we would, in fact, be going at all. Different problems emerged on different days: lack of money, mechanical problems with the coach, no driver booked, you name it.

Yet, I gradually realized, there was another, deeper reason why the camp that week felt curiously half-cocked, in a kind of limbo. It was because there were, as yet, no autistic children on site. Having the children with autism there, I came to realize, was crucial to the camp's best functioning, even its identity. Their absence had not been too critical earlier in the year, because we'd had all that building to do; while in Holland, of course, the autistic kids had indeed been with us. And yet this strange sensation made it more clear than ever why the Mohawk care tradition had evolved. Despite its huge benefits for the autistic children, the care work had above all flourished, over the years, because it was crucial to the scouts. Without the autistic boys the camp was floundering, disoriented, and everyone felt a little strange.

People dealt with this in different ways. For the scouts, it meant they got that much keener on finding jobs, things other than just play. The Cobbett brothers, Johnny and Tim, helped prepare the swimming pool. Christopher Hope and little Terry, a new recruit, helped clean out the bouncy castles, a slithery, slimy mud-infested job, enlivened by shock appearances of frogs, and on good days toads as well, to whoops of glee.

Phil Simpson and Matt Polesden were working on the wood chippings; and here, especially, you could see that recurrent Mohawk characteristic, the way it blurred the dividing lines between things. As with the boys doing the building work back in February, as with the fund-raising at Christmas, it was quite a puzzle to figure out what was work, and what was play.

After all, the chippings lent themselves wonderfully to both. There was, for a start, this rumoured self-ignition, a thought which raised a bright gleam of hope in the boys' faces, though it never happened. What it did mean, though, was that the job clearly had to be done fast, or was it just energetically, or even frantically? However you looked at it, dispersing wood chippings in a rush offered superb scope for hurling huge gobs of material about, or at each other, or at the adults; or turning the piles left by the lorries into superb, instant forts, eagerly attacked and defended; or, if jumped on from above, into wood-chipping 'ponds' in which you could leap and sink yourself, and scream as you drowned; or, if rushed at from the side, into long, skiddy slides, down which you could hurtle to a guaranteed soft landing at the end. As ever, the curious thing about all this play was that it in no way stopped the work; for all the yelling and shouting and falling about, the chippings got spread.

So where *did* the work start and play stop? As I watched them, I found myself remembering the anthropologist Jean Liedloff's description of the Yequana, a hunter-gatherer tribe she lived with in the Amazon Basin. One day the Indians had to carry some canoes across patches of dry ground between waterways. This horrendous (to a Western eye) job, she noted, seemed merely another reason for jokes and laughter to the Yequana. Yet they did the job as fast, or faster, than any whites. Their joy, quite clearly, was crucial to their efficiency. She further noted, incidentally, that there was no word for 'work' in the Yequana language.

In its Mohawk version, certainly, this blurring of the boundaries between duty and self-indulgence could be strangely infectious. I remember the time when Matt Polesden and Tim Fenton, a plump new scout with glasses, asked permission to clean my car. The scouts often did such jobs for the grown-ups. What was plain, from the very manner of their asking, was that they thought we would be doing them the favour, not the other way about.

The only problem, explained Matt, was they needed a source of water, so could I move my car nearer to the tap? I did, but the hose still didn't reach, so I suggested squirting it from a distance. Of course, we could have filled a bucket but that would have been less interesting. What it required – it suddenly seemed very important to demonstrate this to the boys – was to angle the hose at forty-five degrees like an aquatic mortar, then further increase the range by putting one finger on the end. A twitch of a finger tip, I showed Matt, and you could fine-tune the water's landing point to the inch.

So Matt had a go and missed by feet. Then Tim tried and soaked Matt. So I showed them again. Then someone called them both to the other end of the camp and they left me doing it. It was a skill I had perfected watering the garden at home, and I was rather proud of it. These joyous streams of water curled over in great arcs and landed, to the precise millimetre, on the mudguard where I had aimed; or I closed in to point blank range and annihilated one antique, lurking mud-stain, machine-gunning it into oblivion. Next thing I knew, I had been doing it for half an hour. And then I realized what had happened. The kids' world-view had overwhelmed me: 'work' had turned into play.

Later on, of course, the boys came back, tried again, and soon got the hang of it. Reluctantly, I backed off and gave them their go. Later still they came and fetched me, and showed me the work they had done. They had done the job superbly. Not only had they washed the car down, and scrubbed it inside and out, but they had polished it as well. They had clearly taken delight in transforming it, Lazarus-like, from the mud-encrusted disgrace they'd inherited to the twinkling mechanical jewel it had now become. No professional cleaning firm could have done a better job, and their commitment, clearly, had been absolute. Play had turned into work.

Not least, of course, this was because I had left them alone to get on with it, so they had 'owned' the task. Nevertheless, there were times when the decision to walk away was harder, and one got adept at discovering all the very-good-reasons why. I remember another morning when I was standing at the campfire circle, at a loose end myself this time, and saw four scouts carrying some timber planks from one end of the camp to another. Quite hard work, quite heavy lifting, although they could just about manage it. Just the kind of thing, perhaps, an adult could help out with.

Indeed, the more I watched, the more I felt I *ought* to get involved. How could I stand there, idle, and watch these young boys do such a heavy job? I was just about to join then when, from somewhere even deeper, some other, maverick voice told me it would be a mistake. Was it something about the way the boys carried themselves, the way they avoided my eyes? Don't do it, I told myself. But I had no idea why.

Later I mentioned it to John Lee. He laughed in recognition. 'You were dead right not to join in,' he said. Not only would I have deprived them of their work, and thus their sense of purpose, but there was also, he said, a subtler point. It was strange how often, as an adult on the camp, you would get this impulse to join in if you happened, say, to be feeling a bit depressed. And, of course, I had been feeling at a bit of a loose end. Because, whether you realized it consciously or not, you could raise your own spirits by having some practical success. However, as with the shopping list, this was not what the camp was all about.

This was typical of the way John viewed the place: full of the old, libertarian Mohawk philosophy. Yet what was unique about John's world-view was that he simultaneously accommodated the new ways, too. For John is naturally efficient and, within sensible limits, a planner; and yet somehow, he never loses sight of Skip's beloved 'spontaneity'. In John's case this means the crucial capacity to change tack, at the last moment, and do something different from what is planned if it is clear the group mood has changed, vital when working with volatile creatures like young boys. But best of all, he had that extraordinary gentleness and sensitivity which all the scouts, the younger ones in particular, did their macho best to keep hidden. Unsurprisingly, he was a great favourite with the mothers of both scouts and autistic children. Many of them, it seemed to me, were secretly in love with him. They'd have had a problem with John, though: his commitment to the troop was twenty-four hours. He was married to it.

Not least, I came to realize, was this because Skip, over the years, has been a father figure to John, who was brought up by his grandparents and never knew his father and mother. As with so many boys over the years – but especially with John, for whom Skip has a specially soft spot – Skip nurtured him, encouraged him, picked him up every time he lost heart and finally edged him on to do a university degree. A measure of how much John feels he owes Skip and the troop is that three or four years back, when John was still studying, the troop offered John £50 as part payment for his work as a scout leader. After all, they pointed out, he could have been doing a holiday job. But John wouldn't take it. 'I just couldn't accept money from the camp,' he said. 'I owe *them* so much.' The year I joined Mohawk John had just completed his degree, in psychology, from the University of East London, and a picture of John in academic robes, complete with mortarboard, now graces Skip's sideboard in his Beckton front room.

However, what this academic track record also means is that John – who after fifteen years as both scout and scout master has comparable hands-on experience to Skip – has now advanced into another, quite different mental world, that of theory. Not unnaturally, he's especially interested in the theory of autism.

John likes to talk about it; he's interested in the latest ideas; but this is one area where he and Skip part company.

One day I was sitting with Skip, John and a few of the scouts, having a cup of tea on the camp lawn. I mentioned I'd been reading about the Son-Rise Program, an American therapy system for autistic children which seemed to have a lot in common with Mohawk. In particular, Son-Rise laid great stress on intensive, one-to-one care. Far from believing that autism was the kind of 'hard-wired' condition which was essentially inalterable, they seemed to feel some autistic children could advance so much that they could be effectively cured. The founders had based their formalized therapy on the ideas they had used to treat their autistic son. Using those ideas, he had advanced from a virtually dysfunctional 2-year-old with all the familiar problems – remoteness, rages, spinning obsessions, lack of speech – to a remarkable adulthood. His intelligence has been described as 'near-genius level'. He has a degree in biomedical ethics.

John had heard about the Son-Rise Program and he enthused. Indeed, someone from Son-Rise, he said, had come to the University of East London and given a talk. John had loved every minute of it, he said. He'd found it 'fascinating'.

So the Son-Rise speaker had indeed made the heretical link between symptoms and emotions? Absolutely, said John, and elaborated on the thesis. Then suddenly, as John paused a moment, Skip said to me:

'What's your body talk like?'

'Eh?'

'How good are you at reading people's body talk?'

'Average,' I said, wondering where this was going.

'Well,' said Skip, 'look at mine! Look how I'm sitting away from the conversation!'

He was, indeed, presenting half his mighty back to John and me. And the reason, he explained, was that John and I had lost him by getting so theoretical. Even when, as in this case, the theory seemed to back up everything Skip represented.

'Theory frightens me,' he said. 'I have this constant fear that the head is going to take over from the heart. If that happens, in my view, you're dead.' Added to which, said Skip, he didn't know anything about autism anyway; he left it to the boys. 'They're the ones with the vision, the flair, the lack of preconceptions.' And even if he was overstating the case for effect, you could see Skip was defending something he believed vital, something which informed his whole philosophy of life, indeed, not just his philosophy of care.

> our meddling intellect
> misshapes the beauteous form of things
> We murder to dissect.

So Wordsworth put it, the archetypal Romantic. And, of course, this was the point about Skip. In the great Classic/Romantic divide, on one side or other of which nearly all of us pretty much fall, Skip was an out-and-out Romantic. He hated and feared abstraction; he loved immediacy, subjectivity, touch. True, he actually knew a great deal more about autism than he let on. For instance, he had, it turned out later, carefully taped a TV documentary about the Son-Rise Program, and even thought of taking some of Mohawk's autistic children over to the United States to try it out. Nevertheless, he had a profound sense of the dangers of the 'meddling intellect', while what he was in favour of could be summed up, as ever, in his favourite word, 'spontaneity'. It was, he genuinely believed, the key to life. A view that puts him, one cannot but note, at the opposite end of the universe from Microsoft's Bill Gates.

Having said which, the downside with spontaneity (and in fairness, one reason why modern bureaucracy so hates and fears it) is you never quite know how it will work out. Things can just as well go phut as swimmingly.

One day one of the boys asked Skip the name of the trees which overshadowed the campfire circle. Oaks, replied Skip, and duly picked up an oak leaf and put it on the table, explaining that the leaf, above all, is the way to tell a species. Indeed, said Skip picking up another leaf, this second one was a turkey oak – related, but different, as you could tell by its shape. He picked up a third leaf and laid this, too, on the table. This was a sycamore, he said. Look at that lovely broad shape; just like the Canadian national flag.

Now Skip was moving quickly into Mohawk's DIY educational gear, and on to the table came more leaves, all laid out in a row: hazel, ash, pine, larch. Skip expanded into a description of the use to which all the various trees could be put. How oak built the British Navy, how hazel was good for furniture, how ash was good for chariots – the kind of play-chariots the scouts might build at the camp, that is – and how pine was disastrous for cooking. '*Never* use pine for cooking, it makes your steaks stink like toilet cleaner.'

As usual a little clutch of scouts gathered round, and before we knew it, another home-brewed lesson was under way. I was sitting facing the little circle of scouts, just behind Skip's shoulder when suddenly I saw the boys' attention falter, then gradually disappear. Something, way over to our left, was distracting them. What was it?

It was simple enough. One of the visiting lorries, its load of wood chippings delivered, had gone a yard too far backward in its U-turn and had got roundly stuck in the mud. Every time it revved up it got worse. Three of the older scouts, including the inevitable Ian Pool, were already trying to heft it out. Every so often it shifted forward a bit, did a little skid, then settled back where it was first stuck, only deeper. There was even a remote chance it might tip over.

Poor Skip! What possible leaf lesson, however inspired, could compete with a drama like that? Eventually he followed the kids' eyes and saw what was happening. He slowed down and, eventually, stopped. The 'lesson' petered out.

More of a problem was the question that loomed larger every day: what about the French trip? Another downside of 'spontaneity' was that while things were never done unless they felt right, there was always the chance they might never be done at all. There were the routine question marks over the state of the coach, which had supposedly been serviced, but you never quite knew, and the availability of a driver. By late in the week it looked like Michael, the ex-scout leader I'd met in Beckton, might be available, but no one was quite sure. There were subtler worries, too, not about whether we were going but about what would happen if we did.

There were, for instance, worries about Tessa Compton, mother of one of the autistic kids, Leigh. For on this trip Tessa was due to join us. Tessa is a jolly, forceful lady in her thirties who had already worked at Mohawk, the previous summer, as a volunteer. She'd got on fine, but the scouts were nervous. In previous years when parents had come on trips it had been tricky. They tended to have their own ideas, naturally enough, about how their children should be looked after. Nor was it just their own kids. They had ideas about the scouts, too. Before you knew it the troop could get taken in hand. Things could get organized, sensible. Nor was this entirely offset by the prospect of some decent cooking.

So how real were all these worries? I never really knew. All I knew for sure, over the months, was that such dramas were part of the constant emotional framework of Camp Mohawk, always there at some level, not necessarily the most prominent, permanent fixtures like the laughs, the rivalry, the camaraderie. In some weird way I could never quite figure out, I could sense that the love and joy of the place and the various rumbling tensions were somehow interlinked. Take one away and you would lose the other.

In the end, perhaps, what it boiled down to was that at Mohawk organizational worries, like all the other crowding emotions of camp life, were articulated rather than repressed. But what was also true was that they would build and build into an apparent crisis, and then, as often as not, utterly dissolve. This was what happened this time. By the end of the week the coach was fixed, Michael turned out to be available, the autistic kids turned up, plus Tessa, and, at six on the Saturday morning, we were on our way. In the end, as with so much at Mohawk, it all seemed as much meteorological as emotional. Clear skies, dark skies, climax, resolution: the phenomenon was plain to see; the rationale, mysterious.

As we rattled through the early morning lanes, there were three adults on board who hadn't been to Holland: Michael, Tessa and, also, Dave Hamblin, who was, as ever, greeted with cheers by the boys. Some of the autistic children, too, were different. As well as Bernard Naisbitt, who had been to the Dutch carnival, there were also George, Leigh, Teddy and little Brett. And again you got this sense of broad autistic types. Tessa's son Leigh, for instance, pale, dark-haired and retiring, reminded you of the snub-nosed Peter Bell. Eleven-year-old Brett looked tough and butch, the kind of boy who could be *real* trouble, you sensed. His look was accentuated by his crewcut, yet softened by his long, curling eyelashes. As for Teddy, like David Knebworth, we had once again a faerie king. Pale, too, like Leigh and Peter but looking less ill, more spiritual, he had, like Dreamy David, the most exquisite poet's eyes. Grey and dreamy, one eye had a little shot of gold in it, which only added to his enchanted, other-worldly air.

And there were new scouts, too. There was Tim Fenton, for

instance, fourteen years old, plump, lumbering, with glasses. A curiously intense, unsure child, he'd come to Mohawk with a local fame in Beckton for being difficult. He'd been around since earlier in the year but this was his first trip abroad. Unsurprisingly, he had yet to be accepted by the other scouts. Most notably there was little Sebastian, who could have passed for Italian. Small, dark and ineffably cute, he looked like something out of what the art business calls 'genre' paintings. The sort of gypsyish rapscallion, with huge brown eyes, who's tricked out with earrings. Well, Sebastian had no earrings but he had a bright red scarf wound round his neck, Neapolitan style. You couldn't help feeling he was aware of the effect.

So that it was no surprise, somehow, that Sebastian quickly attained high visibility on the coach, as we crossed the Channel and settled into the long cruise southward through France.

Was he aware of his cuteness to adult eyes? I think so. Kids are far more aware of such things than we realize. It is, after all, one of their few sources of power. Like a lot of children – like Pete Pollard on that first trip to Holland – when they first join a group they give a surprising amount of attention to the adults. Irrelevant though the adults may be to the main event – their relationships with other children – they can't be ignored. Get the grown-ups straight first, get them sorted, and they are like a foundation from which you can expand.

So he got straight down to business, and again like Pete, he turned in his seat, faced backwards, and unleashed a charm offensive on the first available adult. As with Pete, because of where I was sitting, this once again happened to be me. The difference was that whereas Pete had majored on cheeky-chappy, charm, Sebastian added in naughtiness.

A volley of questions, first, steadily escalating.

'What's up with your ears?'

'What's up with your arm?'

'What's up with your face?'

And then: 'Twenty-six!'

'Eh?'

'Twenty-six!' A ravishing grin.

'Twenty-six what?'

'Churches,' supplied Tessa Compton, sitting just across the way. 'He's been counting churches ever since Calais.' And, indeed, Sebastian carried on counting them throughout our time in France.

Finally: 'Whassat on your wrist?'

'My watch.'

'Whassat over there?'

I turned. Sebastian nicked my crisps.

Half an hour south of Calais, we branched off the motorway and headed into the services.What's this? More spontaneity? A drinks stop? No – more familiar still – we'd broken down. And to add to the fun, even the problem was the same: it was the wipers.

There followed three hours in which we slaved away in the rain, trying every trick in the book, chiselling things, bashing them, spraying them, while inside the bus John Lee tried desperately to keep the autistic kids occupied. Then we realized the battery had packed up; we must have left something on all the time we'd been parked. But no, a brainwave: there was another battery in the back which should jump-start the main one. It worked! By heroic efforts we finally got back, after three and a half hours, to where we'd started.

At which moment Phil Simpson, who was obviously born for such moments, wandered up.

'Just a thought,' he said.

'What's that?'

'It sounds obvious, but did you realize it's stopped raining?'

He was right. We'd got so involved we hadn't noticed. We piled into the coach and reached Bucquoy within the hour.

In the morning we woke up to an utterly new Bucquoy. Two

months had transformed it. Even in March it had been a welcome break from the Dutch winter. Now, at the end of April, it was a little paradise, a promise of the summer to come. A mere hundred miles south of Dover, it seemed in advance of the British seasons. It was like Berkshire in May.

The farmhouse was bursting with new grass, while the tree that stuck up over the next-door fence, a mere broomstick in March, turned out to be white lilac. In the garden beyond, an orchard sagged with apple blossom; raggedy daffodils pottered around the trees' roots; a red barn and a gaudy, orange and green garden shed glowed in the sun. Ill-tended but homely, the place felt muddled, welcoming and marvellously alive.

The troop quickly made the place their own. Soon Skip was out on his inevitable machine, poised precariously on a mini-tractor towing a grass-cutter, mowing the field at the back. The boys ran wheelbarrow races, dodging and darting in his wake. Michael and Dave stood thoughtfully in front of the bus, poking at the wipers. Tessa Compton took over the dining room next door to the staff sitting room, got out her study books (she was studying the French Revolution for an extra-mural history degree), and made a little kingdom of her own.

For the week, the scouts had been divided into two groups, one run by Ian Pool, the other by Tom Pollard. It was striking how much the two had changed, even in the short time I'd known them. When I'd first met Ian three years earlier, he'd been a child; he was now a foot taller, and looked like the elder brother of the boy I'd known. Barrel-chested and broad, he was now a man. But Tom's change had been more recent. There were money problems at home, and Tom's characteristic expression had long been a preoccupied frown, more or less regardless of what was happening in front of him. But recently he had been transformed. Now he walked around with that same perky, optimistic look I'd seen, at Christmas, on the face of the woodwork-loving scout Dan Knapton, who'd worked with me on the Christmas float. I might almost have thought I'd been imagining it, till others said they'd noticed it too.

But then, it emerged, Tom had every reason to look different: good things were happening. Skip had helped get him get into college to study computing and, on hearing this, a Mohawk supporter had given him a £1,000 laptop. And then, of course, Skip was giving him ever more responsibility in the troop. Skip trusted him. The world was finally looking promising. Meanwhile, it was a reminder of why there is such an art as portraiture. You could see the whole thing right there in his face.

Matt Polesden's change was more dramatic still. When I first met him, back in February, 13-year-old Matt had seemed a rather wan, sad little boy, always on the edge of things, always, seemingly, on the verge of tears. But then he had even greater problems at home than Tom. His mother was on bail, awaiting trial; the signs were she'd be convicted, and he and his brothers would go into care. Yet despite all this, in just two months, some mysterious chemistry had occurred. He'd begun to make friends. He'd palled up initially with Christopher Hope, who'd been marginalized for different reasons – he'd been too bright. Like Tom Pollard, he'd even begun to look different; increasingly the wan look was replaced by an elfin, mischievous grin, and, as he poked you, pinched you and scampered about, you could sense this was the way he charmed his mum.

Nor were such changes confined to the scouts. The autistic boys were changing, too, and on this trip it was Bernard Naisbitt you noticed most of all. For if Bernard's key problem was what the psychologists call passive-aggression, he was quickly losing it. He was eating everything he was offered. He was helping out, domestically. More than once I saw him carry plates across a room, or sweep the dining-room floor. Most striking of all, he was talking, notably with Matt Polesden. But here was a clue to Matt's development, too. For Matt had taken a shine to Bernard, virtually taken him under his wing. His care for Bernard was benefiting both of them. Mohawk therapy, in fact, was once again taking place. But as ever, the question was begged: just who was providing the therapy for whom?

Meanwhile, something quite different was hovering in the background of everyone's consciousness: local history. For the farmhouse, it turned out, was just along the road from all the most noted names of the Battle of the Somme; Thiepval, Pozieres, Beaumont Hamel. Moreover, it was situated just back from the British front line during the great German attack in 1918. It surely would have been a bivouac for British troops. The local landscape, so undistinguished and yet so appealing, was just the kind that a First World War poet like Siegfried Sassoon describes so poignantly; its muddled, unpretentious charm only underscoring the enormity of what was happening just down the road. Added to which the curiously old-fashioned manner of the scouts, both young and old, further added to the sense of historical déjà vu. They talked, and looked, so very much like their great-grandfathers.

Gradually, it became clear that these connections were more direct than might have seemed. Skip's grandfather, it emerged, had gone off to the war in 1915 and never returned. For years his family only knew him as one of the countless thousands who simply disappeared, with no known grave. But not any more. When Skip first bought Bucquoy he had gone one day to visit the great memorial arch at Thiepval, just five miles away, which is devoted exclusively to soldiers without graves. Thousands of their names are engraved upon the arch. Skip carefully checked the lists for the appropriate regiment and time, and there, rediscovered after eighty-five years, was his grandfather. 'It was one of the happiest, and saddest, days of my life,' says Skip.

Not that much of this seemed to interest the scouts; but then the local history has a way of thrusting itself on you whether you will or no.

One morning we went out on a variant of the classic Mohawk therapy, the walk with autistic children. There were a dozen of us. The line-up included myself, Dave Hamblin, Ian Pool, Fred Robinson, and several of the boys with autism. Out we snaked into the village street, then walked a mile or so west into the country. We found a cart track off the main road, and headed slightly uphill; then the cart track turned into a path. Soon we had left the village behind, and were in a vast cornfield.

It was a landscape that could have been designed for battle. Like the Wiltshire downs, it was all about light, space and wind. The great hills rolled ever onwards like slowly undulating breakers, while here and there a smudge on the horizon suggested a village. It was exhilaratingly, fatally, open and unprotected; nowhere on earth, except possibly a desert, could there have been a place better suited to the traversing of machine guns.

And yet, that morning, it felt full of joy and freshness, remote as could be from the horrors of eighty-two years ago. Larks burst out of the field either side of us. The new, green corn looked almost fluorescent. The poplars towards Bucquoy glowed in the steady sun. It was the first day of our holiday, most of the group was under fourteen, and the sap was rising in us, as in the landscape all around. The kids laughed and yelled and chased each other. Even Teddy, most ethereal of boys, seemed half-awakened out of his trance. Walking hand in hand with Dave, he was grinning happily. 'We're friends, aren't we!' Dave told him. 'We'll jump up and down!' And Teddy jumped and shrieked and cackled with the rest.

Then suddenly the scouts were in a huddle by the side of the path. I joined them. They were peering at a rusty, earth-encrusted First World War shell, standing upright at the path's edge. It had, presumably, been put there by the farmer. When shells are ploughed up locally, as they still, remarkably, are, they are stacked at the edge of the field, picked up and brought back to central collection points, then blown up. I pulled the boys back from it, but now their interest was awakened and they began to look for more. Two other shells were quickly spotted, and then another, then one was seen in the semi-ploughed limbo-land just off the main path, half-buried in the earth. And then another! They were everywhere! ''Ere!' said little Sebastian, in tones of outrage. 'Someone bin fighting a *war* round 'ere or something?'

What a chance for one of those Mohawk educational moments! I was off in a rush into the dread majesty of the great 1918 German attack, which had been preceded – as we could see before our eyes – by the greatest bombardment in military history; but the boys weren't interested in grand strategy. They were only interested in the 'bombs', as they called them. Not only did they poke them, and pick them up, and try to dig them out of the ground, but soon Pete and Fred, with the cheery, genial air of kids playing ball, started throwing them from one to the other. As I yelled at them, I spun round to find two other scouts doing exactly the same, and as I turned again there were three of them running happily along the path in a line, chucking a shell from one to the other to the next like they were a rugby three-quarter line.

Dave and I were the only adults. Dave was still hopping and jumping around with Teddy, some way behind. So it was down to me. So what about all those fine ideas of children's 'freedom'? One must be joking. I went apoplectic. 'These bombs could kill us! Touch one more and I'll kill you!' I yelled. It so happened we had heard, that very morning, about an accident at one of those shell collecting points, an explosion in which two people had been killed. Adult interference? It was a question of pure survival. The scouts were absolutely not going to do it, not for one moment more.

But the boys didn't see it like that. For a start, of course, they could see no connection between these earth-encrusted lumps of iron, like long-lost garden ornaments, and anything that might go bang. Then it was the first time, too, since I'd been with them, that I'd pulled the adult card of responsibility and authority. You could see it in their eyes: I wasn't even a proper member of the troop. What right had I?

Not to mention the most urgent question of all. Ian Pool spoke for everyone: 'What's up then?' he said, with withering contempt. 'You scared or something?'

You bet I am. What a way to go: two men and ten kids, last casualties of the Great War.

But the boys disagreed, and even though I finally got them to take the sanity option, and leave the bombs alone, our relationship, which had been steadily improving, went into a nosedive. Especially my relationship with Ian Pool.

Yet all it meant, in one way, was the end of my honeymoon period with the scouts, and the beginnings of real relationship. For anger is quite as much a part of Mohawk as camaraderie. The point is all emotions are allowed and given full vent, rather as they are among children, and different feelings surface at different times. The formal logic of these swings can be mysterious; the emotional logic, flawless.

And even during this one short trip to France, what a maelstrom was boiling away beneath the surface! For a start, I wasn't the only adult Ian Pool had fallen out with; he very soon got cross with Tessa Compton, too. As did Tom Pollard. For Tessa, as feared, quickly started trying to organize the kitchen, and as Ian and Tom were involved in serving up the meals, the fur flew. Then there were the rows among the adults. Dave Hamblin kept up a constant, whingeing rearguard action against Skip. (Their relationship was a strange combination of joviality, resentment and mutual dependence.) Tessa, also, quickly clashed with Skip. Not least of their differences was Tessa's insistence that the autistic children should be fed according to their diets, which was by no means Skip's natural pile-'em-high, fry-'em deep philosophy.

Added to which there were problems, too, with the outside world. Shortly after we arrived Skip sent off the first of a flood of faxes to the garage which had serviced our coach, and which had, it's fair to say, so signally failed. Poor little scouts and autistic kids (that was the faxes' tone), out here in a foreign hell. How *could* the garage have let such a terrible thing occur? How *would* the authorities view it, were it ever to be known? But then such disturbances were routine at Mohawk. They co-existed, weirdly, with everything else.

Nor did any of this prevent Mohawk's great love, the planning of trips out. As ever, they weren't lacking in ambition, if arguably light on logic. Having travelled thus far down from the coast, the word got around that one really great trip would be to go on a little local railway which the French had reactivated, complete with old-time steam engine, way back on the coast.

So off we went. Despite the long distance, this time we actually managed to avoid getting lost. Until, that is, we reached the little seaside town itself, a place of around 5,000 souls but with a street plan that owed a lot to Hampton Court Maze. Our destination, naturally enough, was La Gare. But possibly because regular use stopped thirty years ago, or possibly because of our pronunciation, none of the locals we spoke to seemed to have a clue what we were talking about. Eventually, in the Mohawk tradition of using all talents available, and because I'd been to Oxford, Skip suggested I tried my French.

I asked in the town centre, they sent us to the suburbs; I asked in the suburbs, they sent us to the esplanade; the esplanade sent us back to the town hall. 'C'est magnifique, mais ça n'est pas la gare,' I wittily observed, but no one got it. Undeterred, after devoted research I finally found a woman who gave us impeccable directions and we were there in five minutes. So impressed was Skip by this that he made me trip interpreter on the spot. So flushed was I by my new-found status that I didn't dare admit I'd found the only café owner in town who spoke fluent English.

Everyone loved the steam train. Above all, of course, the autistic children, for whom all trains are an especial delight. But no one loved the train as much as Teddy, who was coming out of himself with alacrity on this trip.

He was behaving in ways no one had seen before. For a start, there was his conversation. As the train sped along, he bombarded everyone in earshot with a string of questions about the engine, the coaches, the track. Then there was this 'withdrawn' child's burgeoning need to touch and hug. He sat happily on Dave's lap, arms round his neck. When Dave had to pop momentarily into the next carriage, Teddy instantly moved over and sat, just as trustingly, with me. It was as if the trust he'd achieved with Dave reached some psychic critical mass and spilled over. For I hardly knew Teddy, and this was a boy who was, like so many autistic children, 'scared of strangers'.

It was a virtuous circle: the more Teddy touched, the more he talked; the more he talked, the more he touched. And now he launched into a string of questions of that faux-naive kind that Einstein said most people stop asking at six. Getting his inspiration, clearly, from the view out of the train window, he asked: why do rivers run? Why do trees grow? And then – evidently inspired by a certain linguistic problem detectable among the adults earlier – why do people speak differently in different countries? Why? It was curious, autistic children are supposed to be so concerned with mechanics, with the mere prosaic 'how' of the world, yet all the questions Teddy asked that afternoon, however simply phrased, were philosophical: they were questions of 'why'.

A great deal of this development, it must be said, was down to his burgeoning relationship with Dave, who was shaping up, on this trip, as Teddy's mentor. Teddy refused, for instance, to go to sleep at night, until Dave read him a story. What was it about Dave? All the boys loved him, and the autistic kids above all; yet he had never studied childcare in his life, and was innocent of autistic theory. Or was that the whole point, as with the relationship the scouts themselves had with the autistic children? What became ever more plain, as the summer wore on, was that Dave, like the boys, was above all an observer. Lacking all forms of preconception, he simply saw, intensely, what was before his eyes. Added to which, he was acutely sensitive to atmosphere; his ability to feel, as much as to see, was critical. It seemed no coincidence that it turned out Dave was, also, very good with animals. When he was younger he'd kept horses, as well as greyhounds which he'd raced.

So successful, indeed, was this trip that it inspired a follow-up two days later. An ardent perusal of brochures found yet another fabulous place to go – a French theme park – and once again, the fact that it was about as close to the coast as you could imagine without actually getting on the ferry back to England was no discouragement.

So despite my frantic protestations, and in my new role of trip interpreter, I was commissioned to ring up the theme park to check its opening hours and prices. I got this receptionist. Who would have thought it, she seemed so nice! When we got there, three hours later, the place was closed. The opening hours she and I had discussed in such detail must have referred to a different day. Not that anyone seemed to mind. If anything, I felt as if I'd passed some rite of passage. So what should we do now? So what else? We went straight to the beach and spent the afternoon there having a wonderful time, a kind of non-stop, all-in, anyone-can-join wrestling match that lasted four hours.

Indeed, the spontaneous trip to the theme park which led to the spontaneous fight on the beach was so enjoyable that on the way back the scouts started a singalong. A sure sign, as with Skip, that they were in a good mood. Pop songs, scout songs, movie themes, all rattled out one after the other with scarcely a pause for breath, until suddenly Skip grabbed the coach's public-address microphone. With his familiar, quavering vibrato, and an expression as serious as when Michael tells a joke, Skip turned round in his seat and sang 'The Alphabet Song', the most golden of oldies, in which each line starts with a letter introducing a new charm in the beloved: A for adorable, B for beautiful and so on.

It was just the kind of old-time, high-camp song you might have imagined Skip would like; more surprising was that the boys seemed to like it, too. But there again, boys do live in a time zone of their own. At any rate, they were soon belting it out like they were on the end of the pier in 1935. Gradually, tentatively, the autistic boys began to join in, too. First Teddy, then Tommy, then Leigh, Tessa's son. Leigh, in particular, did especially well, throwing his head back and carolling with the best, encouraged, as always, by the ever-solicitous John Lee.

It was a flood tide of enthusiasm and exuberance, and a reminder, too, of the strange, crabwise way a community like Camp Mohawk works. The scouts were in such an infectiously good mood – and thus able to give the autistic children such good 'therapy' – precisely because they themselves had had such a good time, however accidental, on the beach. Yet the strangest moment was still to come.

Skip always liked to stretch people beyond their limits. Now he decided to stretch Bernard Naisbitt. On a flood tide of jollity, he turned to Bernard, who happened to be sitting up the front, thrust the mike into his hands, and asked Bernard – lonely, unsure Bernard, who can hardly string a sentence together without huge encouragement – to sing solo, and to sing to all the coach.

Bernard looked flabbergasted, then terrified, then pleased, and then he started singing. Off he, too, went into 'The Alphabet Song', struggling bravely through the letters to mounting cheers from the scouts; he finally made it right through to the end.

He sat down to thunderous applause. He was an utter, unprecedented success.

When we got home, I congratulated Skip on his choice of song.

'Yeah, that one always goes down well with the autistic kids,' he said. 'Funnily enough, I don't like it much, personally.'

Predictably, with that degree of euphoria, the reverse mood-swing had to follow; and the next day it duly happened, with an explosion of outrage over the faxed response of the garage, which had come in overnight. 'It don't make sense,' said Skip. 'They're saying they tested the part before they fitted it; but now could we send them the reference number please, so they can get a new part. If they need the number, and they got the part before, how come they don't know the number already?' It got worse. 'I mean!' yelled an outraged Skip, waving another fax, that evening. 'Now they're asking for the coach's make!' And this from the garage which had serviced Pegasus for years. And off went Skip's response, and back whistled theirs, each incoming fax drawing ever shriller gasps of outrage.

If outward relations were in crisis, so were domestic, because the rumbling discontent among the adults gradually built throughout the week. It began to escalate, in fact, like a five-act drama, and by Thursday we were heading for the pay-off. Skip was getting more and more irritated with Tessa. Tessa was getting more and more fed up with Skip. He reminded her, she said, of her father. John was getting quietly and ruefully fed up with constantly being blamed. According, that was, to arch-gossip Dave. Dave himself, as always, was getting fed up with absolutely everything. Dave, whether at home or abroad, always combined his vast, unpaid commitment with a constant, humorous, charming, but utterly remorseless, drip drip drip of moaning.

By Thursday night, in fact, we were heading for Clash of the Titans Two, the showdown between Tessa and Skip. The kitchen wasn't big enough for the both of them. The atmosphere was toxic; you could measure it by the way everyone disappeared. The staff room was empty. Michael had bailed out upstairs. Dave had 'popped out for some fags' and had been away for over an hour. Skip was sulking in his tent, i.e. his personal sitting room, just down the corridor. Indeed, Tessa, however temporarily, was left in possession of the field. She sat there quietly knitting, but it couldn't last.

And then came yet another of those weird, inexplicable, meteorological releases of tension. Later that evening, Dave finally returned, looking apprehensive. Shortly after, Tessa went off to bed. Coincidence being the wonderful thing it is, Skip promptly reappeared from his sitting room. Tentatively, at first, we all shared some tea, then some beer, then a sudden rush of spirits and wine. Sensible as ever, and concerned for the boys, John went up to the dormitory, but Dave, Skip and I accelerated, and very soon got utterly slaughtered. In Dave and Skip's case this took the form of a wild exaggeration of their normal tendency to tell jokes. Joke joke joke they went, rat-tat-tat one after another, without remission or reprieve, while all three of us gradually disappeared under the table. At two o'clock, we finally crawled away to bed. When we woke up in the morning it was as if the atmosphere had never been. All was genial. We liked one another and forgave one another as well. But then as lovers know there is more than one way to defuse a row.

And the kids benefited too, for the gestalt psychologists are right. Just as the boys' good mood had spread from the beach to the coach, and then on to the autistic children, so the adults' reconciliation, mysteriously embracing Tessa too, quickly spread to the kids. By the evening, the whole troop was in the best of moods as we set off for the climax of the week: a supper at Le Poppy, that same restaurant where we had lunched back in March.

* * *

Little did we know, as we innocently set out, that even by Mohawk's high standards we were due to get more lost this time than ever. After all, we weren't talking Antarctica here, merely a brief round trip into Albert, around twelve miles away, where we were to pick up a bargain-priced barbecue which Skip had promised a friend back at home, then on again to Pozieres, location of Le Poppy, which was about four miles east of Albert. Piece of cake.

Or was it? We started happily enough. Indeed, we even, extraordinarily, had a map, albeit one hand-drawn by Skip. We had Dave on board, and Michael, and Tessa, and we'd all been to Albert before, so what could possibly go wrong?

First intimation of difficulty was when we turned out of the farmhouse and headed straight off down the Arras road, i.e. the opposite direction from Albert. But this, explained Michael, was what it said on Skip's map. Then we turned towards Thiepval, which was in another direction again. But this, too, was OK, said Dave, because he'd come this way just yesterday, and it had led to Albert then. Soon we came to a crossroads and neither Dave nor Michael were absolutely sure. Dave leaned, on balance, towards the left; Michael rather fancied a turn towards the right. They compromised; we went straight on. 'Hang about!' said Dave, a moment later, 'Let's try this road to the left.' He could swear he recognized it, it gave him a really good feeling.

As a mode of direction-finding it was surely unique, because, in the end, what counted was not what the signposts said, or even how the land looked, but rather, the feel. If a road felt good we went up it; if it didn't, we passed it by. It had something in common, too, with the lore of the ancient alchemists, who believed that human nature being what it was, nobody ever performed the same experiment twice. Inevitably, each one was different. Thus if you carried on long enough you'd find gold, in the end, by pure process of elimination. We tried the same thing with roads.

After half an hour we were rattling along brilliantly and the scenery was getting better all the time, but there was no sign that we were any nearer to Albert. We seemed stuck, somehow, somewhere west of it, in an endless spiral of flower-fringed lanes. Yet still we persisted, with weird resilience. There were highs and there were lows. At one moment, to cheers of recognition, we saw an inn we knew a mile away across the valley to our left. Ten minutes later, to groans of disappointment, we saw it sailing by on our right. Soon, the half-hour had turned into an hour, and we were still meandering. What was striking was the resignation shown by both scouts and autistic children. They acted as if this was a perfectly normal journey. (Well, at Mohawk, I guess it was.) Nick Smith and Pete Pollard lay with their heads on each other's shoulders. Matt Polesden pulled his T-shirt up over his head and slept soundly, like a canary covered by its hood. 'One hundred and twenty-nine!' suddenly sang out Sebastian. He was still counting churches.

The climax came after an hour and a half, when Dave's sterling certainty that we were finally in the Albert suburbs was exploded by someone spotting Albert's famous church tower exactly behind us, so that we were evidently speeding away from it at sixty miles an hour. We reached a roundabout. The debate began as to which we way we should turn off it, left or right. Round and round we went, in a long, lazy trajectory like an orbiting satellite, while the row raged on between the adults. Eventually Tessa, who had been holding herself back with an effort, intervened. For Tessa, it swiftly emerged, had got a map! And what made it worse, we were on the right road within minutes, and in a quarter of an hour we were in Albert. And, of course, we bought the barbecue and were soon on our way to Le Poppy.

Even so, it struck me later that there was a curious symbolism in all this. Here, on the coach, were all these autistic kids, full of nameless terrors and various obsessive languages of control, a major one of which was their obsession with maps; while all around them were the Mohawk crew who were so dauntless, whose keynote was spontaneity, but who seemed to feel equally threatened, in their own way, by . . . maps.

We finally made it to Le Poppy an hour late.

Our entrance was a triumph, because the scouts had changed into their uniforms. They rarely wore these, not being of a very paramilitary frame of mind; but when they did, as now, they looked delightful. They had Oxford blue shirts, tricked off with green neckerchiefs. In particular, little Sebastian, who had, of course, a natural feel for neckerchiefs, looked especially fine. A stir went round the customers as we walked in.

We were greeted by Arthur, Skip's long-time French friend who looked after the farmhouse on the Trust's behalf. Arthur knew everyone within twenty miles and had booked the evening specially with the proprietors. Arthur was, in fact, half English. Both he and his father had worked for the Commonwealth War Graves Commission. Arthur was now retired. Arthur had designed the garden at the Thiepval war memorial where Skip had found his grandfather. Nevertheless it would have been hard for Arthur to look much more French. Ruddy-cheeked and amiable, sculpted, seemingly, exclusively out of curves, he was prone to much the same alternations of warmth and sudden wrath as Skip. You could see why they got on, and why the scouts called Arthur 'the French Skip'.

Le Poppy's owners had prepared a long, white-clothed table, prettily tricked out with flowers. Arthur sat at one end; Dave sat at the other; the rest of us disposed ourselves down either side. The autistic kids, as usual, were strung out between us. I ended up sitting beside Ian Pool. You could tell how our relationship had declined by the way we both sat there in stony, mistrustful silence, each more uncertain than the other how to break it. Scrabbling around, at one stage I asked Ian if he was feeling 'hungry'. He looked offended. 'No!' he said roughly, and left it at that. What had I said? It was only later I realized we'd had one of those weird misunderstandings people have when they're estranged. Ian had clearly thought that I'd said 'angry'.

But none of this was evident to the French customers. You could see it in their eyes: what a charming group of English boys, so well dressed in their nice scout uniforms, too! It's always good to see young people have fun.

Such Mohawk evenings often start like that. Not least, as we have seen, because it's no easy matter to notice, at first, that some of the boys are autistic. In this case the honeymoon period lasted a good half-hour, right through the first course, in fact. Then, slowly but surely, you could see these large, invisible question marks rise over our fellow customers' heads. Was there something strange, after all, about these nice English boys?

The first quiver – that I noticed, anyway – was when Ronny started playing a tickling game with the scout next to him. It was sweet enough, in its way, but, of course, it was more what you do when you are three than when you're eleven. Then Brett suddenly turned round, picked up a bread roll and lobbed it hard and unerringly over to one of the nearby French families, where it whistled low across the table like an organic cannon ball, taking out a salt cellar and a butter dish en route. Next, Ronny, encouraged by the tickling, suddenly left his chair and took a flying leap into the lap of a nearby, middle-aged French matron and covered her in kisses. He was rescued by an apologetic Fred.

But the fatal moment came with the arrival of the chocolate mousse. OK, perhaps chocolate mousse was not the *very* best dish to serve to autistic children. Smearing the mousse around on the tablecloth was one thing, and there was plenty of that. But the moment of climax, the time when you felt the whole room freeze aghast, was when Brett took a good scoop of mousse in one hand, lent across the table, and rubbed it into

Tom Pollard's hair. Quel horreur! Vie de ma vie!

At which moment, there was, of course, only one thing to do. Some of us got up, walked over to different tables and breathed the magic words: 'Pardonnez-moi, ils sont autistiques.' And, as consistently happened at such moments, throughout our visits to France, the customers were instantly transformed from outraged hostility, to sudden, extreme sympathy. Instead of looking appalled, they watched enthralled. They were patently admiring how well the scouts could cope. Indeed, by the end of the evening one French gentleman, with that ceremonious air you see so often in France, walked up to Skip and, in a small, semi-public speech, enlivened with many a gracious gesture, declared how remarkable it was to see autistic children integrated in this way. *Surtout*, how wonderful it was that they were being looked after by other *boys*. 'You would not,' he said, with one last, imperious gesture, 'see such a thing in France.'

But there was still one final triumph reserved for Teddy.

For Teddy, who by now had become still more attached to Dave, was sitting down his end of the table, at Dave's right hand. Behind him was a dining French family, with a little girl of around Teddy's age. Understandably, given Teddy's extreme physical beauty, the little girl showed every sign of being attracted to this charming English boy.

With the aid of the adults around them, they quickly began to communicate. So what, you could sense the French family thinking, if Teddy seemed not very talkative, even a little shy? His shyness, surely, only added to his charm; and then his lack of conversation was doubtless down to the fact that he didn't know French. In short, the scouts got the distinct impression that not only did the little girl fancy him, but that neither she nor her parents ever twigged that Teddy was autistic.

By the time the meal was finished, they'd become such good friends that the little girl leaned over and asked Teddy if he would write down his phone number, so they might meet again. This was done, with all due grace. As the scouts left, the little girl very prettily waved Teddy goodbye.

Outside the scouts cheered Teddy to the echo. Who'd ever have thought it – Teddy'd pulled!

Teddy's experience on this trip, rather like Bernard Naisbitt's, had been a steady upward progress of success. Yet his most memorable moment happened the day the troop went horse-riding.

Horse-riding? Here was yet another Mohawk activity which an outsider might have assumed would be beyond autistic boys. After all, these were children who were, some of them, doubly incontinent, unsure of their calculations of size and space, chronically anxious. Were these the children to try something which might scare even 'normal' kids, let alone children with their difficulties? Yet this brings us up against yet another of autism's paradoxes. For some autistic kids are actually rather better at certain kinds of physical activity (notably anything involving balance) than ordinary children. Added to which animal therapy, as it is called in the trade, has a long and distinguished history in the treatment of disabilities.

The outing was blessed from the start, because the April showers which dogged our trip most of the week suddenly stopped. The riding school was about six miles along a straight road from Bucquoy and for once we didn't get lost. By the time we reached it, it was a golden spring day. The water which lay everywhere from the earlier showers only enhanced the effect, like varnish.

The riding school itself, lit by the morning sun, made the heart leap. A huge, redbrick edifice perched heroically on the side of a hill, it looked more like a hotel, or even a château, than a school. It faced out across a rich, fat valley, full of budding greenery and bright meadows, which belied the windy ridge from which we had just driven down. For the Somme landscape is a place of secrets, by no means merely the wild and windswept downland it first seems. True, it's like this on the ridges. But between the endless rolling hills, lie villages, full of flowers, which seem almost in a separate climate. One such village lay just opposite the riding school, down in the valley. In front of it rushed the River Ancre, not slow and ponderous like the muddy Somme, but fresh and clean from the April floods, swift as a brook.

The scouts decanted from the bus and were greeted by two French teachers, dark, swivel-hipped Katie and tall, bronzed Jerome. Both had taught the scouts before and greeted them like old friends.

Hips revolving in a way which seemed to deeply interest the older scouts, notably Phil, Katie led the way into the stables which formed the right-hand wing of the building. Inside we found a row of horses, specially chosen for today's event. The idea was we'd start with preparation, i.e. simple grooming and saddling up. Then we'd have basic riding instruction in the hall next door. Emboldened by this, hopefully, we would go out into the sunlight, and take a slow, circular ride through those golden, tempting meadows.

It sounded fascinating but it also sounded quite ambitious, especially for those autistic children who had no experience of such things. The mere look of the place, inside, was daunting enough. Tall, dark and vaulted like a church or a Roman bath, it was full of just those pungent sounds and smells which autistic children hate. Sure enough, they soon began to look twitchy. Bernard Naisbitt, encouraged by Matt, stepped timidly up towards one six-foot equine monster, and poked it tentatively with one hand; it shook its head and shifted its haunches six inches; Bernard leapt back. Tessa's Leigh wouldn't even go near the horses, but watched them nervously from the shadows. As for Brett, a more proactive boy, his chosen protest was to sit straight down on the stable floor, complete with horse droppings and hay.

Nevertheless, after several false starts, and with infinite patience,

Katie finally got Brett, very tentatively, to stroke a horse, and all seemed well, until – bang! Brett socked it straight on the snout. Good God! What would it do? Bite? Kick? Or even bolt? Not a bit of it. I was standing just close enough to see the horse's expression. He didn't look angry, or even afraid, he simply looked appalled. He reacted as if Brett's behaviour had above all been déclassé, a breach of manners. As indeed it was.

Nor did it bother the serene Katie and or the noble-browed Jerome, who were used to dealing with autistic kids, and who continued, placidly and steadily, with their teaching. When the grooming was completed we split into groups. Mine moved into the stable next door, where we began the next, still trickier stage: first steps in riding.

Jerome stood with a horse in the middle of the floor and invited volunteers. The scouts were happy to try, first Phil and then Troy Northcote. Both, evidently experienced, did fine. They even – this was the riding school's tradition – did basic circus tricks: standing on the horse's back, jumping off while the horse was moving, and so on. Then Jerome had his first shot at an autistic child. Would Bernard like a go? No, Bernard would not. 'He might bite me,' Bernard explained, with undeniable logic. But after ten minutes' gentle encouragement from Jerome, Bernard was finally tempted out from the shadows into the middle of the ring and even, a first for Bernard, went so far as to touch the horse. Already an advance.

Meanwhile, as Jerome's attention was distracted by Bernard, the scouts started chatting, then laughing, then mucking about, little Sebastian, in particular, doing Kung Fu punches around the room. But Dave stopped them in a flash, even though he, too, was busy helping Bernard. He caught them, in fact, just at the moment it was needed, neither so early that he was stifling them nor so late that the lesson swung out of control. Indeed, as Jerome continued to concentrate on Bernard, from that moment Dave virtually took charge.

It was as if he had developed several parallel minds. With one mind – because he, too, was still helping Bernard – he anticipated Bernard's every fear; with another, he sensed the mood of the horse; with another he read the ebb and flow of the boys' moods; with yet another he knew the exact moment when Jerome, too, had reached the end of his much-abused patience, and the scouts' unending chatter actually interfered with the work. More, Dave acted instantly each time to set things right. So fast, in fact, that he plainly never thought about what he was doing. Like a racing driver or a tennis champion or any one of us jumping off a hot stove, it was as if the messages only ever got as far as his spinal cord, never to his brain, and his reactions were purely instinctive. He was like a humming, fizzing top, full of sudden certainty and authority. So much for uncertain, whingeing, moaning, hesitant Dave!

Even so, it was Teddy, yet again, who turned out to be the hero of that riding lesson, as Jerome finally turned his attention to him. Far less nervous than Bernard, but still looking wary, Teddy was quite quickly persuaded to sit up on the horse. Slowly the fear went out of his face. He smiled one of his slow, deep, warm, intensely beautiful smiles. Jerome had a rope attached to the horse's head. He fed it out and had Teddy walk round him in a radius of twenty feet. Still Teddy looked happy, like a boy with a secret treasure.

Then Jerome raised the stakes. Maybe Teddy would like to try some tricks? I for one was amazed. Riding was one thing, trick-riding, for an autistic child, was surely quite another. But no one seemed bothered, least of all Dave, who had been on such trips, with such boys, over many years. And with due encouragement Teddy was, remarkably, encouraged to stand up on the horse's saddle. Even more remarkably, Jerome began to walk the horse slowly round, and still Teddy looked OK. Finally, incredibly, with Teddy still standing up, Jerome put the horse into a gentle gallop.

It was one of those moments when you really do doubt the evidence of your own eyes. Here in front of us, was an autistic boy, a kid who was supposed to be clumsy, unsure, above all lacking in confidence and trust, especially in a new situation and with strangers, galloping merrily round a stable, standing up, on a horse. It seemed impossible.

But the scouts weren't bothered with any of that. They just looked delighted, and very proud. Nice one, Teddy, brilliant, well done! They roared their applause.

However, the most memorable moment of all was still to come.

With the introductory session finished, we went out into the valley, and soon, in a column of a dozen, horses and riders, we headed down the hill towards the village. There soon developed one of those magical times when everything in the world, and everyone in the group, seemed happy. On either side stretched huge, bright yellow meadows, bursting with new grass. Apple blossom bent over us. We splashed through the stream. We reached the village centre, a mass of little gardens ablaze with flowers. Few of the flowers looked foreign, they just looked bigger, somehow, and more luxuriant than those at home.

At the head of our group walked Katie, leading a horse. Dave brought up the rear. Each stride that Katie took, hips swinging a foot, seemingly, from side to side, felt less like a woman walking, more as if some giant was slowly swinging a sack of grain, like a huge pendulum, back and forth. There was a wonderful generosity in her swooping, plunging strides. But if Katie moved differently from English women (and perhaps it was just our mood that made it seem so), it was only one of many moments in that wonderful morning, so typical of the first few days in a foreign country. Each detail, however mundane, was somehow fascinatingly, piquantly different from its equivalent in the UK. As we reached the brow of the hill, Bernard Naisbitt suddenly started yelling 'Oat, oat, oat!' Rubbernecking around for the oat field I saw a 'goat' in a nearby meadow. It was hitched up to two horses. Apparently, said Dave, locals did this so that if one horse had to travel, and there was no room in the horse box for its companion, the goat could go instead to keep it company and provide reassurance.

Indeed, so fresh, curious and optimistic did it all feel that Phil evidently felt inspired to have a crack at Katie. His chat-up line was unusual. It consisted entirely of questions. Nudging his pony towards her, he asked: 'Do bombs go off?' This enigmatic inquiry was inspired, presumably, by our shell-strewn walks. It mystified Katie. 'Sometimes, yes!' she replied. 'Do horses fall over?' he asked next. 'Zey 'ave four feet!' replied Katie, a little wildly. But Phil kept on coming. 'Do they die?' he asked. 'If they fall over, I mean?' 'Only if zey are falling on zere neck!' replied Katie, with a look that made me wonder what the French was for 'you always get one'. But at that moment there was a low whistle from Dave.

He was bringing up the rear with Teddy, leading his horse. And, I should repeat, it was the sunniest, silkiest day. The scouts were happy, giggling helplessly at Phil and Katie's exchange. Teddy's horse must have felt warm and friendly beneath his knees. It was moving with a slow, amiable and luxuriant roll, a horse version, almost, of Katie's movements, seductive, repetitive, hypnotic.

Dave grinned and pointed at Teddy's face. He pantomimed a snore. Teddy was sitting upright, complete with gentle, seraphic smile. He looked more than ever as if he were in a trance. Yet he was riding beautifully.

Nevertheless, there was a very good reason why he looked strange. He was asleep.

Later, Dave said something surprising. Every time he'd been out riding with autistic children the same thing had happened. At least one autistic child had fallen asleep on a horse. Why should this be? Surely because the children were so relaxed. And yet, what a huge degree of relaxation they must achieve to get this effect, especially in children who are so naturally afraid!

Little wonder, perhaps, that 'animal therapy', over the years, has recorded like phenomena. In particular, they have been described by the late E. Royds, who was, for many years, riding adviser for the then National Society for Mentally Handicapped Children, now Mencap.

Royds was a profound believer in work with animals. Describing the effects of such work on severely handicapped children, including children with autism, he wrote:

> Data obtained from 3 different schools, hospitals etc., and a total of 86 children, show that after regular pony rides 73–75% of the children whose behaviour was rated 'very poor' originally (and this is a euphemism for the real bottom of the barrel) improved to such an extent that life outside an institution might be considered for them. The greatest improvements concerned self-confidence, sociability, speech, and relief of tension, the child becoming more relaxed and contented. Possibly the most remarkable improvement, almost certainly the most significant, is the improvement in speech. There are 27 cases I know of, 14 I have heard myself, of children speaking their first words ever from the saddle.

How natural, then, that Teddy should have had the experience he did, and that kind, gentle, instinctive Dave should have been leading his horse. But Royds made another point, too.

For Royds felt that even the most ill-tempered horse would mysteriously change character once it was being ridden by an autistic child, seemingly sensing, as he put it, that 'here is a being who is not going to boss me but needs my help'. And there was yet a further point, arguably the most intriguing of all.

There can come a time, said Royds, when such co-operativeness can fade away, and the difficult horse will once again act up. Royds, paradoxically, took this as evidence of the autistic rider's improvement. He felt that the horse sensed the rider's increasing independence, even dominance. The horse no longer chose to make allowances.

SEVEN

However eventful the earlier months had been, they were all, in a sense, a preparation for the six-week summer camp at Wargrave, climax of the year. For this was the time when staff, scouts, autistic children, adult volunteers, were together long enough that every relationship could move to a quite new level of intimacy, as more and more inhibitions were dropped.

Now we were at the start of the school holidays and the end of July, queen of months. We were in high summer. True, it was not quite the summer we might have expected. For days on end there was an ominous, louring heaviness in the air, as thunderstorms rattled and rumbled along the horizon. Every so often there would come a brief, uncertain shower which poured a little and then petered out, as if it had lost heart.

Yet in its own way, this wet and womb-like soupiness felt as relaxing as the sun. Perched up on its hillside Mohawk always felt parental, the place you returned to, the place that enveloped you in its embrace. It was just that this time the embrace was strictly maternal, warm and damp.

But if the closeness of the Mohawk community intensified, so, as ever, did the rivalry. Skip's rumbling discontent with the inadequacy – or worse still, the adequacy – of the new leadership had gathered pace during the summer. He found all manner of things to complain about. What, he had said to me around June, did Clare and John think they were going to do about the new catering requirements? We'd built the facilities but we needed trained staff, and we didn't have them. Time was ticking on. What were they going to do? Here they were merrily signing up autistic kids for the summer and we might never proceed at all. We might be (that phrase again) closed down.

Added to which, there was Skip's rumbling discontent with the way John was handling the boys. He was, reckoned Skip, holding the troop together by 'the wrong glue'. He was getting them to do things by being nice to them. Saying they could play this game, go on that walk, enjoy this outing, if they did what he required. It wasn't so much that he should be stern with them, it was that the energy should be coming from the boys themselves, not from the leadership. 'The kids have got to own the place,' said Skip. 'It's got to be driven by their loyalty, their sense of pride.' Otherwise, before you knew it, Mohawk would be something else, 'a care home where boys help out'.

Which is where Skip got interesting. To many people, surely, 'a care home where boys help out' might not sound too bad. But not to Skip. What made Mohawk unique, he said, what created its so-called 'magic', so creative for both scouts and autistic boys, was the scouts' sense, above all, that it was their own place; that they were making the running, they were setting the rules. So different, inevitably, from the priorities of grown-ups. And this sense had innumerable knock-on effects. Above all it gave the scouts that sense of relaxation that was crucial for everyone on site, but most especially for the boys with autism.

Then, as ever, there was Dave. Of course, Dave wasn't happy – he never was. It was as if the psychic fuel on which Dave operated, the way he released tension and found energy, was a constant nagging suggestion, to whoever was in earshot at the time, that he was being exploited. As usual, his complaints had some basis. Not only was he being overworked – constant driving, for instance, ferrying stuff up and down to London, the occasional weekend, even, driving volunteers to France – but he was, as a volunteer, dramatically ill paid. At best he got the odd petty cash bung, or petrol money for his trips. But what bothered him most was that he felt unappreciated. And what I gradually realized was that this had as much to do with his deprived past, as with his Mohawk present.

From the age of seven to fourteen Dave had been brought up in a care home. His mother had been separated from his dad and, in the view of the 1950s Berkshire social services, she'd had more children than she could look after. One had to go. It turned out to be Dave. The experience had given him a lifelong sense of being undervalued but it was also a key reason, as he himself said, why he was so good at looking after boys. Much like those deprived scouts who made the most exceptional carers, Dave had a huge, instinctive sympathy for anyone who felt done down. And his emotional history meant, too, that he had a further huge incentive to do the work well. Because while he rarely felt appreciated by the adults, notably Skip, he did feel appreciated by the boys, especially the boys with autism, who he found he could make laugh. 'I don't know if I help *them*,' said Dave, in language that sounded strangely familiar, 'I do know that they help *me*.' He was, indeed, very similar to the scouts.

Meanwhile he whinged on, and a lot of it was directed at John, whose fatal talent it is to be a sympathetic listener. But then John got it constantly from all sides. He got it from Skip, as we have seen. He got it from Skip on Clare's behalf, because when Skip got cross with Clare, as in the catering row, he would often aim the actual ear-bend at John, the softer target. Likewise, John was simultaneously getting gyp from the kids. For the kids were as scared of Skip as Skip was wary of Clare, so any resentments they felt at Skip's ever-escalating criticism were taken out, yet again, on John. 'I'm the meat in the sandwich,' said John. 'I'm fed up with it.' But that, as usual, was as far as John's rebellion went. Along with the fatal virtue of approachability he was, just as fatally, intensely loyal.

Indeed, so at variance, and so different, were the Mohawk adults that you found yourself wondering how the whole thing worked at all. Until, that is, you realized that it was these very differences that were the secret of their strength. There's a lot of talk, these days, about 'teams', mostly artificial and unreal; yet at Mohawk, the most row-prone organization imaginable, where half the staff at any moment weren't speaking to Skip and the other half weren't speaking to each other, there had evolved the most genuine, if unplanned, team of all.

It was a magnificent fluke. Skip was the driving force, the charismatic figurehead who could persuade the whole world to come to Mohawk's aid. Clare was the bureaucrat, the steady organizer. Dave was the wild card, the comedian. John was the gentle carer, embodiment of that almost Christlike love and tenderness which was so critical to the Mohawk spirit and went so strangely with the more rumbustious spirit of Skip and Dave, especially when they'd had a few spirits. All human life was there. And not only was each, in their own way indispensable, but the whole, mysteriously, exceeded the sum of the parts.

By July that team was being added to. Come summer, like migrating birds, there came the flocks of volunteers. There was me, for a start, whatever that was worth. There was Rod, like me, in his fifties. 'You two could be brothers,' said Ian Pool. Rod was on secondment from Waitrose where he worked. He was a quiet, unprepossessing man who spent most of his time doing carpentry, taptaptapping exterior cladding on the huts. Then there was, most memorably, 19-year-old Carrie-Ann. Now here was something unprecedented on the camp: a quite gorgeous, sexy girl with huge brown eyes (she was half Indian). Add to this the sweetest and most gentle of natures, and she was, taken all round, the ultimate Beckton boys' fantasy, their tragic femme fatale. And there she was, in the middle of us, a permanent fixture on the camp. She commuted in but slept over some nights.

Not that any of the boys had a clue what to do about her. They were bowled over, but they were so young; so that the typical expression with which they greeted her was a frown. Their other ploy was to try and wrestle with her, or throw water at her. I never did establish whether Carrie-Ann found this as flattering as she should have done.

As if to counterbalance Carrie-Ann there was also 22-year-old Diana, and she was made of sterner stuff indeed. She would have made a fair young power-station manager, say, in the halcyon days of the Russian Revolution or a quite passable French Resistance heroine during the war. She had a degree in biology, was fiercely logical, and, for all her good nature, was most emphatically *not* about to take any lip from the boys. Quite quickly, the boys began to resent this. Indeed, she soon became the boys' chosen symbol of adult unfairness. A view which was itself, arguably, extremely unfair, as in one way she only made up for the laxity of the rest of us. This was Skip's view, certainly. Had we been more firm, reckoned Skip, then Diana could have been more easy going. As it was, the boys said she was 'always moaning' and, one horrible afternoon, they even let her tyres down.

So it was fortunate that one other volunteer who joined us that summer was a woman who, like John, somehow encompassed the virtues of all of us, and who, again like John, drew us together. This was Sheila, Skip's cousin, from Australia. Sheila was a retired nurse, in her sixties. She'd flown over the previous year to work at the camp, loved every minute of it, and resolved to return. She was a short, placid-looking woman whose mild manner concealed such gravitas that the scouts never even thought of trying anything on. And yet, simultaneously, there was something else about her which made the boys adore her and elect her, however unconsciously, as mother figure of the camp. They brought her their troubles.

Well, that was what they did in fact; on the face of it, however, they brought her their ailments. Her staff role, naturally, was first aid. But the giveaway had been the previous year, when after the first three days of Sheila's 'surgeries' Skip had had to close them down through excess demand. 'What a surprise!' said Skip. 'First day we had three casualties, second nine, third fifteen.' When she'd left at the summer's end, the boys had cooked her a special meal, lined up along the drive, and cheered her out.

Yet as so often with adults who children love, it was quite a question why they'd grown so especially fond of her. But there were clues.

At any given moment, seemingly, she would be sitting out on one of the white chairs, in the sun, knitting. She said little; she listened a lot. Above all she exuded a quiet, enveloping calm. Eventually I thought I understood. In her own Australian way, she had, once again, recreated the Beckton front room.

And with the new blood, and the resulting shift in emotional balance between the adults, came a related shift in our relationships with the boys. The advent of the women was the big change. It meant the men, mysteriously, became more like the boys' co-conspirators. Maybe there was something in what Skip had said. We found ourselves playing with them more, telling them off rather less. But, perhaps, things were changing anyway. Ian Pool, for instance, was getting a great deal friendlier to me. Why? I didn't know, but I had my suspicions. For I, in turn, was getting ever friendlier with Dave Hamblin, and it was my strong hunch (though I never asked either of them) that Dave Hamblin, who had huge emotional credit with the boys, was sticking up for me.

Certainly Ian Pool's behaviour, again without explanation, changed dramatically, albeit in the usual tangential, at-one-remove male ways. He started hitting me, a sure sign of favour. He began pinching things off me when I wasn't looking, especially notebooks, which stuck out at a tempting angle from my back pocket. His biggest coup was the time he called my name, I turned round, and there he was, standing stock still, grinning. In triumph, he slowly produced, from behind his back, not just my notebook but my entire shoulder bag, which he had somehow secreted off my body without my noticing. And the message of the grin was plain: I was forgiven everything, even my wimpishness about the shells in France.

But then the bust ups and reconciliations between scouts and adults always took these indirect, at-one-remove forms. First came the row; then the mutual sulk, sometimes lasting for days. Finally (to my amazement at first – why the scouts should even care what we adults thought?), time and again it would be the boys who made the first reconciliatory move: a pretend theft, maybe, an attempted throttling, an offer of sweets. The one thing you could be sure of was that it would never be made explicitly, but always in code.

However, if one should develop any exaggerated sense of one's importance to the kids there were a thousand little incidents, daily, to put you straight. Typical were the times when they'd use you as a prop for play. You'd be standing there, having a sensible conversation with, say, Rod or John, when suddenly there would be five little boys all dodging and darting around you, all shrieking with delight, and all of them, quite evidently, in their own, entirely separate world. For despite the grave import of our adult conversation, for all the mighty issues we were trying to put to rights, it was plain how the children saw us at such moments: they saw us as trees.

And yet the divisions in the camp, young and old, male and female, were in some ways more apparent than real. As an emotional unit the place was one, and what happened at one end of the camp among the adults could quickly affect what happened the other end among the boys. And vice versa.

One late July day Skip was standing near the campfire circle when, as he put it later, 'things began to sound wrong'. After forty years working with boys Skip's hearing has become rather like that of a mother with a new baby: some subconscious monitoring system sorts the good sounds from the bad. The brilliant, smiling Nick Smith, usually so good at caring for all manner of boys, had been assigned to look after 10-year-old Henry. Now he was shouting at him, and it didn't sound right. Alerted, Skip followed the sound. 'I could see immediately,' said Skip, 'that the chemistry had gone wrong.' Nick was walking away from his child, leaving him alone.

Not that Henry was an easy boy. Small, dark and pale, he was one of those snub-nosed kids, a bit like Peter Bell, who always looked on the brink of tears. Even so, there was no particular reason why he and Nick should have fallen out. 'As I say,' said Skip, 'pure chemistry, like any other friendship.' After forty years, said Skip, he never knew why one relationship worked and another failed, it simply happened, and when it happened you had to adapt. So Skip pulled Nick off caring for Henry, and on a hunch, replaced him with 15-year-old Jon. In this case, the chemistry, no less mysteriously, clicked. For Jon himself was not the easiest boy on site. His father and mother live apart, his father in France. There is a deep, almost despairing resentment in Jon, an acid sarcasm. And the other thing that was interesting, and very Mohawk, was that fixing them up was *all* Skip did; after that he left them to themselves, and wandered off.

This curious decision triggered off a whole sequence of further events; and each stage was emblematic of the workings of the camp.

The boys had erected a marquee to provide a little more covered space for activities. A couple of days later I wandered in there and found Jon and Henry. Jon, in one corner, looked bored and semi-detached. He sat in a chair thirty feet away from Henry, who was being played with by a clutch of other scouts: Fred Robinson, Troy Northcote, Chris Smith, Joe Beckford. For the moment they had taken over Henry's care from Jon. This was, in fact, routine. The boys regularly look after each other's charges, like an extended family. But more remarkable was the way in which they were playing with Henry.

In one corner of the marquee was a big container full of hundreds of plastic balls, one of those devices that give the effect, almost, of an ersatz swimming pool. Its plastic sides were pumped up to around three feet, so that you could dive into the balls like water, roll around in them, even vanish beneath them should you wish. And on the edge of it stood Fred, cheered on by the others, and in Fred's arms was Henry. Every minute or so Fred would hurl Henry bodily over the side of the 'pool' into the balls. With a crash and a floundering shriek, Henry would vanish from sight. As so often with the scouts' autistic care, this would have been wild enough with any ordinary boy; with a child suffering from autism, presumably fragile, it looked bizarre.

But Henry loved every minute of it. He shrieked and gurgled with delight. 'One, two, three!' cried Fred, with the routine, almost bored air with which people throw sacks down from a lorry, and into the ball pool went Henry and disappeared. Out he came again pleading for more. 'One, two, three,' cried Fred again, and hurled him even higher. Henry looked even more pleased. Eventually, to maintain the interest, Fred began adding a kind of spinning motion to his throws, a movement which made it impossible for Henry to have any idea which way up he was going to land. He loved this, plainly, best of all.

While this classic of Mohawk childcare was unfolding on one side of the marquee – here were boys treating autistic boys as if they were just like any others – what was happening the other side was, if anything, even stranger still. For there, sitting on a canvas chair, was another autistic boy, Philip, in the care of Stevie.

Stevie is a big amiable black kid, fifteen years of age. And, watched unconcernedly by Stevie, Philip was eating leaves. 'He likes them,' said Fred, taking a brief rest from throwing Henry around. 'He eats leaves in the garden at home, his mum told us, and she lets him.' Indeed there was a tree in his garden, said Fred, that Philip had stripped bare. Moments later Stevie, who had popped out of the marquee for a moment, reappeared with not just leaves, but a whole two-foot branch of a tree. Then Chris Smith, too, came running up happily, with another. Both were for Philip.

There's a lot of talk, these days, about 'entering the autistic child's world', however bizarre that world may be, as a way of re-establishing some form of human contact. But what adult carer would have done anything like this? And even if he did – and certain advanced schools of autistic care do advocate something comparable – no grown-up could have matched Stevie's style. There was no training, no self-consciousness about Stevie: he merely saw what Philip wanted, worked out what was required, and fetched it.

And then, as if to underscore the extent to which the session broke all known rules, it veered off yet again. For Philip, it turned out, still wasn't happy. But this, it emerged, was because he, too, wanted to be thrown into the ball pool, like Henry. So now all the boys were co-opted into manhandling both Henry and Philip, not to mention each other, and what with the diving, and falling, and the plastic balls getting thrown around, one soon hit Joe on the head. He picked it up and threw it back, and next thing everyone was at it and the whole thing had metamorphosed, magically, into an all-in, all-comers battle of the balls.

It was wonderful. However, the autistic boys were completely forgotten, as the scouts started fighting among themselves. And next, the scouts decided, it would be funnier still if they attacked the only available adult, i.e. me. As I started defending myself the mayhem became complete as everyone in the marquee started hurling balls at everyone else.

Then Clare walked in, and everything stopped dead. She was furious. Not only, she said, were we not paying attention to the autistic children, but we were fighting. Not only were we fighting, but we were throwing the plastic balls. Not only were we throwing the plastic balls, but we were hurling them all over the marquee, which made them filthy.

All of which was supremely sensible. The subtler point, that the autistic kids might be benefiting by the playful atmosphere, even when they weren't joining directly in the play, was one that it felt hard to argue at that moment. So we stopped, and lobbed the balls gently back into the ball pool where they belonged. And as we did so, I couldn't help complimenting Joe on the power with which he had bombarded me. Some of his hits on my chest and arms had been real stingers. He played tennis and it showed; the power in that barrel chest, that eye to aim. Why, I said admiringly, some of those shots had *really hurt*.

Funny how kids react sometimes. Joe seemed quite put out. A lion a moment earlier, he was now a penitent. His voice quavered. 'Sorry, Ian,' he said.

Clare's intervention had been dramatic but it's worth noting that Skip's had been more important still – even though it had, in one sense, been entirely passive. Of course, he had done the initial swoop on Nick, and then the reassignment, typically intuitive, of Henry to Jon. Yet beyond that he had had no direct input at all. He had left everything to the boys. He'd merely trusted them. But that was the point. By absenting himself he had let the boys create their own, anxiety free culture, so different from grown-ups'. That, in turn, had helped them help their charges. At his best, in fact, Skip could be a fine illustration of his own ideal, that of the adult 'who's seen and not heard'.

This creative passivity, in fact, was one of the keys to Mohawk, and crucial to the camp's often dreamlike air of relaxation. For while that afternoon in the marquee was exceptional, similar moments were happening all the time. I remember them as a series of pictures, all different, and yet all, in their own way, symbolic.

It is late afternoon and Nick Smith is running across the camp with a message for John. There is no practical need for him to be running at all and yet, as he reaches the middle of the camp, he accelerates, exultantly, into top speed. His long legs stretch out into great, loping strides and the main feeling you get, as you look at him, is his sheer animal delight in his own body.

It is early morning and Fred is taking Philip into breakfast. He looks down at him and mutters something encouraging in his ear. The boy smiles up and grasps Fred's fingers; they walk slowly off together, hand in hand.

It is lunchtime, warm and sultry, and someone is blowing bubbles. Sixteen-year-old Jeff Pollard, the tough, boxing-loving brother of Pete and Tom, chases a bubble across the campfire circle, jumping and clawing at it like a toddler.

I am walking with Jon and a couple of autistic children in Pear Field. Suddenly Jon stops and picks up a pheasant's feather. There is a quite new look of gentleness, even reverence on his face. 'It's still here!' he says. It turns out he'd noticed the feather a week earlier, and here it is, still in the same place. An autistic boy walks over to have a look. It's a male feather, Jon points out, not female, you can tell by the colours.

It is morning, and Pete Pollard and his friends, including two autistic boys, are playing football. Pete takes ten steps back, makes a mad rush at the ball and hammers it. He slices it and the ball goes into this beautiful swerve, sailing straight between Skip and an autistic child's parent as they stand there talking. Skip roars like a bull; the parent looks aghast; the kids, including the boys with autism, scamper off delightedly, shrieking with laughter.

Summer was indeed the season when the camp really got into gear. One reason, as we have seen, was all that time on site. Another was that the long, school-holidays' camp successfully insulated the scouts from their other lives. For there was a monastic quality about Mohawk. The place, remote on its hill, created its own world, with its own very particular scale of values; not qualitatively different from everyday life, but different in emphasis. For whatever the shouting and yelling and downright piggishness, even when Mohawk was at its mad, bad, chaotic worst, its basic ethic was always clear: that love and trust were the basis of human actions. This gave everyone a remarkable feeling of something benevolent underpinning everything else. Just being there felt extraordinarily good. It was noticeable how casual visitors would hang around. How different from the 'global market economy' outside!

Yet it was more than that. The place had always been a retreat, too, from people's individual lives. This was so for Dave Hamblin as much as for the scouts, for the scouts as much as for the autistic children. You didn't have to know people's backgrounds to sense that we were all to some degree Jekylls and Hydes, living out different, and rather better, characters on site than elsewhere. You could see why John Lee even talked about the scouts being, as he put it, 'polluted', if they spent too much time away from the camp. His very use of such a word was another reminder of the camp's neo-religious psychology. But then, as far as feel and flavour went, John Lee – gentle, devoted, self-sacrificing John – would plainly have made the very best kind of medieval monk. As for Skip, hard though it sometimes was to remember it, especially when he'd had a few, he had, of course, once thought about becoming a vicar.

It was revealing, too, to see what could happen if Mohawk's isolationism broke down. The previous summer, for instance, the normal six-week, sleepover summer camp had been suspended. New safety criteria, demanded by social services, had proved temporarily beyond Mohawk's resources. While the autistic children had indeed been able to come in during the day, they'd gone home at night. The knock-on effects, reckoned Skip, had been considerable. Even six months later, when we went to Holland, he'd thought the scouts were still not back to their normal standard of care. I'd seen rickety moments, in Holland, myself. Yet now, with this year's summer camp once again full-time, the emotional web was being rebuilt. The autistic boys were on site twenty-four hours. Both scouts and autistic children could create their own, unique worlds. The place was once again, in all essentials, a 12-year-old's kingdom, and it worked.

Why did it work? Why were the scouts so good with the autistic boys? I asked myself those questions time and again. Slowly, I began to stumble towards some answers.

Crucial, it seemed to me, was the most obvious point of all: that because of their age, the boys were so much closer, psychologically, to boys with developmental problems than adults. For childhood, even conventional childhood, really is another universe from teenagerdom, let alone adulthood. We underestimate the immensity of the gulf. The scouts can relate to kids who chew leaves because there's still part of them that wants to do the same thing. Equally, they can understand why an autistic child, walking along the street, will suddenly leap at a lamp-post and start shinning up it like a tree. This, too, was something they recently did, a point on which they differ, it must be said, from 35-year-olds. They understand how autistic kids can have such intense hatreds of smells, colours or foods. For the scouts' senses, too, are still so acute, compared to adults, that feeling not merely put off but nauseated by, say, spinach or curry, is no strange abstraction, it's a routine, day-to-day experience. They understand why an autistic child can go ballistic when asked to do some, to an adult, quite trivial, inoffensive thing because they feel just as angry at such moments themselves, though they have learned, just about, to control it.

One of the trickier moments in France happened when little

Brett, the boy who socked the horse, lost it in a major way in the dormitory, head-butted Rob, and cut him badly on the lip. Rob's reaction was as illuminating as it was brave. No, he said later, it didn't bother him, because he'd understood what was going through Brett's mind. Brett had got it into his head that he wanted to go home. This was why he'd headed for the dormitory – to get his bag. He'd decided that the scouts, notably Rob, were trying to prevent him. So he'd seen red and started hitting out.

Rob said he'd have felt exactly the same himself. He clearly meant it. What adult could honestly say this?

Yet it is more than mere 'understanding'. At times it is almost as if the boys share the autistic children's strange patterns of perception. One day, on the bus, one of the autistic boys unaccountably started crying, hands jammed over his ears. 'What's the matter?' I asked Troy. 'It's that aircraft over there,' said Troy, without a blink, pointing to a light plane buzzing faintly half a mile away. This amid all the cacophony of the bus. The boy nodded agreement; but Troy had never read that passage in Annabel Stehli's book when she described the noise from the air vent, yards away from her car, amid all the New York cacophony, that disturbed her autistic daughter.

Little wonder, perhaps, that Skip reckons such lucidity tails off with age and that his carer scouts are over the hill at fifteen. Michael, all of twenty-seven years old and one of the camp's best carers in his time, agrees with this. Michael joined at the age of eleven, and, as an adult, worked as Skip's scoutmaster for four years, doing the same job as John Lee does today. Yet all his experience, he says, is now as nothing. 'I used to understand autistic children,' he says, 'without even trying. But not any more.'

However, this instinctive understanding of autistic boys' minds, this leg up, compared with adults, into their world-view, can be double-edged.

While it meant the scouts sympathized with the boys in one way, it meant, too, that they could be stern. Like poachers turned gamekeepers, they saw, and policed, the many moments when autistic children tried it on. Observing, with a grin, one of the autistic boys suddenly feeding himself, after earlier presenting himself as incapable of doing any such thing, one scout said: 'I saw what happened! He got distracted and forgot to pretend.' The scout was right. A moment later the boy recovered himself and went back to his 'disabled' ways.

Then there was the time when young Henry started rattling the canteen windows, again while he was eating. As with all kids, any acting out above all happens at meals, that time of intense, symbolic acceptance or rejection. Ian Pool, so ready to kiss an autistic child in his friendly mood, was like a foghorn. 'Stop now!' he yelled. The boy, terrified, jumped a foot and stopped right away, and he did not muck about for the rest of the meal. Skip, who happened to be watching, nodded approvingly. 'With autistic kids,' he said, 'there's a difference between genuinely autistic behaviour, which they can't control, and plain naughtiness, which they certainly can.' He could spot the difference himself, he said, up to a point, 'but the experts are the boys.' And the scouts' ethic, albeit unconscious, was clear. Playfulness, yes: game-playing, no.

And yet, whether sympathetic or stern, the most striking thing about the scouts' relationship with the autistic kids was their cool, their refusal to be fazed. That moment when Bernard filled his pants at breakfast, en route to Holland, was typical; such incidents happened constantly, throughout the year, and I never saw a single scout get thrown by them. Matt Polesden, for instance, calmly washing the excreta off an 11-year-old, said he regularly toilet-cleaned his younger brother. Hugely more tolerant than grown-ups, with a far wider span of activities they permitted themselves, let alone the boys they looked after, their typical reaction to 'bizarre behaviour' (as the autism literature calls it) was curiosity, tinged with humour.

Never having built up the rigid structures in which adults live, they weren't afraid to have them knocked down. Nick

Smith, in particular, would recount tales of 'bizarre behaviour' with delight. He described, for instance, one famously 'difficult' boy who simultaneously loved both bikes and dirt. One way he combined both joys, said Nick, was to pile earth up around a child's bike so that the bike could stand up without moving, a kind of cyclic sandcastle. He would do this for hours. Nick plainly found it fascinating.

Indeed, sometimes the scouts' capacity for fun, their determination to apply the pleasure principle to every aspect of their lives, could be almost ruthless. One day we took the autistic children to a local theme park, where everyone went on rides. The deal was, the scouts could go on the rides free, if they were accompanying autistic kids. At one ride, through an organizational hiccup, a group found itself short of an autistic boy. Unabashed, a scout duly pretended to be autistic himself, for twenty minutes – tantrums, screeching, the lot – so his whole group could get the ride. Disgraceful! And what adult would even think of such a thing! Yet undeniably witty, and rather fun.

One day I was standing by the campfire circle when Joe Beckford came up, he of the exuberant lifestyle back in Beckton. 'What day of the week is it?' he asked. It's easy to lose all sense of time during camp. 'Tuesday,' I replied. 'Tuesday . . .' he repeated, 'that's two more days . . .' 'What are you waiting for?' 'Thursday,' said Joe. 'That's when my boy's coming.' My boy: he was counting down the days to the arrival of the autistic child he would be looking after, much as he might have been counting off the days to a holiday.

It was curious. At that very same moment, coincidentally, my own daughter was counting off the days to the arrival of her first pet rabbit, and there was something in Joe's tone that sounded the same. It wasn't that he saw his autistic boy as a pet. It was, like my daughter, that he saw this new relationship as above all something to be looked forward to, a privilege – a promise, in fact, of pleasure.

Although there was one way, perhaps, in which Joe's view of his boy was pet-like. He saw him as a source of play. This typical Mohawk boy's perception is reinforced by autism's theoreticians. For play, and its first cousin humour, are widely regarded, professionally, as crucial for autistic children. Notably, for instance, by John Richer, consultant clinical psychologist at the John Radcliffe Hospital, Oxford, in whose catchment area Camp Mohawk falls. 'Humour and playfulness,' says Richer, 'create the kind of non-pressurized, non-judgemental atmosphere in which autistic children can really grow. It helps them relax, feel allowed to fail (a sure way to get them to succeed), but, above all, it creates an atmosphere in which the children can feel loved for themselves, not for their performance.' Yet play and humour, it must be said, are possibly more of an aspiration than a reality among adult care-workers, not always the very jokiest people in the world. Whereas to young boys they come naturally all the time, without trying.

They even come to children with autism.

One day we were sitting in the canteen waiting for lunch. Phil Simpson, with his normal flamboyance, was doing the cooking. He served up a plate of sausages and chips for a little autistic boy called Jimmy, dark-haired and puffy-eyed. Phil had made it specially. Jimmy turned it down.

'But he asked for it!' yelled an outraged Phil. 'With his Makaton book!'

Makaton is a communication system that helps autistic children who lack speech. In its book version, little stickers are put into a book to signify words and phrases. The notion is that the boy starting with, say, an 'I want' sticker, puts them in a row on the page and thus builds up a sentence.

'Ask him again!' said Phil.

So, helped by his minder, Jimmy once more hunched over his book. He took rather a long time. Phil read out the results.

'I want,' he said, 'chocolate, coke, ice cream, sweets, orange juice, tea, hot drink, cold drink, curry, swimming pool – oy! He's taking the mick!'

And, indeed, he was. He ended up getting sausages and chips. But trust the scouts to pick this idea up and play with it. That evening Troy, inspired by Jimmy's ploy, gave an even longer list to Carrie-Ann, who had taken over from Phil when his shift ended.

'Lollipop,' read Troy. 'Big dinner, small dinner, sausages, curry, meat, fish fingers, burgers, eggs, ice cream . . .'

'Are you really going to eat all that?' said Carrie-Ann.

'Me?' said Troy, in mock astonishment. 'Moi? How could you possibly imagine such a thing? It's for my boy!'

Even so, it's possible to get a bit carried away with the splendours of the scouts' perceptions. One day Johnny Cobbett was chatting to me about David Knebworth, and, in particular, his obsession with knocking over bikes. On at least one day of David's life, reckoned Johnny, he had cured him.

'Instead of steering him away from bikes outside shops,' said Johnny, 'I allowed him to go free. I let him wander up to them if he chose, make his own decision. And you know what? He was fine; he never even knocked one over once.'

Wonderful, I thought. Now here, if ever, was the power of expectation. Precisely because Johnny had not tried to prevent David doing it – and thus, apart from anything else, put the idea into his head – he had left the bikes alone. What intuition!

But when I told the story to John Lee, he grinned. 'You might be right,' he said. 'Myself, though, I'd take a more cynical view. I reckon Johnny left David alone precisely in the hope that he *would* do something with the bikes; but then, unfortunately, from Johnny's point of view, nothing happened after all.

'In short,' said John, 'Johnny told you the story he knew you wanted to hear. But what he'd really wanted out of David was some action.'

* * *

By early August a new factor entered the cosmology of the camp: the prospect of another trip abroad. For on 6 August we were off, once again, to France. Or were we? Because there was something else familiar about the trip. As ever, it was unclear whether we would be going at all.

It was as if each Mohawk crisis, to maintain momentum, had to be a little bigger than the previous one. This crisis, certainly, looked real enough. As had happened before and been resolved, we did not have a driver. Not, this time, within a week of our departure but, due to leave on the Sunday, we didn't even have one by Thursday night. Michael was unavailable. Wild suggestions flew around. Maybe Clare could drive? Not possible. She was indeed doing her HGV but was not yet qualified. What about Dave? No good either. He could drive the minivan but had no qualification for anything like a coach. Maybe the adults could take the kids out in their cars, four kids to a car, a kind of convoy? I flapped about for a bit, checking my insurance, then we dropped that idea too. Maybe we could hire four taxis for the week? Yes, we really were getting that desperate. Maybe . . .

Of course, the still more pressing question was why all this had to happen, on every trip, in such a melodramatic way. In part, of course, it was the downside of Mohawk's instinctiveness but gradually it seemed obvious it was more. Increasingly, it felt like Skip, consciously or unconsciously, more or less contrived such crises. For in the end, of course, what they did achieve, however bizarrely, was to focus attention on the man in charge. And for all Skip's theoretical 'retirement' that man continued to be – at moments like this, certainly – Skip Howgate. Encouraging, perhaps, should you have any lingering doubts whether you are still indispensable.

This time, certainly, it went right to the wire. We never did find a driver – a volunteer, that is – we had to hire one. So the very day we were meant to be leaving I drove down to the station, plus a couple of scouts, to pick the driver up. He wasn't there. He'd missed his train. He arrived, eventually, looking utterly shattered, with the air of a man who'd really hammered it the night before.

His name was Steve, he was tall, thin and levantine-looking, and he was fantastically pissed off. He was, apparently, having trouble at home.

Looking miserable, Steve supervised the loading of the bus. The autistic children arrived and were given their seats. The scouts shrieked and fought their way on board to join them. Once again, we were on our way.

EIGHT

As we decanted from the ferry at Calais, slipping quickly into our familiar Mohawk travelling rhythm, it struck me that this new trip should only accelerate the growing intimacy of the summer camp, because nothing made Mohawk more self-contained than our foreign visits. Largely isolated from our foreign hosts, not least because of our language problems, our attention focused ever more squarely on each other. And from this, in turn, came greater understanding.

Perhaps this was why character change, also, seemed to accelerate in France. Certainly, almost everyone – even, as we shall see, our new driver, Steve – showed sides of themselves that seemed quite new. These changes seemed most striking in those I knew best. But then it's not just the innocent eye that sees clearly. Experience, equally, means you see things that may be invisible at first encounter.

Thirty miles short of Arras I saw Ian Pool move up the coach into a seat just behind, and across the aisle from, Bernard Naisbitt. After a bit, he caught Bernard's eye and smiled; Bernard smiled wanly back. Then he made a face; Bernard grimaced back. Then Ian lifted his arm, leaned forward until he was six inches from Bernard and, gently but firmly, hit him on the shoulder.

Bernard looked aghast. He turned and caught my eye with wild surmise. Above all, he looked disoriented. Why was Ian, hitherto so friendly, so suddenly hostile? In a fine illustration of the autistic child's difficulty with anything other than the out-front, obvious agenda, he had interpreted Ian's behaviour as an attack. He clearly had no idea that this was Ian's round-the-houses way of being friendly. A punch from Ian, indeed, is like a stroke from anyone else. Ian hit him again, and Bernard looked more terrified still. Then he hit him again, and while Bernard continued to say nothing, his face, round eyed and astonished, said it all: 'Help!'

But Ian saved the day. Realizing this particular language of communication wasn't working, he changed tack. Now, instead, he told Bernard to hit him. Go on, he said, putting his face right up to Bernard's, hit me, hit me! And eventually in evident near-desperation, Bernard did just that. It was not a hit, exactly, more a dainty, rather feminine little . . . poke! And it worked. For Bernard, however blunderingly, was now drawn in. He'd grasped the spirit, if not the logic, of what was going on. Moments later, they were even talking (well, just a bit); a sure sign that Bernard was feeling relaxed.

Would Ian have adjusted his behaviour so readily back, say, in March? I doubt it. The more time he spent with Bernard, the more he liked him; the more he liked him, the more he understood.

For all of us, closeness and perception went hand in hand.

By late afternoon we had arrived at Bucquoy, but now a new problem arose: where would we all sleep? With new helpers like Sheila and Carrie-Ann, with fifteen scouts, with five boys with autism, not to mention old lags like me and Dave, it was quite a question how everyone would fit in. In the end, Dave and I got outplaced clean out of the main building into a caravan. The caravan was in one of the barns, and stank of mildew and superannuated rats. Outraged, Dave for once in his life did more than whinge: he launched a revolt. Amazingly, it succeeded and he got back in the farm.

This left me alone. Frankly, I wasn't too bothered. At least my isolation meant I'd get some peace. But it was a measure of my growing relationship with the scouts that *they* were. 'I feel really sorry for you, Ian,' said Nick Smith, 'down there in that manky old caravan.' Indeed, unasked, Ian Pool and Matt Polesden even cleaned it out for me. And Ian's involvement was a further indication of how his relationship with me, too, had changed. From anger, it had moved to genuine friendliness. And there was more. One day I noticed him staring at me, having been struck, apparently, by my preoccupied air. 'You worry too much, Ian,' he said. True. As well as friendliness there was something else – a strange protectiveness. From wicked uncle, seemingly, I had turned into younger brother.

As the troop grew close, in fact, we all began to see each other more realistically, complete with problems. And we adults, certainly, did have problems. Not least, as I had suspected, our new driver, Steve. That first evening I joined him at the local bar. Poor Steve! Few men could have given a more convincing portrait of misery. It wasn't just that he talked about his own domestic crisis, though he did. It was more the way he talked about everything else in the world – as people do, when they feel sad. Women? Grasping, game-playing, ruthless. The typical coach tour group? Chaotic, demanding, quarrelsome. Modern life? Cut-throat, uncaring, psychotic. The universe, as seen by Steve that evening, was a very dull and hopeless place indeed.

In short, for excellent personal reasons, Steve was deeply depressed. Yet the way Mohawk functioned meant that Steve, who was sleeping on site, would be very much part of our group. Young kids, let alone autistic kids, are not the easiest people to be around when you feel low. I wondered how he would cope with the week ahead.

* * *

The next morning we decided to kick off, as usual, with a walk. But this time we would add in another factor that the scouts, especially, enjoyed: a quiz. John Lee had photocopied an educational quiz based around the village sights. The idea was we would all walk around Bucquoy, use our powers of observation, and tick the appropriate boxes for the bits we saw, the church, the supermarket, the village dog, etc. To do this we were split up into groups. John Lee assigned me to Matt Polesden and Bernard Naisbitt.

It was a funny moment when he told us. Matt gasped, jumped up and down, and spun on the spot; Bernard blinked furiously. I thought they were cross. The truth, it turned out, was the very opposite: they were delighted. Young boys are not the only ones who underrate themselves. Mysteriously, Matt, in particular, had taken a shine to me. I had no idea why; it's not as if I'd done him any particular good turns. Yet come to think of it, that may have been the point. I certainly hadn't interfered, or set him or any of his friends to rights, for their own good.

What I had done, in fact, was remain quietly in the background, a vaguely amiable, if slightly droopy, presence. But what had also happened, as we have seen, was I had come to like them; a feeling which I must have betrayed by a thousand smiles and glances, the most certain currency of all. How many of us, especially kids, dislike people who like them? While for the boys' part, they, too, had been expressing friendliness, but in subtler ways still. True, there was the occasional overt gesture, like the caravan-cleaning. Yet mainly it was, as usual, signs and mirrors. The only clear indication that they liked me was that they were always, somehow, *there*. They followed me around like dogs. The Ian Pool/Bernard Naisbitt incident on the bus was typical. Why were Bernard and Matt, let alone Ian, sitting so close to me in the first place? In the end, as with all Mohawk relationships, it came down to pure chemistry.

But there was more. In bringing Matt, Bernard and I together,

Skip and John were acting in the classic Mohawk tradition. Far from making an abstract, impersonal decision, they were building on a dynamic that was there. While all I knew, consciously, was that increasingly I found Matt amusing, and that Bernard had a beautiful slow smile, Skip and John understood better. They knew they had something on which they could build.

Doing my level best, like a good researcher, to observe others, it was amusing to realize I had been so effectively, and unbeknown to me, observed myself.

What was certain was that the assignment worked. For with me hovering discreetly and slightly droopily in the background, off we set in the morning round the village, the odd couple plus one, with Matt noting down the questionnaire answers with all the wild, mysterious enthusiasm with which young boys treat quizzes. Bernard seemed, as ever, uncomprehending of the event's fine print but blissfully happy with its overall feel.

He certainly picked up on Matt's cheerfulness. The two of them smiled, just as they moved, as one. And here was yet another of those pictures that I found myself remembering months afterward. For that morning, and throughout the week, whenever Matt and Bernard set off together, whether out of a shop door, or off along the street, or just getting up from a park bench, smack! Matt's hand would clutch firm hold of Bernard's, like mother and son, and they would proceed together as if umbilically joined.

Of course, their growing relationship had been plain even before we went to France; but in this rarified, holiday atmosphere it intensified. And as so often happens when an autistic child feels safe, Bernard's behaviour, even his symptomatology, began to change. That afternoon we went back to the riding school. Once more it was idyllic; once more the village glowed with flowers; once more we met the lovely Katie; once more the lovelorn Phil Simpson goggled. This time, however, not only was Bernard persuaded to ride, but he actually galloped; while at the height of the session there was a reprise of the incident on the bus.

Bernard started talking. With Ian Pool it had only been a few words, but this time Bernard was chatting away quite merrily to Dave Hamblin, who was, as ever, helping to lead his horse. It was, in fact, almost a rehash of the phenomenon recorded by the Mencap riding adviser E. Royds, quoted in chapter six, when he described the twenty-seven cases he'd encountered when non-speaking children had recorded their first speech on a horse. Nor was this all. When I chatted with Clothilde, Katie's assistant, at the session's end, she mentioned that Bernard's horse was rarely as well-behaved as he had been that day, but that she'd long since noticed that the worst-behaved horses were transformed once they had autistic children on their back. 'Really!' I said. 'Had she ever read Royds?' 'Mais non,' she replied, 'who he?'

And Bernard managed one further achievement. One should recall that Bernard, like so many autistic children, rarely sees things from any point of view but his own. As the session ended, he walked over to Katie and, as a thankyou, shook hands. Katie looked astonished, then laughed, then threw her arms around him and hugged him, placing two smacking kisses on his cheeks.

Nevertheless, if Bernard and Matt had elected me their prime parent for the trip, this never precluded anyone else from taking over the role. One day I noticed this rowing, wheedling thing going on between Steve the driver and Matt. Steve had elected to clean out the coach, and in a vague, haphazard way, young Matt seemed to be helping him. Or was he? The main thing happening seemed to be a series of barked reprimands. 'Come on, you pillock,' Steve would yell, 'surely you must have used a brush at some stage in your life.'

Gradually this curious friendship seemed to extend till Matt seemed to be helping out Steve full time. Predictably, Matt clearly assumed this meant Bernard would be involved as well. Hand in hand, as ever, both Matt and Bernard attempted to work.

Not that this threw Steve. He still barked at Matt and teased him. This was clearly his parental style. But, just as much, he started being distinctly encouraging, especially with Bernard.

Matt hosed down the bus, the kind of wild and whooshy job which was right up his street. But Bernard couldn't help with this. Unusually for an autistic child he was afraid of water. So Steve set him to sweep out the bus instead.

But Bernard couldn't do this either; he just couldn't manage the motor skills involved. Most especially he had difficulty with the bus steps, because he had to back down them at the same time as he swept them. The job meant, in fact, he had to do more than one thing at once, so often anathema for children with autism. So Steve stood at his shoulder and, speaking with infinite gentleness, broke the process down into manageable, sequential parts.

'There you are, Bernard,' he said, 'that's it! First, hold the brush like this; next, draw it back into the pan, so; next, back very slowly down the steps. That's very good, Bernard, that's lovely! Beautifully done!'

'Now!' said Steve. 'Put the contents into the rubbish bin!' He showed Bernard how to make the twenty-yard journey to the rubbish dump. Soon Bernard had twigged the whole sequence, and worked away with delight. Meanwhile Matt was having the time of his life, smashing storms of water into the side of the bus at one foot range which bounced back, showering him and everyone else within twenty yards. Then, inadvertently, he shot water over the bus roof, arcing it beautifully to land on Skip and John. As the roars began and the laughter followed it became more and more like a party, less and less like work. By the end of it, indeed, so infused had Bernard become by the pleasure of it all that every time he went to empty his pan, he skipped the few yards there and back to the bin like a child of three.

Later on, predictably, all pretence of work finally vanished as the hosing 'accidents' turned into a full-fledged water fight. At the height of the scrap Steve suddenly nudged me in the ribs and pointed to Bernard. Bernard was round the back of the coach, away from the others, hosing down the bus. And this was the boy who was so afraid of water! No doubt, I said, the party atmosphere had relaxed him, but Steve thought there was something else as well. From watching Bernard's reactions to the water fight, he reckoned it was above all uncontrolled water that frightened him. In the hose, of course, his water was strictly under his control. 'Maybe Bernard's a bit like my Dad,' said Steve. Apparently Steve's father had nearly drowned in a beach landing during the Second World War and, ever since, the unpredictability of water had terrified him.

Bernard's progress was indeed remarkable, and yet it was Steve's own transformation that was most dramatic of all. He'd found an extraordinarily effective distraction from his own difficulties. Indeed, from then on, and throughout the following week, he seemed more fascinated by the autistic kids than any of us. He was another man from the tortured soul I'd met in the bar.

If our growing closeness meant our emotional peaks were higher than before, it meant, as ever, that our lows were deeper, too. Quite promptly, at the end of our very first full day, on Monday night, we were off and away into the week's opening row. The starting point (one is tempted to say, the rationalization) as so often, was mechanical. It was Skip's new – well, 5-year-old, second-hand – car. He'd driven it over from Beckton, accompanying the coach. En route, in Mohawk's great tradition, it had given him gyp. On arrival it had stopped dead. Some said Dave had inadvertently put diesel into the petrol hole, but this turned out to be malicious. Soon after, the blame became more firmly fixed, as usual, outwards. Skip had been sold the car by a neighbour for nine grand. The fault, it was decided, was his.

So once again the phones glowed hot as Skip entered into yet another cross-Channel motor row, but by the evening it emerged that even if the neighbour had wanted to, he couldn't give Skip his money back, he'd already sent it to his brother in Pakistan.

'Would you believe it!' declared Skip, as the situation was reviewed, on the garden chairs, in a sunny corner of the courtyard. This rapidly became where the adults gathered every evening, plus drinks, to review the day. Dave was there, and John Lee, and Sheila, looking philosophical. We had been joined, too, by the rubicund Arthur who had popped round to welcome us to Bucquoy. Spruce and amiable, humorous as ever, Arthur's attitude to this latest crisis, it must be said, lacked reverence. He was shaking with laughter. 'Always it ees the same!' he said. 'Always your vehicles are breakeengk down. Skip, please tell me, why are you always driving such rubbeesh?'

Every so often Dave would get up from the table and dart over to the car, which was parked ten yards away. He would examine it for a minute, follow up the latest wild theory advanced at the table as to what might be the matter, check it out, find that wasn't it, and come back.

After one such sally his face suddenly took on a knowing, glowing look. 'I've had an idea,' he said.

'Gawd help us,' said Skip.

'No, look, you remember we've got that other motor, back in Beckton,' he said. 'The Omega. I know it sounds funny, but seriously, why don't I nip over to England and fetch it here?'

'What?' erupted Skip. 'Go all the way home?'

'I'd come back,' pointed out Dave. 'It's not that far. I could be back in twenty-four hours.'

And there you had Dave all over. He was constantly complaining about being overworked; he would regularly put in those thirty-hour sessions for Skip back home in England, followed by forty-eight hour sessions of wall-to-wall complaining, and here he was putting his own head, as he so often did, when you thought about it, into the noose.

'Well, said Skip, 'if you really . . .'. And before we knew it the idea, skipping round the table, had developed a life of its own. Why shouldn't Dave go, after all? It wasn't *that* far; couple of hours up to the ferry, two hours across the sea, two hours more up to London. He might quite enjoy it. You forget how close London is, if you look at it on the map (not that anyone ever looked at maps). It's further to Paris . . .

Within minutes, in fact, there was a weird steam up behind this strange idea. As much as anything, it seemed to me, it was the time of day. We were in a mood to look for entertainment, this seemed like a laugh, and that was it.

Skip seized the moment. 'Well, if you do go,' he said, 'you'll need to go as soon as possible.' Indeed, given our commitment to return within the week, given the awkwardness of ferry times and all – Dave really ought to leave *right now*.

What! Dave looked aghast. Now this he hadn't bargained for. It was nice here in the sun! But now the whole group got behind this idea, too. If he was going at all then he must go immediately. It was now or never. Overwhelmed, Dave said he would; then he changed his mind and said he wouldn't; then he changed his mind again and said he would.

'Dithair, dithair, dithair,' cried Arthur. 'Always you are dithairing, Daveed! Get a greep on yourself, man! Make up your mind!'

In the end, reluctantly, Dave agreed to go. But it rebounded on Arthur. Because frantic consultation of timetables soon revealed that he could just make a late ferry if only someone could run him in to Arras station *at this very moment*. The only person who could possibly do this, at this very moment, was Arthur. So twenty minutes later, our pleasant, wind-you-down evening drink vaporized as three key members, Dave, Arthur and Skip, who had decided to go to the station for the ride, suddenly shot out of the farm doors. Spontaneity was routine at Mohawk, but this was absurd.

* * *

Suffice it to say Dave then disappeared. The plan was he should ring in when he got to Calais, or at the very least when he got to Dover. In the event, he was last seen boarding the train at Arras. We heard nothing from him throughout the following day.

The next evening, however, he suddenly reappeared, as usual unforewarned. He had, indeed, successfully fetched the Omega from England. It was parked out in the yard. But, said Dave, you would not believe his journey! There were very good reasons why he had never rung.

He'd been travelling non-stop, he said, for twenty-four hours. Where should he begin? There was the train that Arthur recommended, for a start. Arthur had said there'd be just the one stop; in fact there'd been twenty-four. Dave had counted 'em, and in one place he'd leapt out by mistake and the doors had closed behind him, vawhoomf! 'And there I was, stuck out on the platform!'

Dave sat, the hero of the hour, in the middle of the staff room, surrounded by sympathetic faces. Sheila, especially, seemed concerned. She clucked around him, gave him biscuits, brought him drinks.

'But I was lucky, wasn't I,' said Dave. No sooner had his heels touched the ground than he'd leapt back into the train again, quick as a flash, and caught it. Even so, it had been so slow that by the time it got to Calais he'd missed his ferry and he had to wait three hours for the next one. Then when he got to Dover it was already the small hours and he'd had to wait again, so that he didn't get to London till 7.30. He was travelling or hanging around all night. And *then* he had to get the Land Rover and drive straight back, so he never got no sleep, and he'd hardly eaten anything either. As he talked, his mood gradually built to a crescendo. The whole thing was utterly ridiculous, he'd never been so pissed off in his life. He'd finally had it up to *here* with Skip and the camp. This was finally *it*, the bleeding *end*.

Sheila gave him tea. Momentarily, he seemed mollified. Seconds later, like a returning tide, he was off again.

He wasn't the only one, he said, who was fed up round here. Oh no! Because Skip and Arthur had had this furious row just before they dropped him. You wouldn't believe what Arthur had said. 'I have had it up to here with your stupid cars!' he had yelled. 'You are driving me crazee, crazee!' Red in the face he was, waving his arms, until, finally, he had said 'You are . . . worse than the Irish!' The ultimate insult this, apparently. A reference to the Irish military group who'd owned the farmhouse before Skip bought it and who Arthur had also dealt with.

'What you really need,' said Sheila, who for the moment was once again entirely the nurse, 'is some proper food. I'm making toad-in-the-hole for the boys. Why don't you have some?'

'Oh no, I couldn't possibly do that.' said Dave, 'That's for the boys.'

Pause.

'I tell you, this time this is *it*. I'm making a stand.'

Pause.

'Did you say toad-in-the-'ole?'

'Yes.'

'Are you quite sure the boys will have enough?'

'Yes.'

'Well, just a bit, then.'

And he had his toad-in-the-hole.

Shortly afterwards Sheila sent him to bed, but now the row caught hold and quickly spread. Soon Clare was involved and then John Lee and Ian Pool and even Tom Pollard as, like a forest fire, it fanned out among the boys.

Indeed, by the evening it was involving everyone, with its epicentre, as usual, in the kitchen. Who controlled the kitchen controlled Mohawk. It was like TV stations in third world revolutions. With Dave in bed, and Skip temporarily disappeared, the women seized the power. And they were blaming Skip. Sheila, who was of course Skip's cousin, and had known him before her family emigrated to Australia, said he'd never been any different: charming, gifted, full of warmth and bright ideas, but capable of quite breathtaking thoughtlessness. 'Seventy per cent genius, thirty per cent child,' she said. But then, she pointed out, he'd had no brothers and sisters; his mum had spoiled him. She was a jolly woman, his mum, and she'd played the piano, semi-professionally, in pubs. It was her belief, said Sheila, that she'd felt guilty at leaving Roy and had spoiled him as a kind of compensation. Even so, the bottom line remained that Skip's key problem was his failure to come to terms with his retirement. It was having terrible effects on his mind.

And on this much everybody in the room agreed.

As for Skip himself, he'd bailed out two hours earlier. His response, as usual, to revolt among the natives was to retreat back to his personal sitting room, and shut the door.

Around ten o'clock, however, Phil Simpson came looking for me.

'Skip wants to see you in his sitting room,' he said. 'He says to bring some beer,' he added.

So off I went duly armed with beer bottles from our store. Predictably, given the request for beer, Skip wasn't about to start in on me; rather, having fallen out with everyone else, he was looking for emotional support.

He greeted me royally. 'You like music, don't you, Ian,' he said, shoving a video of Andrew Lloyd Webber's *Celebration* into the TV. We opened the first bottle; and in the way such things go, having started off with a detailed outline of his viewpoint, Skip cheered up a bit and started reminiscing about the past. He certainly did love music, he said. Now here was something he bet I didn't know. Did I realize he'd once been a champion ballroom dancer?

I didn't, though he was just the sort of person you might have expected to love dancing, especially in his younger, lighter days.

'Oh yes,' he said, 'I used to do it twice a week. I had all manner of adventures.

'I mean,' he said, 'there was the time when I was working as a publisher's rep and I fished up one night in Cardiff, with nowhere to stay.

'I found this B and B, I booked in there, and I started chatting with the landlady. I said I'd heard there was a dance hall down the road and I thought I'd go there later on, have a bit of fun.

'Well, as soon as I said that, this lady began to look very interested and she said that she, too, had been an enthusiastic dancer, but had given it up since her husband died. But now I'd reawakened her enthusiasm, could she possibly come along too?

'Cut a long story short, she duly came, we had a wonderful evening, and when we got home she told me it was the happiest evening she had had for months. I never saw her again, but later on I heard down the grapevine that she and her husband were ballroom dancing champions of Wales and after that evening she'd started dancing again and regained all her former enthusiasm. Wonderful really.'

And indeed it was; and it was a reminder, too, of Skip's unique charisma. For all his virtues, I could not imagine John Lee, for instance, telling a story like that. You could see why Skip had been such a magnet, both for his supporters and for all those generations of scouts, over all those years.

Warmed by my obvious interest, Skip became confiding. 'I know I've been difficult this year,' he said.

'But there's a very good reason.' His manner became more confidential still. 'It's my retirement,' he said. 'It's getting to me. I just can't bear to let the scout troop go. God knows I've built it up over all these years. It breaks my heart to walk away from it. It's me.'

And there was another thing, he added. None of the troop understood that it was this, above all, which brought about his moods.

'No one at all?' I asked.

'Not a soul,' said Skip.

By now, however, I knew the Mohawk patterns. With a storm like this the calm would surely follow. Next morning, it duly arrived, announced, as usual, by an ear-cracking carolling from Skip. The row had been resolved. Why? The answer, as usual, remained mysterious. However, the word was out that late the previous night Sheila had pulled rank as a relative, told Skip just how badly he was treating Dave, and ticked him off.

Skip's good humour quickly filtered down to everyone else and we launched into one of those days when it really felt like God was on our side. The sun shone triumphantly, the Bucquoy gardens, as ever, seemingly, a month in advance of England, were full of fat, floppy autumnal flowers, while a stealing mist promised a day of unusual heat. The idea was we'd do a quick scoot into Arras, have a bite of lunch and a bit of a drink, and look round the town.

As always, I was assigned to Bernard and Matt, while for our mooch round Arras Phil Simpson was attached to us as well. But Phil, unlike the rest of us, was feeling unhappy. It wasn't that he disliked either Matt, Bernard, or me, he explained, it was just that he wished he'd joined a group that was 'more exciting'. Oh dear, I thought, let's hope this doesn't lead to aggravation. I'd done taking fed-up kids around French towns and it could be quite extraordinarily hard work. There had been one half-hour with four scouts and two autistic boys in an Albert toy shop which will stay with me for ever, as it will, I'm sure, with the toy shop's owner.

Unbeknown to me, in fact, this thought must have been written plain on my face, because as we walked towards the town square, I heard a cry of 'It's good to see a man who loves his work!' It was Skip, chortling with glee, already ensconced in a pavement café. He'd read me perfectly and it was yet another reminder, if one were needed, why he was so good at group dynamics.

The really curious thing was I was only half aware of how I felt myself.

My nervousness was not unreasonable. True, the walk began amiably enough, as my three boys wandered in and out of shops, cruised up and down the stalls in the town square, and bought, or nearly bought, a range of shiny trinkets. Then they all bought sweets, the sine qua non of childhood shopping. Then Matt bought, for 20 francs, a ring with 'M' stamped on it. Next he remembered how dearly he wanted a wristwatch and there followed a long traipse round every watch shop within half a mile, with Phil Simpson swiftly getting very irritable indeed. Indeed, so fed up did he get that eventually I suggested I bought them a drink in the town square, and Phil began to perk up.

Little did we know what the great scoutmaster in the sky had planned! As we sat there, rubbernecking around, trying hard to convince ourselves how interesting we found a provincial French square, young Matt, with a ready eye for the flotsam of the street, suddenly pounced on a discarded lottery ticket. Mysteriously, he quickly decided it was a winning ticket that someone had inexplicably thrown away. Closer examination showed that it was, of course, a dud, but it put the thought of lotteries in our minds and a moment later we noticed we were sitting right outside the shop which sold the tickets. And there, in the window, was a poster giving the lottery ticket odds. Wild excitement! For now the boys were utterly determined to get some bets on and, subject to the usual caveats, I let them. It was their money, for heaven's sake.

So both Matt and Phil bought 5 franc tickets. They opened them up and examined them. They'd won! Matt, to his bubbling delight, had come in at six to one, winning 30 francs, but Phil had won, it said on the ticket, 500 francs. I examined and re-examined his ticket, so incredible did it seem. A hundred to one! It was beyond belief. It was the biggest percentage win I, for one, had ever been near. We checked with the pay-out lady to sort out the obvious mistake; but no, she said, it might indeed be a win and got on the phone to head office to check. Mais oui, it was!

Phil always had a broad, characteristic, Cheshire cat grin. This time his face expanded so fast and far I seriously wondered if it might not burst open with the strain. The smile never left his face for the rest of the day. Nor was Matt entirely left out. With his budget bumped up by his winnings, and subbed a little by me, he bought the watch he'd coveted earlier but couldn't afford. It was purple and black, Matt chose it by colour, and he stroked it and caressed it like a pet dog. While as for Bernard, he had, as usual, a limited reading on the technicalities of the situation but was well aware of the general atmosphere, one of amazed joy.

Phil made me swear I wouldn't tell Skip. Skip has firm views on the boys gambling. He reckoned his best ploy would be to convert his winnings into pounds, then surreptitiously take them back to England. He hinted darkly at a deal with Steve the driver, who apparently needed the francs.

But the strangest thing was the way these flukes kept happening around Mohawk. It really made you wonder if there was not some fairy godmother, some guardian angel that watched over our every action. It sometimes felt like it.

But then even as hard-headed an operator as Napoleon used to ask, of a new general, 'Is he lucky?' Some times and persons do genuinely seem blessed. And when Mohawk was on a roll it seemed to affect everything.

That evening Arthur suddenly reappeared. For a man who, according to Dave, had so very recently sworn that his relationship with Mohawk was, finally, at an absolute end, he seemed to have made a remarkable recovery. For he was quite back to his old, smiling self, and as a peace offering he'd turned up with a vast crate of drinks: a local beer plus a local aperitif as well, which he proceeded to mix up into some kind of killer cocktail. He handed these round to everyone at the table. Gradually, however, we pieced together his story. Apparently Skip had told his wife Maureen about the row on the phone, and she, in turn, had rung up Arthur to make peace.

Arthur was very fond of Maureen. Like everyone around Mohawk he felt deep respect for her unstinting support of Skip, not to mention her constant, generous concern for the welfare of the boys. Skip's career had meant constant financial uncertainty, plus recurrent absences at times most families use for leisure. Yet far from discouraging him she had herself become a mother figure to innumerable scouts. John Lee was a case in point.

So a phone call from Maureen was a major diplomatic event. It had worked. And now, once again, everyone was in a good mood. Not least Sheila, who had been given a superb bunch of flowers. I asked who gave them to her. She told me John Lee. How typically generous of John, I smiled.

It was a balmy, golden evening, the sun turning the farmhouse roof to deep crimson, the light flashing off the leaves like glass. And with Mohawk once again at peace, it was one of those moments when you felt how truly Mohawk was a real community: the adults chatting and mildly squabbling over their drinks; Phil and Steve the driver engaged in discreet negotiations behind the coach; Matt Polesden and Bernard Naisbitt planning something dodgy with the hose; little macho Pete Pollard sitting on the grass, at our feet, announcing one moment, 'You could make a wicked daisy chain out here, there are masses of daisies', and a moment later, when Arthur went to the loo, 'I wonder if Arthur brought me a bomb.' A place for everyone, and everyone in their place.

Nevertheless, if Arthur had promised Pete a 'bomb' it didn't look like he'd remembered. But in every other way that evening he was a star. His shoulders heaved at tales of how we got lost every time we drove anywhere. He gave advice on the intricacies of local food and drink. He was a constant fount of tales about the war. His father had been in the Resistance.

Truly, Arthur was indeed 'the French Skip' with his warmth, his tall stories, his sudden angers and still more dramatic reconciliations. Emboldened by his drinks and our own ever-mellowing good mood, the group stumbled into theme after jokey theme, until, by one of those strange conversational meanders which you can never account for later we blundered into, of all things, my daughter's joy at her new rabbit, and how hard it was to get her to look after it, and clean it out.

'I hope you're doing the injections,' said Skip.

'Oh yes,' I said, 'unquestionably. Whatever injections the rabbit needs, it will have them.'

'No, no,' said Skip, 'the injections for your kids. If they're not vaccinated they could catch myxomatosis!'

'Really!' I said. 'I never knew human beings could catch that!'

At which the whole table erupted with delight. It was, of course, a tease. Sheila called out at the top of her voice: 'I don't believe it! He's an absolute innocent, that man!' But there was something strange about her tone: she didn't sound jokey. In some weird way she actually sounded annoyed. Was I imagining it? If not, how on earth had I offended her?

But the moment vanished in a storm of jokes and shortly afterwards we moved inside to the boys' dining room, a huge ninety by thirty foot ex-barn that Skip had christened 'the baronial hall'. It had a huge, open fireplace and, as the night was chilly, we lit a log fire and sat around it, drinking. Skip was right back on his most genial form, making plans to hold weekenders here for adults from Beckton, joking, teasing, in his most expansive, Christmas mode. And, yet, I still found myself wondering what on earth had I done to offend Sheila. Why all this fuss about a goddamned rabbit?

However, this had to remain a mystery as our trip, its momentum restored, proceeded ever more happily onward from that moment. The next day we drove the long haul up to the sea, choosing, as usual, the same beach. It may have been a struggle but it was what we knew, and there was a conservative streak in Mohawk that always brought us back to whatever worked. The kids fought each other on the sand for four hours. They attacked the adults, and we had a picnic. They fought each other on the sand for two more hours. They attacked the adults again, then we drove home, scouts and autistic children singing all the way.

But on the Friday we did something different. We devoted a whole day to First World War history, a rare event at Mohawk. For although the adults in their different ways were fascinated by it, the children so very often seemed bored. Nevertheless, Skip and John, in their constant observation of the kids' moods, must have picked up something positive at the prospect of battlefield visits, and, riding as ever on the back of the kids' enthusiasms, decided to do it.

So off we went in the morning to nearby Beaumont Hamel, where the kids ran and shot and scampered about in the three square miles of preserved trenches, without, it must be said, showing very much sense that they were different from the beach. Come the afternoon we went on to Thiepval, scene of a disastrous 1916 attack during the Battle of the Somme. Thiepval's memorial arch was, of course, where Skip's grandfather was remembered.

This time, for some reason, it seemed to catch the boys' interest. Had we finally moved into an emotional gear which could cope with such serious events? Or had the adults simply got better at making it all sound interesting? Steve the driver, certainly, did his best. Steve had often driven round this area on other trips, and had learned to give his passengers what they wanted. He announced, for instance, that in the German cemeteries the soldiers were buried upright, facing towards Germany, so that they could walk back – at the resurrection, presumably. It certainly went down well with the boys, and had the added advantage that there was little serious prospect of proving it one way or the other, without, that is, several hours' work, and a good few shovels and picks.

Whatever the cause, the boys seemed suddenly curious, quite changed from their uproariousness at Beaumont Hamel. They gazed in awe at the gargantuan arch, with its crowded names.

As they walked away they started talking about it.

'I'd have *loved* the war,' said Fred Robinson, the thin wiry boy who looked exactly like a First World War private anyway. 'It must have been so exciting. Those trenches we saw this morning were *wicked*. Did you see *Saving Private Ryan*? There you are, wandering along, and all of a sudden you've been shot in the head!'

'Which was first?' asked Troy Northcote. 'The Vietnam War or the First World War?'

'The First World War, stupid,' said Fred. 'An' my dad says that was the worst war of all, even worse than the Second. It'd be different if we had a war today though, it'd be a doddle, 'cos nowadays everyone's our friend.'

'Yeah,' said Troy. 'They'd all come in on our side, wouldn't they, America, Russia, France, Germany . . .'

'Barbados, Jamaica, Serbia . . .' said Fred.

'St Lucia, Antigua, Sierra Leone . . .' added Troy.

Meanwhile Bernard Naisbitt had been standing with Matt Polesden, gazing thoughtfully up at the arch. Suddenly, he spoke.

'What's that?' he said.

'A memorial,' said Matt.

'What's a memorial?'

'To remind us of the war.'

'What's a war?'

'It's when people get mad and fight each other and there's a battle.'

Bernard was looking increasingly baffled.

'What's a battle?'

Matt gave it a go.

'It's, like . . . Imagine if there were some people in this wood here, and other people in that wood over there, then suddenly the ones over here start yelling and shouting an' then they all rush over to the ones over there and kill them.'

Bernard Naisbitt looked amazed.

'What they do that for?'

But for the adults, Thiepval meant only grief. Most notably it was affecting Sheila, whose great-uncle's name – Skip's grandfather – was, of course, up there on the arch.

'He just . . . disappeared,' she said. 'He went off to the war and his family never saw him again. No body, no grave, no nothing. Disappeared. His wife, my great-aunt, was just thirty-two. She was left with six kids.'

Then Sheila started talking about her own bereavement.

'My husband was seventeen years older than me,' she said. 'We had twenty-five wonderful years. He was seventy-two years old and I think he sensed he was about to go, even though he was active. He'd say, if I do go it doesn't matter, I've done all I need to do.'

In a level voice, Sheila went on: 'It was during the day. He was sitting there, asleep in his chair. I spoke to him and he didn't reply. I spoke to him again. He was still silent. I looked more carefully and I saw his eyes were open, but there was nothing there.

'I screamed to wake the dead. My neighbour got in such a panic she climbed straight over the fence to get to me. My husband died in hospital five days later.'

And there had been other deaths, too.

'My father died suddenly, as well, having a sleep after lunch. And my son, Ian, he died in a car crash. It was really strange, he spoke to me on the phone just before it happened. His last words were, "I love you."'

The memorial was more powerful than we realized. Silent, we walked back to the coach.

It was remarkable, the intimacy into which Sheila and I had

stumbled. There was no trace, seemingly, of the irritation she had shown, so inexplicably, the night before. Maybe she felt the difference as well. Perhaps this was why, as the evening unfolded, she told me other confidences as well. To be honest, I can't remember exactly what she said. All I know is that by the end of that last night of our French trip, I had understood a further, rather crucial, piece of Mohawk news. Dave and Sheila, I learned, were lovers. They'd been keeping it under wraps, with some sense that people might think it was inappropriate; but finally they had decided to come clean.

Of course, the flowers that Sheila had been given the other evening weren't from John at all, they'd been from Dave. Most of the other adults, more streetwise than I, had long ago grasped their relationship, though they'd pretended not to. I'd missed it altogether, which was why Sheila had got so exasperated, and why she'd felt, in an understandable, if rather curious transference, so irritated at my innocence in a quite different context, that of rabbit care.

Startling news! And yet, with the ease of hindsight, how obvious, for those with eyes to see! Now I remembered consciously the moments I had only sensed before. The way, for instance, that Dave and Sheila, on some pretext, had gone off together on their own for four hours during that seaside visit and, more importantly, how they had looked. Then I remembered, too, all the solicitousness Sheila had shown to Dave after his nightmare journey, not to mention the time, shortly afterwards, when I had come into the staff room and found them sitting together. Both were lying on couches at opposite sides of the room, but each perfectly mirrored the other's body talk and posture, and they were deep in conversation. I'd sensed my redundancy and left. I'd assumed they were discussing Skip. They weren't. They were an item. I was right about their need for privacy, but wrong about the reasons.

Nevertheless, this news was wonderful. Here were two tender, loving people, both in their early sixties, both single (Sheila had been bereaved, Dave's marriage had broken down), both deeply lonely. Now they had found each other, by doing voluntary work to help others! Why, even their faults dovetailed, a key element in any relationship. If Dave whinged, Sheila bossed a bit. They fitted like gloves.

That evening, our last, we had an end of trip party. Arthur was coming and once again, before he arrived, Pete Pollard was going on and on about his promised 'bomb'. Not that I'd ever heard him mention it to Arthur directly. All the Pollard brothers found it hard to ask for things and would even turn down little gifts like sweets or ice creams. But like all kids who act like that their need, in fact, was greater rather than less. I really hoped that Arthur would bring that bomb.

At seven o' clock, in swept Arthur's car. First thing, he opened the boot and got out Pete's beloved 'bomb'. I could have kissed him. Not that Pete showed any exceptional gratitude. He thanked him, but not effusively. I never did find out whether Arthur knew just why this should be, or how much a gift like that had really meant to Pete.

Once again, the evening swiftly disappeared into alcoholic uproar, with now a new, rich theme for badinage: the Sheila–Dave relationship. With all this to celebrate and with it being the last night and all, this was, even by the high standards of Mohawk, quite a party. By one o'clock everyone but myself, Steve, Sheila and Dave had collapsed into bed. By 1.30 Sheila gave up and went to bed as well.

Then through the alcoholic swirl I gradually realized that there was this intense thing going on between Dave and Steve. For Dave, being Dave, couldn't enjoy his success and leave it at that. He had to complicate it. He was going on and on about this string of problems. Sheila had asked him to visit her out in Australia. Of course, he wanted to go, but would it be wise? Would it work out? Would he and Sheila get on as well out there as here? What would her relatives think? Come to that, he was skint, where was he supposed to find the fare?

In vino veritas. It isn't just your own life you can see more clearly under alcohol, but those of others, too. It seemed plain to me that these objections were a smokescreen. What Dave was really saying was that he didn't feel worthy of what life was offering him. He didn't deserve it.

Steve seemed to read it this way, too. Dimly I saw that he was trying to talk Dave round. Does drink coarsen people? Not necessarily! Steve's gentleness, even delicacy, was remarkable to see. It was just like that time when he had encouraged autistic Bernard.

In the end Dave surrendered, temporarily at least, and agreed if nothing else to consider the possibility of happiness. And yet what was plainer still was that it was Steve, in fact, not Dave, who was benefiting most from the exchange, in ways that had become quite familiar during the previous few days.

Not that anybody had done anything for him. Rather, he'd done things for other people. His cure, in fact, had been simple. He'd cured himself. The ultimate joiner, from the start he'd helped in every direction he could. He'd even done the cooking at one stage – some years back he'd worked as a chef. The side of his character that had emerged during the week simply had nothing in common with that desperately cynical man I'd met five days before.

Steve's own comment was succinct: 'I've learnt a lot,' he said, 'on this trip.' Few words, much meaning.

NINE

With our trip to France finished we returned again to Mohawk, this time for the camp's final fortnight.

Even in a week the place had been transformed. For now, once again, Camp Mohawk was as I first remembered it; not budding and hopeful as it had been back in May, nor warm and sultry like July, but at the height of its summer glory. The bracken was bone dry, the earth like stone. The leaves, as if weary, had lost their plastic sheen of spring; olive-grey, they were on the very edge of autumn. The fields, too, looked tired, as if burned out by the heat. The dominant tint was dun, almost khaki, the colour of rabbit's fur.

And over everything lay this inch of white dust, that same dust so characteristic of any English summer up to the 1920s, when the roads were tarmacked. It settled on the tables and chairs; it stuck at the back of our throats; when the wind gusted it whirled in great spirals up to the sky. When Dave drove the Land Rover up in the morning he would come trailing clouds of glory, great swathes of billowing white smoke, stretching back fifty yards.

And yet for all the joy of this summer warmth the finest moments, curiously, came neither at noon, nor even at evening, with its sunsets so readily viewed from our vantage point on the hill. Rather, they came at dawn. To wake up in a tent at Mohawk was something special. First the grey fingers of light would come stealing in; then there would build this sense of expectancy, of some imminent, almost awful event. Suddenly, as if turned on by a switch, the first bird would sing, followed by another, then still another, until, in a rush, every bird in the world. Then after ten minutes, just as suddenly, all would stop.

As the sunlight strengthened, the treetops would glow like tapers, and a strange timelessness would come upon the camp. It was as if the place had drifted back two centuries; as if some magic process had placed us in the backdrop of a Reynolds painting. Above all it was a feeling of recognition, as if the forest were some good, old friend, long missed and now returned. This was when it was possible to lose all track of time, and half an hour, an hour, could vanish without explanation.

Then, at last, the first shafts of sunlight would strike the tent wall, making firm orange rectangles that grew brighter by the minute, and normal consciousness would reassert itself. The day would begin.

Only later did I find out how many of the boys, too, would be awake at this hour and would regard these early morning moments as most precious of all. Occasionally, indeed, they would even leave their tents and sleep in the open air, the better to experience them. Although their enjoyment of the dawn, it must be said, was more striking than their description of it. All Christopher Hope, for instance, could say was that 'it seemed to take for ever', but maybe this was more eloquent than it seemed. Perhaps he, too, was trying to describe the dawn's strange timelessness.

And if the landscape felt sated, like a power that has reached its zenith, so we, too, felt our own strange lethargy. It was not typical of Mohawk. We would greet each other with yawns, our conversations would be punctuated with more yawns, while even a forty-yard stroll down to the swimming pool would seem an effort. When boys disappeared they'd no longer turn up in the woods, which is where they'd have been earlier in the year, but in their tents asleep.

Was it the weather? It was in part, but it was more. For a start, of course, we were simply getting tired. In the natural rhythm of the Mohawk year, which started with the fund-raising before Christmas, we were already into our ninth month. At this summer camp alone, there were scouts who hadn't been home since July.

But there were subtler causes. Skip, for instance, was finally showing serious signs of retirement. For days on end he would stay in London, and never come down to Mohawk at all. The result was the kind of uncertainty, among both adults and scouts, that children feel when separated from their parents. Uncertainty, too, can make people feel tired. But our feelings were a reminder, too, of just how crucial Skip was to the camp's energy. Whatever his mood, he had always been the fountainhead of ideas and inspiration, even when his ideas, sometimes, were somewhat bizarre. Now, under John – for it was John, rather than Clare, who ran the camp day-to-day – there was an uncharacteristic calm. In its own way, it was delightful and it was certainly different, but it had its limitations. The bottom line was plain: Skip Howgate, the man who, above all others, needed to feel indispensable, was sorely missed.

Given this, it was lucky that we found an energy source from another quarter. For it was at this stage, in the last few weeks of the summer camp, that we met a whole series of disabled boys who were quite different from those who'd come before. Tricky though they often were, they were undeniably stimulating. Earlier boys had all seemed variants on a theme, whether snub-nosed boys like Peter Bell, faerie kings like Teddy and Dreamy David, or little tykes like Brett, the one who socked the horse at the riding school. But these new kids were one-offs.

There was, for instance, Tony Hampshire. Tony suffered from the curiously-named Fragile X syndrome.

You could see Tony was unusual; it was something about his head. His hair brushed neatly back, his jawline firm, his eyes authoritative-looking, he looked anything but underdeveloped; he looked, if anything, disproportionately mature. Indeed, his head looked like that of a middle-aged businessman, on the body of a boy. He seemed wise beyond his years. And at one level, the explanation was simple. The head of a Fragile X syndrome child *is* larger than usual, it is one of the condition's key symptoms. But beyond that, as usual, the mysteries begin.

A Fragile X sufferer can demonstrate many autistic difficulties – biting, arm-flapping, speech problems, extreme withdrawal – but while 15 per cent of Fragile X sufferers do indeed suffer from full-blown autism, Fragile X has been recognized as a separate syndrome for the last twenty years. Above all it is distinguished by its causality. For while the genetic causality of autism proper continues to be debated, with Fragile X it is beyond any doubt. The cause is a defect in the X chromosome, which may be passed from one generation to the next.

Nevertheless, the precise mechanism of this process is Fragile X's greatest wonder.

Parents, for instance, may be carriers of the condition without actively suffering from it themselves. However, their children may well be victims. This is indeed the case with the Hampshire family. And so, also, their children's descendants may be sufferers.

The complexities multiply. A woman carrier, for example, has a fifty-fifty chance of passing the Fragile X chromosome to her children. Of these, the sons are most likely to be affected, while for daughters the chances are one in three. Men, too, can be unaffected carriers of Fragile X, and here the processes are different again. They pass on the chromosome to all daughters.

These daughters, though themselves unaffected, may give birth to affected children.

More complex still, any sons of male carriers will be completely unaffected as they do not receive the X chromosome from their father.

What a hand to be dealt by fate! Fragile X affects about 1 in 4,000 males and 1 in 8,000 females; so that the chances of Tony's family being involved were devastatingly low. Nevertheless, that was what biology had decreed. However, one further difference between Fragile X and mainstream autism is that there will rarely be any symptoms in other family members. (This is by no means the case with autism.) Certainly, both Tony's parents were as able and loving as you could wish. Perhaps this, in turn, has some connection with the other thing about Tony that struck everyone at Mohawk: his friendliness.

For while some sufferers from Fragile X are indeed withdrawn, others most emphatically are not, and Tony belongs firmly in the sociable camp. So cheerful was he, as he wandered round the camp with his jaunty, rolling gait, that he swiftly gained a kind of local celebrity, and kids came rushing from all over Mohawk to greet him.

Nevertheless, his language, in particular, remained extremely limited. He had little more than half a dozen words. But what was charming, and, predictably, instantly charmed the scouts, was that in this minute vocabulary two words, above all, were key: words of greeting.

''Allo mate!' he would cry to everyone he met, accompanied by a massive, perky, utterly captivating grin. ''Allo Mate!' everyone would yell back. And Tony would toddle on his way, leaving a wake of grinning, cheery-looking scouts behind him. So sweet was Tony's manner that even this minimalist exchange could transform the mood of those he met. ''Allo mate!' soon became the greeting of choice among the scouts, the leitmotif of those last few weeks at the camp.

With Tony, too, I have another visual memory. Within half an hour of Tony's arrival, he and his gofer, Chris Smith, with whom the chemistry certainly seemed to work well, were walking hand in hand to the swimming pool. Tony had already, seemingly, happily settled in. The day, like so many that August, was blazing hot, so both were going barefoot. They came to the entrance track, where there are stones.

Suddenly, for the first time, Tony looked unsure. He was afraid, clearly, of cutting his feet. Not so Chris. In a flash, he had lifted Tony bodily off the ground and clean over the stones; even though Chris is, if anything, rather smaller than Tony. And the moment Chris put him down, Tony threw his arms round him and hugged him. And this time he managed a variant on those customary two words. It took a bit of time, but eventually, out it came: 'Thanks, mate!'

And yet, for all the warmth of this boy, and the undoubted pleasure he got from his stay, here was one child of whom it seemed near-certain that he could gain little more than joy for himself, and respite for his parents, from his time with Mohawk. For if ever there was a 'hard-wired' problem Tony's was it. The glitch in his brain is so fundamental that only carefully calculated, Fragile X-specific therapies are likely to help. Fortunately, especially in the United States, such therapies exist, and are constantly being improved.

How different from Edward, who joined us shortly after. For here was a boy whose symptoms seemed quite exceptionally dependent on how others treated him. So much so, indeed, that he rapidly achieved a very different kind of fame. Rightly or wrongly he became the only boy, throughout that summer, of whom carer after carer said: 'This boy has a behaviour problem: he is not autistic.'

Perhaps one should stress therefore, at the start, that Edward has been professionally diagnosed autistic. He is now eight and his condition was established when he was three, at Guy's Hospital, in London.

Yet the carers' reaction was understandable. Time and again, those who worked with Edward, both adults and scouts, would talk with surprise about how competent he was – and how his moments of seeming incompetence so often appeared a kind of pretence, an attempt to manipulate the world about him. It was as if the game-playing element, so often present to some degree in all autistic children, had in Edward become overwhelming.

Not that he was so different in other ways, for instance, physically. Dark and pale, he seemed to fall into that snub-nosed, tearful category, most memorably represented by Peter Bell, the train-loving boy who went with us to Holland. But then Peter too, whose very body talk would often suggest disappointment, even petulance, was also notable for the elasticity of his symptoms. One only has to think of the coming and going of his speech, according to circumstance and the quality of his relationships. What made Edward different was that this elasticity seemed to apply virtually all the time.

His carers were Tim, younger brother of Johnny Cobbett, and Christopher Hope. Christopher was one of the very best observers among the boys. Christopher was the scout, mentioned in chapter one, who had realized that the autistic child I thought was making swimming motions was in fact pretending to steer a car, indicating that he wanted to go home. And Christopher it was who first started reporting back that Edward's autism somehow didn't add up. For a start, he seemed quite competent academically. He was, for instance, an extremely good reader. Then there were his language difficulties. We were used, of course, to boys whose language difficulties seemed strangely contingent on circumstances, especially emotional circumstances, but in Edward this elasticity seemed acute. Most of the time he said absolutely nothing; then suddenly, without warning, he would produce, not merely speech, but little rushes of exceptionally fluent speech, using language which seemed noticeably *beyond*, rather than behind, what you might have expected for his age.

Christopher said that, after many hours of silence, it was in the middle of a scouts' scrimmage that Edward suddenly spoke. 'This is a splendid fight!' he declared. Soon after, he spoke again. Spending time in the canteen, in the corner of which was a piano, he had once more passed a silent hour, tinkering pensively with the keys. Then without warning he turned to Christopher: 'This really is the most magnificent piece of engineering,' he said. These gnomic utterances were not only beyond his years but were also of a very specific bent; there was a certain self-importance about them which would not have disgraced a judge. Or a chief clerk? It was exactly how one might have imagined Peter Bell speaking in his chief clerk mode that time in Holland. Although Peter, of course, was at that time silent. And yet, perhaps, we can see something else in these incidents, something we have come across before. They both happened when Edward was clearly enjoying himself. Presumably he felt relaxed. And the reason for his relaxation, especially in the second case, was plain: Edward was doing exactly as he pleased. He was in control.

It was reminiscent of these 'Willed' chapters 'Willed Weakness', 'Willed Deafness', 'Willed Blindness', 'Willed Isolation', in Clara Claiborne Park's *The Siege*, mentioned earlier in chapter five. For whatever else caused Edward's reticence it plainly wasn't physical, and seemed, as Clara Park speculated about her daughter, more like some kind of deep choice. And this possibility would certainly seem to have been borne out by other behaviours that Christopher noticed.

Because, said Christopher, another key characteristic of Edward's behaviour during his visit was that he consistently threw tantrums. And one quality united these rows: they all involved crises of will.

There was, for instance, a memorable barney in the canteen. The cause? Edward not being offered the cup that he required. Then there were the tantrums Edward threw during an impromptu Mohawk sports day. The triggers were the times he failed to win. There was also the swimming trunks row. Edward had two pairs, but dropped one in the mud. When Christopher tried to get him to put on the clean pair, Edward refused, and wanted to carry on wearing the muddy ones. When Christopher tried to insist . . . row number three.

Especially revealing was the row in the 'white' or audio-tactile room. Edward's carers, Tim and Christopher, had made an impromptu slide out of some floor-cushions. Edward's mood started deteriorating when they wouldn't let him lay the cushions out the way *he* required. But the real row came when he found a pair of glasses, inadvertently left there by one of the scouts. He put them on, and when Tim and Christopher tried to take them back, he began to get angry. When, by a trick, they deftly succeeded, he exploded. 'I can't see! I can't see!' he yelled. He had, apparently, been suddenly struck blind. And his litany of 'I can't see! I can't see!', ever louder, and ever less convincing, carried on until they all had left the room.

In each case, said Christopher, what struck him was that Edward's anger had nothing to do with what might be called a 'legitimate' cause of frustration, a co-ordination problem, say, like the one Bernard Naisbitt experienced when cleaning out the coach in France. Edward's anger was about will. To be honest, said Christopher, Edward didn't strike him as autistic at all. He seemed plain spoiled.

Of course, this was often said about autistic boys, especially when they had the particular knack, which Edward, certainly, had developed pretty well, of winding the scouts up. But what was unusual about Edward was that after he had been there a day or two, everyone on site, quite independently, was saying the same thing: 'I really don't think this boy is autistic.' Tim, John Lee, Sheila, everyone. And they all gave the same reason: time and again, when he refused or failed to do something, the cause, they felt, was less incapacity than choice. In short, interestingly, they seemed to be making a similar distinction to that made months earlier by Skip: between a certain willed defiance, which Skip wouldn't accept, and anger based on genuine incapacity, which he would.

But the most question-begging moment was one I saw myself.

One evening I was in the tent with Christopher and Edward, just as Edward was settling down for bed. Could Edward's imagination, his sense of fantasy, have been stirred by the look of the place, which was undeniably weird? There was torchlight inside the tent, darkness outside. The tent walls shone with a dull, misty sheen as they picked up two further, exterior light sources, the moon, brilliant and full, and the lamps that lit the site. And on the tent walls, their shapes projected as if by magic lantern, were the shadows of leaves, hugely magnified. They looked ghostly, threatening. You could see how any child might have found them scary, let alone a child who was at all excitable.

Having said which, Edward played the situation for all it was worth. This was one of his talkative phases. First of all, he declared, he was afraid of the dark. However, this didn't stop him using the light from a torch to make the place more scary still by making shadow pictures on the tent wall. 'Oooh, a horrible crocodile!' he said. 'Ooooh, a monster! Frightening! Fierce!' Then he gave a yell. By this time, one should note, the other boys were trying to get to sleep. Next, he declared, the tent was now *so* scary – not least, presumably, because of his shadow shapes – that he wanted something to calm him down. He wanted a 'jam sandwich'. Sorry Edward, said Christopher, it's too late, the canteen's closed. 'I *want a jam sandwich*!' yelled Edward, 'and I want it *now*!' And when Christopher still refused, Edward said his mummy always let him have one, at which Christopher relented, and somehow rustled one up. Edward sat there eating it, triumph in his eye. We found out later, from Edward's mum, that she did not give him a jam sandwich at night. First round to Edward.

But the climax was yet to come. After ten minutes' silence, Edward suddenly sat bolt upright in bed.

'AAAAAAAAAARRRRRRRRRGGGGGH!' He shrieked. 'AAAAAAAAAARRRRRRGH!AAAAAAAAAAAAARRR-RRRRGH!'

The tent erupted. 'What's up Edward? What's the matter, mate?' The boys tumbled out of bed and rushed to his side.

'I've had a nightmare!' yelled Edward.

'It's all right mate! Don't be scared! We're here! We'll look after you!'

Five seconds silence. And then: 'Only pretending!'

'AAAAAAAAAAAAAARGH!' But now it was the scouts who were screaming, and they were screams of wrath. And they weren't pretending.

So it was unsurprising that Edward won himself his Mohawk reputation of being the one kid whose autism wasn't real. And yet it turned out to be only another example of the endless mystery of autism, of its fluid, paradoxical elusiveness. Some weeks later I interviewed his mother. And it quickly emerged that Edward did indeed have a whole range of familiar autistic symptoms, not all of which had been evident at the camp.

He was, for instance, much given to 'bizarre behaviour'. Typical was the time he elected to take a bicycle chain on a shopping visit to Sainsbury's. As his mother pointed out, this would be acceptable in a child of three, but hardly in a child of eight. Then there was his autistic literalism. One day he heard how white blood cells fought 'bad' cells during illness and he quickly became appalled, says his mother, at the battle potentially being fought out inside his body. But most eloquent of all was an incident at his special school. One term they put on a show for the parents. The pupils were encouraged to join in, and put on little performances to help their confidence. At one stage each child came on stage to tell a joke. Edward was having trouble with his timing. So his teacher suggested he count up to five, before delivering the punchline.

Edward duly appeared on stage. 'What trousers do you wear when it's raining?' he asked. 'One, two, three, four, five,' he said, 'drainpipe trousers!'

What behaviour could be more classically autistic?

And Edward even displays typically autistic talents. Intensely visual, like so many boys with autism, he makes his own cardboard cut-out models, designing the patterns himself. This means he sees the necessary shape of each constituent part, embodied as it were within the model. His mother showed me parts he had already cut out, a string of disembodied shapes which, put together, would indeed make the required railway engine. Where he differed from other children, and adults like me, was in the ease with which he could see, without any help, these constituent shapes, which, to a less gifted eye, are hard indeed to connect with the final result.

Suffice it to say that in a range of other ways too, in his rigidity, his love of sequence, his food faddism, his lack of eye contact, he shows a range of familiar autistic behaviours. So why were Mohawk's carers so sure he was not autistic? Were they just plain deluded? Or did they see a truth, albeit a part-truth merely? Were there some aspects of Edward's behaviour over which he had control, others less so? As with other boys, the contradictions multiply. Indeed, they are strangely implacable. To the Mohawk carers, it seemed certain and demonstrable that his autism symptoms were chosen; to others, it seemed equally certain and demonstrable that they were not. The mystery remains.

No other child, all summer, brought with him quite the history of Tariq Aziz, who joined us for the very last week of the camp. Like Tony Hampshire, Tariq was not strictly autistic. He simply had many comparable symptoms, enough, certainly, to put him well within the Camp Mohawk remit. Above all, both he and his parents sorely needed help.

He must have been the sickest-looking boy we saw all summer. Ten years old, shrimp-like and thin, he had the physique of a boy of six; yet he moved like an old man. He heaved himself out of the car with a terrible, slow world-weariness. Then he shuffled slowly across the campfire circle to be greeted by John Lee. He looked like he bore the weight of the universe.

His parents didn't look too well, either. His mother, in particular, seemed exhausted. It turned out this was the first time she had ever let Tariq stay away from home. She was desperately concerned for his wellbeing. Indeed, she had phoned up, earlier in the day, to cancel Tariq's visit, and had been talked out of it by John Lee. Before she and her husband had left home, she'd been physically sick.

Terrible though Tariq looked, his illness remained obscure. True, his problem, like autism, was essentially developmental; but beyond that the questions marks began. His technical diagnosis, said his parents, was 'global development delay'. Yet this was, it seemed, a bit of a label, plucked out of the air by his doctors in some desperation, as they had no clear idea *what* the problem was. All that was certain was his enormous range of symptoms. He was undergrown, underweight, and had feeding problems; he had huge difficulties with language. When crossed, he suffered from furious fits of anger; he would hold his breath and turn blue. Above all, he had virtually no resistance to infection. He was constantly picking things up. He'd already been to hospital, reckoned his mother, around forty times in his short life. That included four operations, starting with open-heart surgery when he was two and a half.

Less mysterious was the effect all this was having on his family. For apart from the more familiar difficulties of a child with developmental problems – at ten years old, for instance, Tariq still needed help to go to the toilet – there were the perils that came with Tariq's susceptibility to illness, for he brought germs into the house. Indeed, reckoned his mother, so susceptible was Tariq to flu, that at one stage he was spending two weeks at home for every week at school. Tariq's father is self-employed. He writes computer programs, paid by the hour, and can't afford days off for illness. Yet he is inclined to pick up his son's infections; given the pressures under which they all live, the father's resistance isn't too good either. So to all the other problems are added financial concerns as well . . .

So it was understandable, perhaps, that Tariq's mother presented John Lee with a long list of instructions as to what Tariq could and couldn't do. 'No swimming pool below 35 degrees centigrade,' said John, running his fingers through his hair. 'All visits to the swimming pool for ten minutes only. No baths or showers – she was especially insistent about this.' Tariq's mother had had a further alarm when she'd delivered him at the camp, as only then had she realized the troop would be sleeping in tents rather than huts. 'He must wear a roll-neck at all times in bed,' she'd said.

Given Tariq's impossible history, given, quite simply, the way the poor boy looked, you could see why his mother felt so protective. But even knowing the scouts' capacity to cope with almost anything, this looked like a tall order. How on earth would they cope? This, finally, could be the one they couldn't handle. The fear was they might very well make poor Tariq worse.

So it was a surprise when I found out who Skip and John had chosen to do the caring. For while the gofer was Chris Smith – quiet, dedicated Chris who wanted to teach disabled children – the carer was Tim Fenton, the plump, bespectacled scout, new this year, who had come to Mohawk with such fame for being difficult. I was frankly amazed. Not only had I seen regular incidents between Tim and the other boys, plus rows with the staff, but I had experienced the full vent of Tim's behaviour just the night before, when he'd been one of the scouts I'd driven over to Wokingham for an evening's swimming. The pool at Mohawk, designed for disabled children, is too small and shallow for the scouts to get a real swim.

Not only had Tim yelled abuse at passing pedestrians, not only had he made several mock-humorous attempts to get out of the car, but when we got back to the camp a whole other caper had taken place. Through an organizational hiccup we'd got back half an hour before anyone else and with just me, Tim and four other scouts on site, they'd moved swiftly into that wild, riot-oriented mode that every teacher knows. As an ex-teacher myself, and in attempt to head things off at the pass, I finished up locking all six of us into the scouts' lounge, where the riot could at least be contained. In the end, after a chase, two fights and a climactic, eyeball-to-eyeball confrontation between me and Tim, he finally simmered down.

OK, so there had not, in fact, been a death, nor even a maiming, but the memory of that evening is with me yet. Was Tim really the ideal child to look after a boy as delicate, as waif-like, as Tariq Aziz?

The upshot, however, was yet another surprise. As with so many things you don't expect, at first I couldn't see it. Then gradually, in a kind of parallel consciousness, I began to realize that Tim was doing something interesting with Tariq. For a start, I noticed, there was that familiar, intuitive thing of physical presence. Tim was constantly to be seen around his boy; hugely attentive, he never left him for moment. More, there was the quality of their togetherness. Like Matt Polesden and Bernard Naisbitt, Tim and Tariq seemed umbilically linked. Their body talk mirrored each other. If they were sitting on chairs in the campfire circle, and Tariq was leaning back, one foot on a table, so would Tariq be. If Tariq was lying down as if asleep as he often did during the day, there would Tim be beside him, stretched out as well. Other times, sprawled across one another, limb over limb, it was hard to tell which leg related to which. Most surprising of all, for a kid as noisy as Tim, was the way they would spend a lot of time in utter silence, just staring at each other.

One afternoon, I came across them in the white room. The white room, with its audio-tactile equipment and New Age music, was always a hit with the autistic kids. They found it relaxing. It was Tariq's second day, so he was already beginning to feel a bit less anxious. The two were there alone.

At one end of the room was a large waterbed. Tim and Tariq were lying on opposite sides of it, separated by six feet. They were silent; they were relaxed; they were mirroring each other's posture, both stretched at full length, leaning on an elbow, facing each other.

The room, which has no windows, was quite dark, which added to the sense of quietude.

All of a sudden, Tim took a flying leap in the air, landed right beside Tariq and sent him, such was the rebound from the water in the mattress, flying upwards, to land back down again with a crash. It was quite extraordinary. I can't think of anything I expected less, or would have thought less suitable for a child of Tariq's delicacy. Yet arrived back on earth Tariq looked utterly unperturbed. Yet this was only the beginning, for now Tim went right up close to Tariq and did it again, and then again, and then yet again, huge jumps, great kicks, wild, plunging rolls, anything to give the maximum possible disturbance to the bed's water. And Tariq duly flew upwards, sideways, backwards, every which way imaginable, like driftwood in a storm.

It looked terrible. I was on the verge of intervening when Tim, catching my eye, declared 'He likes it.' And indeed he did. The more Tim leaped and plunged the more Tariq laughed and smiled. Eventually, both exhausted, they stopped and dropped again into their earlier positions on opposite sides of the bed. Then Tariq, inexplicably, made a quacking noise, much like a duck. Tim quacked back. Then Tariq squeaked like a mouse; Tim squeaked back. Then Tariq crawled over and snuggled up in Tim's arms. Once again they lay there, in total silence, gazing into each other's eyes. Tariq looked like a babe in arms, lost, seemingly, in utter rapture. But most striking of all given everything else I knew about him, was the look of Tim. This deeply anxious boy, for the first time that I, certainly, had seen since he'd been at the camp, seemed utterly at peace.

It is strange how perception works. It was as if that unexpected vision worked as a battering ram on my consciousness, and opened my mind to a whole series of moments I had only half-noticed before. Not only had there been those earlier times I'd seen between Tim and Tariq, but dimly I realized there had been other incidents as well. I'd seen Tim helping with the camp cleaning, picking up rubbish, sweeping floors. I'd seen him hosting visitors: welcoming them, chatting to them, bringing them cups of tea. I'd even seen him helping other scouts with their autistic kids. This new Tim I was becoming aware of had been evolving quite a while.

Indeed, by the time the Azizs came to pick Tariq up at the end of his stay everyone else at the camp was aware of it as well. Tim Fenton was the talk of Mohawk. So here was Tim in an unprecedented role, surrounded by smiling, approving faces, as Tariq's parents sipped their tea and said how lucky they were that this especially caring boy – his name was Tim, wasn't it? – had been assigned to their obviously contented child.

The moment parents come to collect their children is always one of the best times at Mohawk. Nine times out of ten the child's visit has been a success, the autistic boys are self-evidently happy, and everyone, scouts, adult volunteers and parents, all look relieved. The scouts are released from the tension of giving care, the parents from worry that the visit might not have worked out. And this time it was truer than ever. Tariq's mother, especially – not unnaturally, given her worry when she had delivered her son – looked ten years younger. Yet the most striking figure, unquestionably, was that of Tim, who was standing there, hands behind his back, best boy in class, wallowing in the unwonted praise being lavished on him from all quarters. As I watched the scene, I told John what I'd noticed about Tim's development. Was it me, or had this change started long before Tariq came?

Yes, said John, he thought it had. Indeed, both he and Skip had noticed it; and that was precisely why they'd chosen Tim for such a daunting task. Once again, I said to myself, their observation had been acute, way ahead of the rest of us.

Not that the old, turbulent Tim had faded away; he was still there. Nor, even, that some new persona had emerged, quite separate from what Tim had been before. Rather it was as if some yet older Tim had been reborn. A side of him emerged that had been buried, presumably, under years of sadness and stress. Right now, this older, and more hopeful Tim was in the ascendant; tomorrow we might be back to the Tim we'd known. The two characters, for the foreseeable future, would co-exist side by side.

Nevertheless, it was a rebirth of hope.

Perhaps it was the effect, once more, of feeling warm towards a boy, but now I began to see some of Tim's other behaviours in a new light. Those wild scenes that night after the swimming, for instance. As Sheila pointed out, that evening had seen the end of a three-day session with the autistic children, and whenever a session ended, the scouts had a tendency to let off steam. Tim was no different from the rest. He might have been nervous, too, about what was scheduled for the next morning, the coming of Tariq.

Tim was just one of many boys I was getting fond of. And, as ever, the more I liked the boys, the more I understood them. Although, as with the scouts' understanding of the autistic children, this perception was double-edged. While appreciating their virtues, I became more streetwise about their ploys.

I began, for instance, to be less naive about their reasons for doing things, their attempts to manipulate a soft touch like me. Previously, if they had asked me to take them for a walk, or offered to show me one of the hides they had constructed in the woods, I would have felt naively pleased, glad to be liked. Now I twigged how often they had a hidden, if entirely understandable, agenda. Should their project require permission, then my presence would make that permission much easier to get. Should we go out for a walk, that walk might give them the excuse they needed for skipping some chore. Then there was their love of doing good turns, like cleaning cars. It was not that they weren't genuinely generous, it was that there were a lot of other things going on as well. So why did they want to clean cars? Not least, of course, because cleaning gave them access. Once inside – so they could 'clean the interior' – they had entrée to a veritable wonderland of further possibilities: releasing handbrakes, switching lights on, playing radios, working electric windows. This applied even if they failed to borrow the keys. (Of course, they would explain, this would be for entry merely, no start-ups, no mucking about.) For even without the keys, there was the further factor of Mohawk's position on a hill. Who needs keys when you've got gravity? With the handbrake off, they could be rolling.

At first, given their protestations, I let them inside, while keeping the keys, until I twigged the scenario. More than once, when I came back to the car in the evening, it seemed, for the life of me, that it had moved. The boys denied it, so it must have been the fairies; just as it was the fairies, too, who must have produced the dent on its door, on yet another day when it had inexplicably taken wing. In the end, I never did catch them at it. But if I'd any doubts about what was happening they vanished the day I spotted a posse of kids on Skip's mechanical digger, parked up on the high end of the camp. As they swarmed over it, one of them suddenly found the handbrake, released it, and they were rolling, kids hanging on to it like flies. As they moved, they burst into cheers, cheers which swiftly turned to wails as they gathered pace down the hill. Fortunately one of the older scouts leaped aboard and pulled the handbrake on again, thus cheating death.

Nevertheless, our growing friendship was more often positive, and I found the boys far readier than earlier to drop their guard, and speak from the heart. Nor did our intimacy any longer need disguises; it could happen quite naturally whenever we found ourselves alone, notably on walks. I remember a walk with Tom Pollard. He was the scout leader who had been so withdrawn when I first met him, and had been getting steadily more forthcoming throughout the year. Through a fluke of circumstance, on one walk we were left behind by the rest of the group, and he suddenly started talking about how much he enjoyed reading. His favourite author, he said, was J. R. R. Tolkien, of *Lord of the Rings*. What he especially liked about these tales of wizards and dragons, he said, was the way in which the good guys, the elves, were so loyal to each other, and would face death rather than betray their friends. If only people were like that in real life! He didn't know anyone who felt like that, except possibly his brother, he said, the boxer, Jeff Pollard.

Then there was the time when I was walking with Chris Smith, the 11-year-old who helped Tim Fenton look after Tariq. Gradually, haltingly, he talked more and more about his family's problems, about his lorry-driver father's blackout and subsequent unemployment, about the premature death of no less than two of his brothers, one six years ago, of asthma, the other, last year, as a baby. He'd done his best to cheer his mother up, he said, buying her things out of his pocket money. 'You know,' he said, 'rings, sweets, diamonds, things like that.'

And yet there was no doubt that the closest relationship the scouts developed on these walks was with the forest itself. Increasingly, it emerged as a character in its own right. Its spirit, so benign in high summer, would quickly dictate the mood of every group that entered it, and the longer I spent with the scouts, the less fanciful seemed the notion that the forest itself had a kind of healing power, for both boys and autistic children.

Most especially I felt this on one of the last evenings of the camp, when some of us went out for a walk led by John Lee. The group included Troy Northcote and Rob, plus two autistic boys. Quite a crowd, not best known for their level-headedness, yet from the start the walk was unusually calm.

In part, undoubtedly, this was down to the weather, for we were walking in late afternoon after what was surely the most sumptuous day of the year. So strong was the sun, even that late in the day, that the trees' branches, silhouetted against all this brilliance, looked jet black. And yet, by contrast, wherever the sun fell on them directly, they seemed unusually bright. Their greens were fluorescent, their golds had the depth and lustre you more customarily see in seaweed. They felt unreal, as did everything else about that enchanted afternoon.

John and the forest seemed somehow linked. He was like a medium. The normally noisy boys said very little, and when anyone did say anything its content seemed to matter less than its tone. John talked the most, and all his conversation felt amiable. He talked about friends of the camp and how they'd helped us out. He recalled old Alfred, one of the camp's long-dead supporters, whose tree, like Margaret's, is in the memorial garden. He told how, even in his eighties, he'd used to keep an eye on the camp when the troop was away; how every time he visited he'd always bring gifts, not least a bone for Skip's dog; how one day the troop had given him a new bike, and how he'd given it away because he preferred his old one, so fond was he of sticking with what he knew.

It was, in fact, just the kind of deeply amiable atmosphere that autistic children love. Certainly the two autistic boys on this walk seemed utterly content.

Until, that is, we came to a classic, and to an autistic mind deeply symbolic, moment of crisis: a divide in the path. Here was a threshold, an uncertainty, just the kind of situation boys with autism like least. John led the troop one way; then one of the autistic kids, usually noisy but up to now uncharacteristically calm, went the other. When the troop kept going, he sat on the ground. When they still kept going, he threw a tantrum. Some of the scouts tried to cajole him, but the harder they tried, the more frantic he became. Unlike the rest of us, however, John stayed calm, chatting to the other scouts, seemingly unconcerned. Eventually, he walked back to the autistic boy. The rest of us stopped twenty yards along the path; behind us, John stood talking to the boy. After five minutes the child got up and followed us.

I asked John how he'd done it. 'I told him a story,' said John. 'I said I'd had words with the Forestry Commission and they'd unilaterally blocked off the path he wanted to go down. No reason given; they'd simply done it.' A fantastic tale, said John, but that was the point. 'Non-verbal kids often live more in a cartoon, fantasy world than in our reality. So, weirdly, the more fantastic the idea you put to them, the more they may like it. By talking in fantasy, I had been translating the situation into the boy's language.'

And having 'explained', said John, he had offered the boy a choice: he could go down the path that had been blocked off, or he could follow us down the other; it was up to him.

So the final obstacle had been surmounted; for John had abolished any need for a clash of wills. The boy no longer had to dig his heels in, to confront us so he could maintain his sense of self. Predictably, he'd chosen to join our path.

The crisis over, the walk finished off as happily as it began.

We had already met three children – Tony, Edward and Tariq – who were each, in their own way, exceptional, and yet there was one other child who joined Mohawk in those last few weeks who was different again. This was Jeremy Browne, who was, quite simply, the most extraordinary child I have ever met. A view held by many other helpers at the camp.

Jeremy joined us, just after we returned from France, as one of a routine group of autistic children who had come for the customary three-day stay. He was a short blond boy, who looked around nine, with darting, intelligent eyes. At first sight the most striking thing about him, for a child who was supposed to be autistic, was his normality.

He looked fine. He moved easily, even energetically. He had no seeming language problems. Indeed, he was, if anything, unusually fluent. And as he padded around, getting used to the camp, he was followed by the two scouts looking after him: Bob Enright, one of the older scouts, as carer, and Chris Smith, once again, as gofer. They were one of the scouts' stronger teams. Not that it looked like this boy should be too hard, compared to some. It was his lack of symptoms that was striking.

Or was it? Quite quickly, our perception began to change. There was something strange about this boy. For a start, why did we find ourselves calling him 'short'? All boys are short. What we meant was, 'short for his age'. But what was his age? 'Around nine' people said. But why 'around'? There was something indeterminate about Jeremy; even at this early stage, we sensed there was something strangely grown up about this boy, whose actual age, we finally established, was six. Why do I remember him, even now, as ten?

Then there was his use of language. This was the area where we first noticed something specific. For while his conversation was indeed fluent, we soon began to feel he was garrulous. Having grasped that he was garrulous, we soon realized he was a conversational obsessive, a kid who seemed in thrall to a constant, manic need to talk. Nor was this all. His streams of frantic, motor-mouthing monologue consisted almost entirely of questions. More striking still, this verbal interrogation had its physical counterpart, the most furious, high-speed traipsing around the camp. For Jeremy was compulsively checking out every last, hidden corner of his new environment.

If Peter Bell, back in Holland, had felt like a chief clerk, then this boy, as he rushed around, felt like some manic chief executive. The boss, perhaps of some global corporation, parachuted in to a subdivision that was underperforming, rushing from department to department, orientating himself, barking questions, demanding to know precisely what was going wrong and why.

'Follow me!' he cried, to an increasingly alarmed-looking Bob and Chris, as his small, urgent, strutting, self-important figure shot off to the white room, then the campfire circle, then the scouts' tents, then the camp office, then back to the white room again, then on to the swimming pool, where the plastic covering not yet been opened up for the day. 'Unzip it!' he commanded, but even before it was done, he was off up the other end of the camp, a constant stream of questions pouring out all the way, questions relating to previous questions, questions piled on questions, an endless, frantic, autocratic stream of inquiry. 'Why's the floor wet? Has it been raining? Is there something wrong with the roof? Is that a crack over there? Is the roof safe? What holds it up? Is it timber? Where do you get it? Who did the building?' Every so often the questions would spiral off from the concrete and immediate to ever more steepling pyramids of abstraction: 'What causes rain? How does it get in the clouds? What are clouds? Who put them there? What do you mean, God? Who's God? Who made Him?' etc., etc., all accompanied by ever more frenetic rushing about. Within one hour of his arrival an exhausted Bob and Chris, trotting round in his wake, had already been round the camp perimeter three times.

By lunch we'd been for a walk. 'Come on! I'm taking you out!' said Jeremy. And as we walked in single file, along the narrow forest paths, it was Jeremy who led the way. By tea, there was an incident in the plastic ball pool. Both Jeremy and Bob had got themselves stuck. 'Get me out!' demanded Jeremy and as soon as he was rescued he rushed off. If Bob had also needed any kind of help, Jeremy seemed not to have even noticed. Then there was the strange phenomenon of Jeremy's reading. As we sped along a corridor, Jeremy suddenly yelled out: 'Fire Exit!' He'd seen a notice. He could read! 'Can you read, Jeremy?' I asked him. 'No I can't!' he yelled, yet as we sped into the canteen, he glanced at another notice and cried 'Fire Hazard!'

'So you *can* read, Jeremy.'

'No I can't! Can *you*? Where did you learn? *How* did you learn? Open this window please! Not that one, this one! What are windows for, anyway? Why the glass? Why's glass transparent?' etc., etc. The speed, the energy, the rat-tat-tat urgency were breathtaking, as was Jeremy's constant need for control. But most striking of all was that despite all these words not once did Jeremy come within light years of a conversation. He never listened to a word that anybody said. Jeremy had, in fact, invented a whole new style of 'autistic aloofness', quite as cut off as the boys who never spoke. He was isolated, inviolate within a grand moat of his own verbosity.

It was deeply mysterious. Here was a boy, so young and yet so old, who swung wildly from childish petulance to the inquisitiveness of a philosopher, who seemed less a character, in the conventional sense, than the embodiment of some mighty primal force, the kind of exaggerated, caricature presence we know in dreams. Come night-time, a shattered-looking Bob and Chris finally lured Jeremy towards his bed. Through shortage of room in the tents, they were sleeping in one of the huts. They slept on three single beds, Jeremy in the middle. And, of course, as it was bedtime, Jeremy's excitement only increased, because bedtimes, like mealtimes, are some of those highly charged, symbolic moments when autistic children are most prone to anxiety.

Did Jeremy lead us a dance! First he wanted a story; but not

Bob's story, rather one he chose himself. Then he wanted a game; and then, after all, he wanted a story again. Then he wanted to sleep. Then he wanted the lights off in the bedroom, but the light on in the corridor outside. The wall between the bedroom and the corridor had windows, so then he wanted the blinds down on one window, and up on the other. When Chris got out of bed and did all this, he changed his mind, and wanted the blinds *up* where they had just been down, down where they had been up. Then he noticed, as he had in the canteen, a 'crack' in the ceiling and that got him in the most frantic state of all.

'What's that crack up there!' he cried. 'What does it mean! There's another crack over there, too, look! That's two cracks! Why? What's wrong with the roof? What's wrong with the building! Who built it? Was it men? Was it boys?'

When, understandably, neither Bob or Chris saw fit to answer this latest barrage of demands, his whole tone suddenly changed. Till now, his questions, though remorseless, had been delivered with a kind of good-humoured eagerness, an intense but essentially amiable curiosity. But suddenly that switched.

'ANSWER ME MY QUESTION!' he suddenly thundered, and at that moment I caught his eye. It was terrifying. Sharp as a needle, implacable as God, he looked fifty years old. For one dread moment, I knew how Jeremy might be when he grew up, if that degree of curiosity, energy and intensity, depending on how he evolved, ever put him in a position of power. Once again, he felt more like the embodiment of a spirit, an emotional essence, than a little boy. Jeremy the child had disappeared. In his place was the Grand Inquisitor.

Not that he was usually like this. Most of the time he was merely frenetic, as his mother confirmed when I met her at their little red-brick council house, not far from the camp. Jeremy's mother is a small, pale lady with a harassed air. She talks in fits and starts, sometimes beginning at the very moment when you think she's paused to let you speak. Her laugh, too, comes unexpectedly, shrill and barking, almost a hoot. It's unsurprising that she looks tired, given that Jeremy has a fair crop of more 'conventional' autistic symptoms, as well as everything described above.

As with so many autistic boys, he was fine, she said, until he was around eighteen months, when the problems began. There were problems with speech. Until recently, far from his present garrulity, Jeremy didn't talk at all. He had obsessions with order. At breakfast, his cereal packets must be lined up in a row. He had obsessions with diet. He would only have ham and tomato-ketchup sandwiches for tea. He had problems with toilet training, he was in nappies till the age of five. And yet, as the scouts also found, it was Jeremy's hyperactivity, she said, which was hardest of all to take; it was utterly exhausting. All those questions! Her husband, in particular, found them 'frustrating'.

After we'd been talking for half an hour, her husband, who'd been out, came back to the house. Noticeably, he didn't join us. His wife said he was 'shy'. Finally, after about twenty minutes he did come in, and ate a late lunch on the dining table the other side of the room. A tall, beetle-browed man who avoided my eyes, at first he said nothing at all.

Tentatively, however, he began to join in.

Jeremy's questions could indeed drive you crazy, he said. But they had meaning. Jeremy was bright. Indeed some of his questions could be curiously suggestive. 'He'll say "What does green look like? Or blue? Describe the smell, the feel, the taste." Or: "Why does blood circulate in the body?"'

In particular, said his father, Jeremy was obsessed with their house, its physical fabric, the way that it is built. 'I'll tell him it's built out of bricks and he'll say where are they, can I see them? And I'll say don't worry Jeremy, they're there, they're underneath the plaster, and he'll say, what's holding them together?'

I mentioned Jeremy's obsession, back at the camp, with cracks in the ceiling.

'That's typical,' said his father. 'He's got this constant sense that things are falling apart. I can understand it, I've felt just like that myself. I was desperately insecure when I was a boy. I had a father who was always criticizing me, and I never knew how he'd behave from day to day. At any moment, in fact, I felt my whole world might collapse.

'This uncertainty has stayed with me all my life. I've great problems with relationships. I hate going out to meet friends. Indeed, it's not so much that I don't *like* doing it, it's more that I don't know *how*.'

The silent father and the loquacious son have this much in common: both spend their lives asking questions. True, Jeremy's father goes about it a different way. He asks his questions of philosophy. 'Descartes, Berkeley, John Locke,' he said, 'they're all, at bottom, doing the same thing as Jeremy, going on and on about the same question, returning to it obsessively.' Given that the philosophers were indeed pursuing certainty, albeit of a rather different kind, the connection sounded plausible. What made Mr Browne's reading list more unusual, however, was that his last job, before I met him, was office cleaner. Again like Jeremy, his father, too, would seem an unusual mixture of acuity and underachievement.

For Jeremy has more conventional talents to go with all those questions. 'He's very good with his hands,' said Mr Browne. 'He's brilliant mechanically. Above all, he's phenomenal on the computer. He's only six years old and already he's explaining things to *me*.'

Jeremy has one other notable capacity, said Mrs Browne, which might seem to sit quite strangely with a boy who, on the face of it, seems so extraordinarily closed off. 'He's strangely sensitive,' she said, 'in ways that don't depend on words. Above all, he's enormously sensitive to atmosphere.'

This particular sensitivity I was to see for myself, on the last of his three days at camp.

His behaviour was already beginning to change. It was as if, now he had come to his third day, he was getting more used to his surroundings and was settling down. This often happens to boys who stay at Mohawk. 'He's definitely getting less bossy,' said Bob Enright. At one stage, indeed, when Bob climbed a tree, Jeremy applauded him and even gave Bob a hug. Quite a change from how he'd ignored him in the ball pool on the first day.

But it was later on, when Jeremy was at the camp's adventure playground, that the truly memorable moment occurred.

As so often, the surroundings seemed very much part of it. The playground is on the edge of a field, but so dense are the trees that surround it on three sides that it has the quietness and remoteness of a forest glade. Here too, as on that walk with John Lee, every open space was flooded with light; insects rose and fell in the shining air. Yet this time the forest felt more than idyllic, it felt as if we were actually inside a dream. Two ash trees, feathery and eastern-looking, added to the unreal air.

And a particular mood evolved. In part, at least, the spirit of place produced it. As well as Jeremy and his carers, Phil Simpson and Stevie were there as well, plus a clutch of other scouts, and two other autistic boys. At first it seemed just a normal playing session, with nothing unusual. The first unusual thing I noticed was the kids' exceptional good humour; shortly afterwards, presumably connected, their exceptional adventurousness. One moment Phil was swinging on the bars like a chimpanzee, chortling with delight. Then Chris took a flying leap off the wooden tower, ten feet high at least, and landed, rolling over in the leaves: 'I learned it on a parachuting course,' he said, and did it again. Then Bob leaped from bar to bar of a rope bridge. This involved a series of precisely gauged leaps onto twelve separate, slippery wooden planks, six foot above the ground. He managed it all with Tarzan-like adroitness and precision.

The mood – joyous, indefinable – built just like a successful party. Each happy incident bounced off the one before, and gave rise to an even happier one moments later. Diana was there, and a couple of other adult helpers, but they stayed in the background. So the atmosphere built steadily, and soon it began to affect the autistic children, notably Jeremy. He began to connect. Chris suggested he took part in a chasing game and Jeremy agreed. Stevie started throwing leaves at him and Jeremy threw them back. Previously he had always turned down all such offers. Now, not only was he coming out of his autistic aloneness, but he was doing something rarer still: he was playing the scouts' own games, according to their rules and on their terms, rather than his own.

Moments later, I saw him head off for the slide, which he had previously been too scared to try. He still looked nervous, but I gently encouraged him and down he flew, screaming with delight, and when he reached the bottom, he threw open his arms and hugged me.

The party mood involved everyone; but the transformation was above all Jeremy's. And gradually, a weird, maverick thought began to take shape in my mind. Right now, I thought to myself, Jeremy is no longer autistic. Not one of his symptoms currently apply. There is no motor-mouthing, no autocracy, no refusal to join in the games of other boys. At this moment, here before us, we have a normal, happy, friendly – quiet! – boy.

It was strangely like the moment neurologist Oliver Sacks describes in his *An Anthropologist on Mars* when an autistic boy decides to sing a song. He wrote:

> He seemed completely at one with the music, completely possessed – and at this point there was none of the skewed neck posture that is habitual with him, none of the stiltedness, the ticcing, the aversion of gaze. His entire autistic persona, it seemed, had totally vanished, replaced by movements that were free, graceful, with emotional appropriateness and range. Very startled at this transformation, I wrote in large capitals in my notebook AUTISM DISAPPEARS. But

as soon as the music stopped, Stephen looked autistic again.

And Jeremy's experience had a similar upshot, too. For so happy was he that he went up to Diana and asked her whether he could come back to the playground the following day. She looked concerned, for this was, of course, his final evening. And she had to tell him that he wouldn't be coming back, because he'd be leaving the camp.

And Jeremy's questions began again!

'Why can't I stay?'

'Because another boy will be coming in your place.'

'Where will he sleep?'

'In your room.'

'Why in my room?'

'Because he'll need your bed.'

'Why my bed?' And Jeremy was off and away into yet another interrogative torrent. By coincidence, just at that moment, Clare appeared. 'Stop climbing on those bars,' she told Phil and Bob, 'it's dangerous.' Which was true. Then finally, to cap it all, one of the other autistic boys pissed on the grass and Diana said to clear the whole playground.

The joy, the party spirit, the air of supreme confidence evaporated.

Moments later, as Jeremy walked up the hill with the rest of us, every one of his regular symptoms had returned. Garrulity, autocracy, compulsive questioning, everything. Once more, he was autistic.

It was an evening I long remembered, because never had I seen so many of that summer's themes – the power of spontaneity, the danger of well-meaning attempts to establish order, the apparent elasticity of autistic symptoms, their intimate relationship with trust and confidence – so vividly concentrated in one time and place.

And there was a curious little coda to these events, too. As Jeremy's father lived just a couple of miles from me, I would occasionally run into him in town. He was right about his social diffidence. The first couple of times we met he did at least manage to say hello, but only after a visible effort, and only after I'd said hello first.

The next time we met – and I once again said hello – he blanked me totally.

TEN

Neither a child nor a man.

Curiously enough, it was not, in fact, Jeremy's computing talents that most impressed his special school. Sometimes, they said, this is more a generational question than one of capacity, and many children seem brighter around computers, to their parents, than they really are. Nevertheless, unlike many autistic children, they felt Jeremy was at the very least of average IQ. His autistic symptoms, which were indeed lessening, had been masking his natural abilities. He *was*, for instance, learning to read, whatever he said.

More, he did have certain unusual qualities, notably that tendency to ask a philosopher's questions, both profound and simple, the kind of questions Einstein felt most of us stop asking at the age of six. Above all, there were his startling cross-references and connections, as suggestive, in their way, as a poet's.

Such qualities hardly fall within the remit of that most extraordinary category, 'autistic savants'. Nevertheless, the remarkable distribution of his abilities – the way he and, seemingly, his father combine strengths and weaknesses in such strange proportion – does raise the most fascinating of questions: what is the relationship between such weaknesses and such strengths? Is this relationship, at the very least, comparable to those autists who do have exceptional talents? Because savants, too, while almost spookily gifted in certain areas, are full of other, more everyday deficits.

Perhaps we should start with a little context. Jeremy's problems, including the most egregious, have their parallels with other autistic experiences. 'Excessive questioning' is a familiar feature in autism, and Temple Grandin – the adult, 'recovered' woman with autism who has written about her experiences and was much quoted in chapter five – describes it as characteristic of her childhood. 'Constantly asking questions,' she says, 'was another of my annoying fixations.' Donna Williams, also quoted in chapter five, describes something similar, although she calls it 'hyper-connection', connections which tumble one on top of each other, almost breed each other, much like Jeremy's questions. Indeed, in her case, the surging, spiralling floods of connection sound quite terrifying. She says:

> Imagine, the effect of this type of processing on the ability to keep track of conversation. In the short break between two halves of a sentence, there may have been triggered a huge number of tracks, leading to tracks leading to tracks.
>
> For example, at the time the speaker said 'on your way home . . .' an image in the listener's mind may have been triggered of the home she once lived in, which may take her careening down a serial memory path of what was in the loungeroom at that time and who put the ornaments on the shelf and where each of them came from and when they were bought and what someone said at that time they were first put there and what was on the television in the room at the time and how long that programme had been running. In the meantime, the speaker may have continued with 'I want you to take these eggs . . .' at which point the word 'eggs' might trigger a serial memory of an article about

> battery hens that the listener read on the train last week as she drunk a bottle of mineral water which came from French mountains which is where her friend, Peter, comes from who lived there in that house in the postcard that he sent on which he wrote about his cat that looked like the one that . . .

Add in a heavy dose of anxiety and these kinds of connections could clearly form the basis of Jeremy's questions.

Among other things, of course, this 'hyper-connection' is a kind of extreme and out-of control memory, and it is here that we begin to see the connection with certain positive abilities. The Russian scientist Alexander Luria described the mental processes of a memory savant in his pre-war classic, *The Mind of a Mnemonist*. The talents of 'S', as Luria called him, included remarkable feats of mathematical calculation, but also took more everyday forms. He could, for instance, recall a list of up to seventy words, letters and numbers from one hearing, and even repeat them in reverse order.

Yet these memory feats went along with a mind which could, equally, be overwhelmed by remembrance and association. If someone read a story to him at all rapidly his face 'would register confusion and finally utter bewilderment. "No," he would say. "This is too much. Each word calls up images; they collide with one another, and the result is chaos."' The problem he shared with Donna Williams – and arguably, Jeremy Browne – is hard to conceive for the rest of us, whose more familiar problem is remembering. 'The big question for him,' said Luria, 'and the most troublesome, was how he could learn to forget.'

In short, he lacked the profound self-censoring process which, according to one theory of brain development, most of us develop in early childhood, and is the way we cope with the deluge of information life throws at us. We retain a little, in the interest of survival, but forget most. Consciously, that is. Many neuroscientists, notably the late Wilder Penfield, believe we retain everything somewhere in our brains, much like the accident victim who blanks out the last minutes before the crash.

But where such processes become more interesting still is in the wider implications of such failures of self-censorship, failures which are, arguably, what we would customarily call 'gifts'. For here Jeremy's mental processes connect not merely with autistic savants, but, in their most extreme form, with so-called 'genius'. Some gifts, to be sure, are more interesting than others. Calendar talents of the kind exhibited by 'S' are one thing; the exceptional musical memory that Oliver Sacks describes in another of his patients (an amateur musician who could remember Bach cantatas note-perfect) are another. Yet even this kind of memory remains essentially passive and static, and has little connection with what would normally be called creativity.

But there are other kinds of memory, notably, for instance, those manifested by the writer D. H. Lawrence, which combine hauntingly similar mental processes with the intense subjectivity and individuality of art. As his friend Richard Aldington put it, commenting on the extraordinarily detailed description of a Sicilian religious procession in Lawrence's travel book *Sea and Sardinia* (1921):

> How long had he to take all that in? Five minutes? Surely not ten, for even a slowly-moving religious procession is soon past and gone. In that short time he took in and remembered not only the general effect of gorgeous moving colour, but exact details and shades of the brilliant clothes of children, women and men. He never made notes of such things . . . but trusted to the living imaginative memory . . .

Not very surprisingly, there are distinct 'autistic streaks' in Lawrence's character, as described by many who knew him. But what his memory processes seem to share with Donna Williams, with Sacks's musician and with Luria's mnemonist, was that the processes were involuntary. Unlike the rest of us – unlike an actor, say, learning a part for a play, or a student studying a theorem for an examination – he didn't strive or strain, or seek the information out; it was as if the information found him. His 'talent' like the three cases above, was strangely passive.

Such excesses of memory, association and even simple perception, can take, it seems, many forms. Donna Williams describes how the shine of fluorescent lighting can 'cause a visual effect of shooting out streams or sparks of light'. They can, as with Donna Williams and 'S', be visual. 'S' said he 'read' his remembered dates off a kind of internal, mental chart. They can involve sound. One thinks of young Omar, at Camp Mohawk, with his hands over his ears, terrified of the thunderous noise of leaves. They can involve taste. 'S' said that the taste of certain foods could so overwhelm his senses that it could become impossible, temporarily, for him to think about anything else.

They can even involve smell, and it is interesting that one of the most striking examples Sacks gives of excessive ability to smell does not involve autism at all. For just as excess can take so many forms so can its triggers, and autism, it would seem, is just one cause among many. Brain disease can do it. So can an accident, a blow to the head. So, arguably, can inappropriate diet; and so, more predictably, can drugs, the trigger in the case described by Sacks. For his patient, a student, had blown his mind on amphetamines before he woke up, inexplicably, with an almost canine intensity of smell. More striking still, he was utterly delighted by the experience. It was, he said, as if he had been transformed into an entirely new perceptual universe. 'I went into a scent shop,' he said. 'I never had much of a nose for smells, before, but now I distinguished each one instantly – and I found each one unique, evocative, a whole world.' More, he could distinguish between his friends by smell, and he could even smell their emotions – happiness, fear, sexuality – just like a dog. When, after three weeks, he spontaneously went back to normal, he described his recovery as a 'tremendous loss'.

Sacks, indeed, with a use of language which itself implies the positive, describes all these varied entry points to hyper-consciousness as 'portals'. And while some manifestations are clearly horrendous, like the hyper-association described above by Donna Williams, some, just as clearly, can be rhapsodic – albeit, on occasion, almost frighteningly so. A third of those with autism are epileptic. Dostoyevsky described the 'rapture' of the opening phases of the epileptic attacks to which he was prone. 'There are moments,' he said, 'and it is only a matter of five or six seconds, when you feel the presence of the eternal harmony . . . during these five seconds I live a whole human existence, and for that I would give my whole life and not think that I was paying too dearly.'

Donna Williams describes her streams of sparks, Annabel Stehli (see chapter five) her autistic daughter's Van Goghian sense of colour, but one of the best descriptions of such perception seen from the inside is that contained in Aldous Huxley's *The Doors of Perception* (1954).

Huxley describes a controlled mescaline trip he undertook back in the fifties. Here, too, as with Sacks's smell example, the trigger was a drug. But in this case the release of otherwise censored perception was above all visual, which, as it happens, is the sensory language, before all others, of the autistic.

As the drug kicked in, Huxley gazed at a garden chair.

> That chair – shall I ever forget it? Where the shadows fell on the canvas upholstery, stripes of a deep but glowing indigo alternated with stripes of an incandescence so intensely bright that it was hard to believe that they could be made of anything but blue fire. For what seemed an immensely long time I gazed without knowing, without wishing to know, what it was that confronted me. At any other time I

> would have seen a chair barred with alternate light and shade. Today the percept had swallowed up the concept. I was so completely absorbed by looking, so thunderstruck by what I actually saw, that I could not be aware of anything else.
>
> Garden furniture, laths, sunlight, shadow – these were no more than names and notions, mere verbalisations, for utilitarian or scientific purposes, after the event. The event was this succession of azure furnace-doors separated by gulfs of unfathomable gentian. It was inexpressibly wonderful, wonderful to the point, almost, of being terrifying. And suddenly I had an inkling of what it must feel like to be mad.

Do autistic children ever have such experiences? Setting aside the recollected-in-adulthood testimony of 'recovered' autistics like Temple Grandin and Donna Williams, we will never know what goes on in the heads of the autistic children we meet. We can only imagine, for instance, quite what visionary experience the likes of 'faerie kings' such as Dreamy David and the horse-loving Teddy might know. But if, for even only part of the time, their experience is anything like Huxley's, we can see why their expressions might be so faraway and so rhapsodic.

Jeremy's over-inclusiveness, then, is something he shares with other children with autism, with autistic savants, and even with those 'autistically-streaked' people we call creative talents. As he does, too, his other striking quality, his 'autistic aloofness'. Although, like his over-inclusiveness, the particular form it takes in Jeremy's case – the endless stream of compulsive, motor-mouthing questions – is unusual.

Yet autistic aloofness, too, is a mental process which can have enormous creative results. You can see them, potentially, even in Jeremy's frenetic questioning, notably in those questions that so struck his philosophy-loving father, his 'Why does blood circulate in the body?' or 'What does green look like? Describe the smell, the feel, the taste.' For if there is one thing that the cut-off quality of autism does encourage, in its profound disconnection from conventional assumptions, it is originality.

Certainly, originality surfaced, in varying degrees, in many of the other autistic children at Camp Mohawk that summer. It was there in Edward's self-taught capacity to 'see' the shapes required to build his model train; it was there, too, in Teddy's questions about language in France; it was there in his asking, as his mother recounted, why English men so rarely wear bright colours. After all, until the nineteenth century they did, and thereby hangs an important cultural tale.

Then there was the situation, more eloquent still, also described by his mother. One day she was with Teddy in the supermarket. Who does all this food belong to? asked Teddy. Tesco's, said his mother. Shortly after, they reached the checkout. There beside them was another shopper's trolley, whose purchases included a bag of doughnuts. Teddy promptly pinched one and started eating it. When Teddy's mum told him not to, Teddy was mystified; and it was the nature of his mystification that was revealing. Why on earth should the other shopper get cross? After all, his mum had explained that the doughnuts belonged to Tesco's. They didn't belong to the shopper – not yet, anyway!

So at what moment do the doughnuts cease to be Tesco's, and become the shopper's? With classic autistic lucidity Teddy had stumbled across a conundrum that would do credit to an economist.

Linked with this individuality, and clearly nurtured by it, is the intense sense of separation we more normally call concentration. Peter Bell, for instance, buried deep in his train drawings that time in Holland. But this, too, can be associated with those savant abilities which are the upside of autism. One of the best known of the autistic savants is of course, Stephen Wiltshire, whose extraordinary drawing ability has been seen on TV. His ability to concentrate is so prodigious that a friend once said of him, as he was drawing: 'Don't worry, you can talk at the top of your voice if you want to. It won't make any difference – you can't interrupt him – he could concentrate if the house was falling down.'

Yet in this autistic context the word 'concentration' is scarcely adequate. Oliver Sacks described how he observed two mathematical autistic savants, twins, develop a kind of duet in which, one after the other, they exchanged 'primes' – numbers that could be evenly divided by no other whole number than itself or one. As they made their calculations, says Sacks, their demeanour had 'a gravity . . . a sort of serene and meditative and almost holy intensity'. Hardly surprising, perhaps, as wherever their minds were they were certainly not in any familiar, earth-bound place. For by all everyday intellectual standards they should not have been able to do the simplest addition, let alone make calculations as profound as these. For they were innocent of all conventional mathematical knowledge.

And yet, as with autistic 'over-inclusiveness,' 'autistic concentration', too, shades into the concentration we associate with the more conventionally gifted. Along with his recurrent social boorishness, and lack of interest in those who worked for him, Churchill's tendency to shut himself off from people had more positive aspects too. A colleague, during the war, described the arrival of a memo at Churchill's breakfast table. Instantly, Churchill was totally absorbed in it, undisturbed by – unaware of, even – the chatter around him. The result was several minutes of extreme efficiency and a swift response to the memo. D. H. Lawrence, too, could reach depths of concentration regardless of his surroundings. Richard Aldington described him writing at the kitchen table, surrounded by guests, noise and cooking. Yet such writing could include his very best.

The pioneer of autism research, Hans Asperger, coined the phrase 'autistic intelligence'. As Uta Frith puts it in her *Autism, Explaining the Enigma*, 'he believed that autistic intelligence had distinct qualities and was the opposite of conventional learning and worldly-wise cunning. Indeed, he thought of it as a vital ingredient in all great creations in art or science . . . is a dash of autism a mark of original thought?'

'A dash of autism.' The phrase is a reminder of the clumsiness of the all-encompassing label 'autistic', as if autism was something you either had, utterly, or were utterly innocent of. In reality, arguably, autism describes a particular cast of mind, almost a mode, which can exist in otherwise quite ordinary people, and which can come and go, according to circumstance. Nor are the forms it takes exclusively those of 'high art'.

Many years ago, as a reporter, I had to interview a series of record holders who were featured in *The Guinness Book of Records*. They included, of all the things, the world champion knitter, whom I met in her home.

In every possible way she was utterly normal, setting aside, that is, her esoteric, and most remarkable, talent for knitting. As with most other record holders, her entry was initially based on speed; and yet the speed of her knitting was in many ways the least interesting thing about her. Far more striking was the way knitting activated a particular kind of memory. For she had only to knit the most complex pattern once through, she said, and it lodged with her for life.

And it is worth considering just exactly what such a memory feat means. As she moved, at the highest speed, down through the pattern, her memory would be, presumably, mathematical. For as she changed the balance of colours for each line – ten blue stitches, five yellow, six green, ten red, five blue, etc., then the next line, twelve blue, seven yellow, eight green, etc. – she was effectively remembering the longest telephone number in the world. Yet she had no idea how she did it, she said. It just came.

And it was her husband's comments that were most striking of all. When his wife was knitting, he said, he found it scary. Because it was as if the knitting episodes formed a quite separate part of her life; they involved far more than deep concentration. It was as if she dropped, he said, into 'a trance'. For the duration the wife he knew and loved would simply vanish, and be replaced by – what?

What is interesting, in fact, about the positive aspects of autistic processes is less their power, than their nature; for such processes have notable similarities to those of the more conventionally gifted, and above all, perhaps, to those endowed with what we vaguely call 'genius'.

For what does seem plain is that the unusual achievements of autistic individuals are arrived at by qualitatively different processes. Most notably, to reiterate a recurrent leitmotif of autism, such processes are visual. When Edward showed his capacity to dismember, into its constituent visual parts, the railway engine he wanted to copy, his talent was typical. Uta Frith describes an Embedded Figures test in which autistic children – 'retarded' in so many other ways – scored above average for their mental age. More dramatically, Sacks describes the moment when his autistic mathematical twins dropped a box of matches on the floor and yelled out, simultaneously, 'one hundred and eleven'. Where others would have had to count the number of matches, they apparently saw it. They saw it, seemingly, in one simultaneous flash of visual perception, much as the rest of us might see the number of dots on a dice. This particular autistic talent was made much of in the film, *Rain Man*.

But most striking of all, reckoned Sacks, was the way the twins arrived at those other mathematical calculations, mentioned above, their sequences of prime numbers. For here, too, he felt the twins were 'not calculators, and their numeracy is iconic'. In a word, he thought they saw their primes, and read them off a kind of interior mental chart. Just as Luria's 'S' did, incidentally, with his calendar calculations.

Having said which, such visual talents, striking though they are, only partly describe the exceptional processes of the autistic mind. For just as the man who smelled as a dog was, as well, crossing sensual boundaries – experiencing simultaneously sensual experiences that the rest of us keep separate – the twins also were in a similar state of what theory calls 'synaesthesia'. For, apparently, they 'felt' their numbers, they 'tasted' them, they were their 'friends'. Or as Sacks sums it up: their relationship with numbers was not only visual but 'sensual'.

It is curious that a friend of the 'autistically-streaked' Einstein once described, with wonder, the scientist's almost 'sensual' love of physics.

It is process, in fact, not power, that links the minor to the major autistic savant, and the autistic community generally to the strange ways of 'genius'.

And the manifestations of such processes are as varied as there are people. Mathematical savantry is probably the best-known example, but Donna Williams, in her *Autism – An Inside-Out Approach* describes similar processes at work in music. Not only, she says, did music somehow teach itself to her, rather than her having to learn it, but she even found herself creating 'automatic' compositions – melodies dictated, as it seemed, from some external source. All this without learning a formal note.

'By the time I was thirteen, my head was not just filled with mental replays of heard jingles and tunes, but with unintentional compositions, first simple, then progressively more complex. I, however, did not feel like their composer, for they composed themselves of a volition I was unaware of, according to feelings I was disconnected from, and expressing with a depth that I knew myself incapable of.' In the same way, Donna Williams argues, she has produced poetry, paintings, and even sculpture: 'All of these have been what socially is considered a very high standard that would normally require many years of training. Yet none of these involved any conscious learning of the skills involved nor any applied conscious trying in producing these works. It felt, quite simply, that they had a life of their own.'

Anyone who reads this and also saw the film *Amadeus* must be reminded of the moment when Salieri, faced by original compositions by Mozart, found it incredible that his first drafts were final copies. It was almost, indeed, as if Mozart had been taking dictation. Mozart's 'bizarre behaviour', the sort of thing that has led some to diagnose him as Asperger's, was also well in evidence in that film. While Schumann, a severe manic depressive who ended his life in an asylum, described music pouring into him, as it were, from outside. It made him feel, he said, 'like bursting'. Indeed, he often wrote down the sounds he heard – quite literally, a form of dictation. Some of his best work, his *Manfred Overture* and his *Spring Symphony*, for instance, were written in this way. While Handel, describing the unprecedented inspiration which enabled him to write the *Messiah* in just three weeks, was more explicit still. He was, he said, inspired by 'God'.

One day at the camp, Edward, the boy whose 'autistic talents' included such exceptional pattern-recognition, got into a barney at the campfire circle. The problem, explained Fred Robinson later, was that he didn't want the scouts to burn some branches they had picked up for the fire. 'It was strange,' said Fred. 'On the face of it he seemed to feel, like some kids might, that burning branches was cruel to nature. But it was more than that. I got this strange feeling – and others felt the same – that in some weird way he identified with the wood itself, so that if we burned it, we would be burning him.'

Weird indeed. And yet here, too, as with his visual abilities, Edward's mind was working in ways characteristic of other autistic children, too. Donna Williams described how, as a child, 'Walking through the supermarket, I physically felt the pain when someone banged themselves. Around someone with a broken leg, I felt their pain in my leg . . . in the same way, the pain of an animal or even the distress of a tree can be sensed, whether physical or spiritual-emotional.' 'Sensory exploration . . .' she commented, 'is not mental. It is more primitive and somehow beyond the mental. It is the following, not of mind, but of instinct.' Or as Temple Grandin put it, when Oliver Sacks noticed how well she connected with the farm animals: 'When I'm with cattle, it's not at all cognitive. I know what the cow's feeling.' 'The cattle seemed to sense this,' commented Sacks, 'sensed her calm, her confidence, and came up to her hand. They did not come up to me . . . I was struck by the enormous difference, the gulf, between Temple's immediate, intuitive recognition of animal moods and signs and her extraordinary difficulties understanding human beings, their codes and signals, the way they conduct themselves.'

What makes this remarkable is that it is above all empathy that autistic minds are supposed to lack; the ability, put simply, to put oneself in another's shoes. Yet what is being described here – assuming we believe what Donna Williams and Temple Grandin are telling us – is not mere ordinary everyday empathy, it is, as Donna Williams herself puts it, 'an intense uncontrollable empathy'. A strange, more than human empathy which co-exists somehow with the more mundane, everyday empathy she so conspicuously lacks.

Certainly this union of seeming opposites, this linking of excess and deficit, is a constant characteristic of autistic minds. Oliver Sacks describes the savant twins' inability to do basic arithmetic and ability to dream up primes. Donna Williams describes her enormous difficulty, as a child, with the simplest process of syntax and spelling and yet her ability to scan a book and grasp its essence, in minutes. A mildly autistic friend of mine can't find his way across London, yet has explored a remote part of the Amazon Basin. (I am told, incidentally that this tactical orientation problem is often found among explorers, whatever that means.)

Once again, qualitatively different mental processes seem to be involved, processes far removed from our everyday comprehension. It is as if, with the autistic, a strange developmental double-act takes place. Conventional developmental processes somehow fail to kick in; earlier, pre-verbal processes, of egregious power and quality, are retained. And, as ever, to posit such an idea does not mean we weigh down boys like Edward or Jeremy with the burden of 'genius'. Rather we should merely notice the nature of their mental processes; the things they have in common with much more overtly exceptional savants like Oliver Sacks's twins; and then, in turn, with the minds of 'geniuses' – a term which, if it means anything at all, has usually tried to indicate some qualitative difference of mental process, not merely of power, from the rest of us.

Certainly, the experience of 'intense, uncontrollable empathy', an empathy which can seem constantly, terrifyingly, Donna Williams tells us, on the verge of swallowing the receiving mind up, is certainly characteristic of artistic minds, notably novelists and poets. One critic, describing Tolstoy's biography of a horse, *Strider*, noted with wonder that it felt less like description, more as if Tolstoy had actually become – been possessed by – the animal concerned. While the poet Keats described his famous 'negative capability' like this: 'When I am in a room with people . . .' he wrote, 'the identity of everyone in the room begins to press upon me, so that I am in a very little time annihilated.'

This 'intense, uncontrollable empathy' is clearly an immense advantage for a poet or a novelist. George Orwell felt D. H. Lawrence's outstanding quality as a novelist was his capacity to empathize with characters, like Prussian soldiers, who he had no way of understanding from personal experience. There is, also, another art where such empathy, even amounting, indeed, to a kind of possession, is more relevant still: acting.

It was Peter Sellers, yet another of those claimed as one of theirs by the autistic, who once said: 'Looking at myself I find myself singularly lacking in what I regard as the ingredients of a character.' Adrift in an identity swamp, the advent of a plausible part, or character, can be extraordinarily attractive to the compulsive actor, even though the fix will be inevitably short-lived. That the character must be well written enough to be convincing is why good parts are so important to actors. Not that you have to be as eminent as Peter Sellers for the process to work. As ever, what matters is less eminence than cast of mind.

Oliver Sacks described the 'identity hunger' of the non-savant autistic children he worked with, and their frequent love of performance. He saw how, when acting or singing, they could acquire a coherence, physical, verbal, even, seemingly, emotional, quite unlike their everyday selves. He described Stephen Wiltshire singing a Tom Jones song, and how he 'took on Jones's flamboyant physicality, adding to it a flavour of Stevie Wonder'. It was as if, indeed, he had 'borrowed' a complete identity, though this was 'lost the moment the music ended'.

Nevertheless, 'It was as if, for a brief time, he had become truly alive.'

As with all things autistic, every answer breeds ten questions, but it does seem at least possible that the autistic, like the exceptionally 'gifted', have retained some mode of perception that the rest of us have lost, as a normal part of growing up. Poets, perhaps, are better placed than most to remember this earlier mode of being.

'The corn was orient and immortal wheat,' Thomas Traherne tells us, remembering the intense, overwhelming splendour of his childhood consciousness; while Wordsworth, too, felt that

> There was a time when meadow, grove and stream,
> The earth, and every common sight
> To me did seem
> Apparell'd in celestial light,
> The glory and the freshness of a dream.

Both poets and autists, if we are to believe testimonies like Donna Williams's, have retained, at least in some degree, this early, unsullied perception. Haphazard the autists' retention of this other consciousness may be, sometimes peeping through in only strictly limited, even comical areas; yet the nagging suggestion constantly remains, that for all their surface incapacities something remarkable may be alive in them that the rest of us have lost.

As we have seen, one of the strangest manifestations of this 'other sensibility' relates to animals. Both Donna Williams and Temple Grandin report on the extreme comfort they feel in animals' company. Certainly, innumerable forms of animal behaviour remain utterly mysterious to science. No one knows, for instance, how fish or starlings transmit the messages that enable them to swerve, instantaneously, as one; or how a lost pet can find its way home across thirty miles of unknown countryside.

So it is interesting, in this context, to remember that autistic adult we came across in the Introduction – the man who, in his everyday life, couldn't find his way to the corner shop – and the day he navigated three miles of unknown countryside to get back to the Camp Mohawk he had visited once, and loved.

If, therefore, a personality is going to be locked into this earlier, utterly different consciousness, what has to take place? In chapter five we reviewed the arguments over the role of trauma in autistic maldevelopment; and we saw how any sense that emotional factors are a significant cause became a kind of heresy. Nevertheless, whatever their role in autism, it is hard to escape their significance in the strange developmental processes of 'genius'.

Tolstoy lost his mother at twenty-three months and his father at eight years old; Bertrand Russell was orphaned at three; Joseph Conrad (for whom Russell felt a profound emotional affinity) at nine. The First World War poet Siegfried Sassoon, who incidentally himself showed distinct autistic traits, lost his father at nine, when his parents were already living apart. 'I thought I would never stop crying,' he wrote.

And this is to ignore the effects of childhood trauma that stopped short of death. One thinks of Dickens sent out, as a young boy, to his blacking factory; of the economic catastrophe in the household of the young Wilfred Owen; of T. E. Lawrence's beatings at the hands of his mother; of D. H. Lawrence's reaction to the tortured relationship of his parents. Indeed, D. H. Lawrence cited the intense, compensatory love shown him by his mother as a crucial cause of the imaginative empathy that so struck George Orwell. He wrote to his friend Rachel Taylor, just before his mother's death,

> We have been like one, so sensitive to each other that we never needed words. It has been rather terrible and has made me, in some respects, abnormal.
>
> I think this particular fusion of soul (don't think me high-falutin) never comes twice in a lifetime – it doesn't seem natural. When it comes it seems to distribute one's consciousness far abroad from oneself, and one understands.

Something, certainly, has to happen to a mind if the world is to be perceived in these exceptional ways. Studies show that a remarkable 70 per cent of those artists whose work is felt to be original are manic depressives. A bright friend of mine once watched a television film of the ground-breaking psychiatrist Ronnie Laing. 'How strange,' he said. 'Neither a child nor a man.' It was, he felt, as if Laing had somehow retained the direct, unmediated perception of childhood and yet advanced it into an adult language. All children lack the language; most adults, the perception.

A perception which we do indeed associate with the young, but it is an intriguing thought that it may have been common in earlier cultures as well as in our own, early lives. The American psychologist Julian Jaynes argued that 'primitive' cultures operated by instinct rather than mind. Each individual, he believed, made decisions via the kind of inner promptings that later cultures turned into gods. Such unimaginably emotion-dominated human beings might just have maintained in adulthood precisely that acute sensibility, that glowing sense of beauty, that Traherne and Wordsworth mourned.

Apropos which it is interesting to note the word George Orwell latched on to, as he struggled to articulate what he felt was the radically un-twentieth-century nature of D. H. Lawrence's consciousness, so sensitive to natural scenery, so reverent of the 'instinctive' body, so infinitely perceptive, to an almost occult degree, of the emotional states of those he met. Lawrence was, said Orwell, like a creature from 'the Bronze Age.'

Yet perhaps the most striking example of the strange relationship between autistic deficits and savant abilities is that of Nadia, perhaps the most remarkable of all autist artists, who became famous in the 1970s.

Nadia had a familiar range of autistic symptoms. By nine months the few words she had developed had disappeared totally. She was clumsy, poorly co-ordinated and socially impassive. And yet at the age of three and a half she suddenly developed exceptional drawing abilities. Her favourite subject was horses – especially funfair horses – and she drew these with a flair and verve that the most gifted conventional children would normally only develop at three times her age.

Yet strangest of all was what she didn't do. For she completely missed out the developmental stages via which virtually every child learns to draw. Most children start with matchstick figures and geometric shapes, develop gradually into tadpole figures, then move on to something more recognizably animal or human.

Nadia completely left out all these stages. Somehow, she

leapfrogged straight into an adult way of drawing, without any of the preliminary processes at all.

In short, looking at Nadia in the round, and taking these startling abilities along with her equally striking deficits, it is surely hard to talk, in the conventional way, about Nadia's developmental 'problem'.

More plausible, surely, must be to think in terms of her developmental condition.

It's a cliché in Hollywood, that world HQ of both acting and identity crisis, that performers who go into analysis can get cured yet lose their talent.

Something similar can happen to those with autism. Nadia, for instance, was given therapy which helped develop her conventional abilities, notably language, but she lost her exceptional talent to draw. As the writer Nigel Dennis commented: 'We are left with a genius who has had her genius removed, leaving nothing behind but a general defectiveness. What are we to think about such a curious cure?' Likewise, the mathematical savant autistic twins, who so delightedly swapped primes, were treated and separated 'for their own good', with the result that they, too, can now pass muster socially, but they have lost their savant talent.

Nevertheless, many others with autism – notably Donna Williams and Temple Grandin – have developed in ways that seem a huge advance on their childhood and without any especially evident loss. Donna Williams, for instance, has not only improved her language and social skills a thousandfold but is now an internationally famous authoress, while Temple Grandin is one of America's foremost designers of animal management systems. And as for the majority of autistic children, they would seem even less likely than the talented Temple Grandin and Donna Williams to put in peril any special abilities. Assuming, then, that for most children conventional development, where achievable, is desirable, how far would a regime like Camp Mohawk's be inclined to contribute to it; to do more, that is, than provide strictly shallow, temporary change?

First of all we have to remind ourselves of the obvious: Camp Mohawk is exceptional among those who care for autistic children because the carers are children. So that it is worth noting, at the start, that Camp Mohawk is not alone in advocating what is known as 'child therapy'. Nikolaas Tinbergen, for instance, felt that 'children can no doubt play an important part as co-therapists', especially normal children, while Temple Grandin felt 'autistic children should be with normal children as much as possible'. There have, too, been other practical expressions of such 'co-therapies'; notably the Yasuda Life Welfare Foundation nursery school in Tokyo, which has run programmes which integrate autistic children with normal children, achieving excellent results.

Even so, Mohawk remains in certain ways unique, above all in the stress it lays on the scouts' freedom and sense of autonomy. For Mohawk remains, in many ways, a children's place. And the fact that the scouts feel this has a number of knock-on effects. For a start, as we have seen, it puts the scouts themselves in a relaxed frame of mind, and this sense of relaxation conveys itself to the autistic children. More, as Dr John Richer, consultant clinical psychologist in paediatrics at Oxford's John Radcliffe Hospital points out, it encourages them to behave in ways quite natural to children, but different from adults.

'Children PLAY,' he says, 'they are not orientated toward results. Even if what they are doing does fall within the category of what adults call "useful" – like, say, helping an autistic child to speak – they are not burdened by adults' anxieties about outcomes and performance. "Manana, manana!" – that's the attitude of kids. "If it goes wrong, so what, if we enjoy it? And what's 'wrong', anyway? If we enjoyed it, it's probably right."

'And this is extraordinarily good for children with autism; because one of the deepest things about them is their profound, instinctive pessimism, which can give rise to unthinkable anxieties.

Above all else, kids value, not what they are doing, but the person they are doing it with: the friendship. For the autistic child this is most important of all.'

Nikolaas Tinbergen goes further still. 'Autistic children,' he says, 'are even more in need of a playful atmosphere than normal children.'

And if you consider that most crucial subdivision of 'playfulness' known as humour, then this, so characteristic of Mohawk, is especially stressed as desirable by theoreticians. As Tinbergen puts it, arguing forcefully for the therapeutic power of humour among autistic children, '"Laughing together" (in the young as in adults, and even if it has to be done at one's own expense) is one of the most effective and satisfying bonding mechanisms of our species.' Humour, in fact, brings people together: the heart of autistic therapy, surely.

And what is especially valuable about Mohawk's humour is its naturalness. Forget the ponderous jokiness of properly-trained social workers, proving with graphs, and statistics, and colour-coded pie-charts, the psychic benefits of a good laugh. At Mohawk, rather, it is a lifestyle that is humorous, sometimes hopelessly so, from the dread jokes of the adults, through the dire jokes of the kids, to the compulsive story-telling of everyone; and then, even more fundamentally, the natural clowning and humorousness of the main characters. A lifestyle, indeed, in which humour is less incidental than fundamental. Reverenced, almost, and with very good reason.

Equally, the scouts' ability to observe means they are better informed. They screen in the kind of things children care about: what's for supper, what's the best route up 'John's Tree', can a bicycle stand up by itself if you pile earth around it. They screen out the things they don't: the six o'clock news, the new lounge suite, the hoped-for promotion. They know better how to act, in fact, for the simple reason that they have better information. They are aided in this, as we have seen, because their own minds work in ways not so very different from the kids they are observing

Jeff Pollard's comment on that time Edward pretended to have a nightmare in the tent was typical. Had we considered the possibility, asked Jeff, that Edward was simply repeating, as autistic children do, something he'd picked up from a video? Even at the advanced age of sixteen, Jeff still retained some of the thought processes of a kid of eight. Later on, Edward's mum said that from her experience with Edward, Jeff was probably dead right.

And what such understanding further means, very naturally, is that the scouts are superbly placed for the most crucial moment of all; the moment when real emotional contact takes place between carer and autistic charge, however bizarre that moment, initially, may seem. Oliver Sacks described one such time when he joined the mathematical twins, in their swapping of primes, by interpolating one of his own. 'They both turned to me, then suddenly became still, with a look of intense concentration and perhaps wonder on their faces . . . then suddenly, simultaneously, they both broke into smiles.' That was strange enough, yet it still remains, somehow, within the broad parameters of adult understanding. Rather stranger, and closer to the weird Other Universe of childhood, must have been the time described by Elisabeth Tinbergen, Nikolaas's wife, when she broke through to an autistic child by noticing, then answering, his rhythmic clapping. Yet there are limits to what even the most imaginative adult is likely to understand, and this is where the scouts come in. What adult would have viewed the chewing of leaves as a natural conduit of dialogue, as Stevie did that time with Philip?

What is clear is that everyone agrees such moments of contact are crucial. Or, as Bruno Bettelheim puts it, the autistic child 'must feel that we are with him in his private world and not that he is once more repeating the experience that "everyone wants me to come out of my world and enter his".' Nor can there be much doubt that having children around can be extraordinarily helpful in such processes, even when the perception is made, overtly, by an adult. John Lee described how he made his first significant contact with one, highly withdrawn, autistic child. The child reacted to a 'brrrrr' sound made by vibrating the lips. The boy made the same sound himself when he was happy. Need one add that there were plenty of scouts around at the time.

Undoubtedly, a key advantage the scouts have when working with autistic children is the way in which they are like them mentally – much closer, certainly, than adults. So it is curious that in another way the key gift they can give the autistic children is their difference. The difference, that is, between great confidence and great fear. We've already seen this in the quaint example of the maps; the autistic children's obsession with them, the scouts' instinctive revulsion at being planned. But there is another area of difference, equally symbolic, equally strongly felt on both sides: the whole business of touch.

Touch! What could be more symbolic of warm, instinctive, rough-and-ready Mohawk? Little wonder that Skip, trying to sum up Mohawk in a phrase, once said, 'At Mohawk we just teach our boys to cuddle.' Or that the mighty, and mightily unverbal, Ian Pool, furiously massaging the neck muscles of everyone in sight, also sticks in the mind as a classic Mohawk icon. As, of course, does that moment from chapter one, when little George, in his distress, was bounced from boy to boy until he finished up in the arms of Mickey, whose only verbal contribution was 'Woshermatter?' Mohawk knows well what lovers know when they close their eyes to kiss: touch is a profound language and the deepest truth, deeper, even, than looks, far deeper than words.

And yet the received understanding about autistic children, for years, was that they were, above all, averse to being touched. As

Lorna Wing puts it in her introductory manual for families with autism, *The Autistic Spectrum*, some autistic children 'will pull away even from gentle, affectionate touches', while Donna Williams, writing from the inside, goes further still: 'There was something overwhelming that always seemed too powerful in giving in to physical touch. It was the threat of losing all sense of separateness between myself and the other person. Like being eaten up, or drowned by a tidal wave, fear of touch was the same as fear of death.'

Touch, in fact, like everything else in autistic life, becomes symbolic. It can come to embody the terror Bruno Bettelheim noted in his patients who 'shared one thing in common: an unremitting fear for their lives'. In the end, love, death and touch can become inextricably entwined in one all-enveloping love–hate relationship. But as the father of one autistic child described by Nikolaas Tinbergen pointed out, one should never be fooled by an autistic child's rejection. 'Autistic children need above anything else love. The more they reject loving approaches the more they need them.'

Given all of which, how does one explain the reaction of these desperately touch-needy, love-needy, touch-terrified individuals when plunged into the exceptionally tactile culture of a place like Mohawk? John Richer, certainly, finds it entirely natural that such children should react positively. 'There are, broadly, two ways to approach autistic kids,' he says. 'One is with extraordinary care and delicacy; this can work. The other, curiously enough, is to be highly intrusive and direct. This works too.' It is the second, of course, that is the scouts' way, and presumably accounts for their success. A success which is linked in spirit, surely, to that described by Clara Claiborne Park, and recorded in chapter five, when the visitor who had no pre-knowledge of her daughter's disability plunged in and related to her like any other child. With the result that her daughter, also, for the duration of that visit, reacted normally, like any other child.

Perhaps predictably, given all of the above, there is a long-standing tradition of touch as quite consciously conceived therapy for autistic children. Usually known as 'holding therapies', the best known is probably that of the American Dr Martha Welch, who has been practising her particular version since the mid-seventies. Martha Welch falls firmly in the 'psychogenic', or emotions-as-cause, camp of autistic studies. As she put it in one of her papers: 'autism is caused by faulty bonding between mother and child'. She believes that this faulty bonding will almost always be expressed by a failure, on the part of a mother, to hold her child. And, because the experience of holding and being held is so fundamental to a child's psychic health, overcoming that failure can stimulate the most dramatic improvements. Thus her therapy encourages the mother to hold the child, even if neither are used to this, and even if the child – furiously – objects. Each session must last until the child moves from resistance to acceptance. Which means, predictably, that some sessions can last hours.

Equally predictably, because of the element of coercion involved, holding therapy is highly controversial. While most autistic practitioners now allow the process at least some value, many reject the compulsive element; while others (a recurrent problem with all autistic therapies) argue that the remarkable results claimed by Martha Welch and her supporters lack convincing independent verification.

Nevertheless, her case histories are deeply suggestive. She describes, for instance, one case where the autistic child's mother was unquestionably disturbed, even to the extent of carrying a knife to the child's nursery. For two months Welch worked effectively with this woman and her child, then one day, after Welch had returned from a long absence through illness, the mother disappeared. In desperation, Welch contacted the mother's own mother (grandmother of the autistic child) and went to see her, at the City of New York day-care nursery the grandmother ran from her home. Welch describes the result:

> The child's mother was furious with me for invoking her mother's help but did agree to participate in weekly sessions. Later she was able to tell me that she was angry because my long absence had caused her to miss me and had made her realize that she wanted me to hold her. This realization opened the floodgate of feeling she had for her mother. In our sessions with the grandmother, the two women told each other how much they longed to be close, how much the daughter wanted her mother to hold her, how jealous she was of the babies in the day-care program who were getting the grandma's care and attention, and how much the grandma missed the babyhood of her six children and wished to return to that time. A breakthrough came when the grandma physically embraced the mother on Mother's Day. The mother finally experienced the holding she had been missing all her life. Within a day or two the autistic child uttered his first words, even though he had not been present at the session.

Most striking, surely, is the child's reaction: a remarkable short-circuiting of all familiar cause and effect.

Nevertheless, the most memorable instance of the crucial importance of touch to autistic children must lie in the story of Temple Grandin, the recovered autistic who has turned up so often in these pages.

For a start, she exhibits, in its most extreme form, the autistic paradox of touch. On the one hand, she declares her familiar autistic terror. As early as her first year, she says, when her mother tried to hug her, 'I clawed at her like a trapped animal.' While as a child she could not endure 'tactile stimulation – not even loving, tactile stimulation'.

On the other hand, simultaneously, 'I craved tender touching. I ached to be loved – hugged. At the same time I withdrew from over-touch as from my overweight, overly affectionate, "marshmallow" aunt. Her affection was like being swallowed by a whale. Even being touched by the teacher made me flinch and draw back. Wanting but withdrawing.' At the age of ten, she says, she scored a 9 out of a possible 15 on the Ayres checklist for tactile defensiveness.

'Tactile stimulation,' she says, 'for me and many autistic children is a no-win situation. Our bodies cry out for human contact but when the contact is made, we withdraw in pain and confusion.'

So what to do? Suffice it to say Grandin deployed her 'autistic aloofness', or originality, to come up with the most remarkable self-help solution imaginable. As an adolescent, she designed her own 'squeeze machine' which would give her the reassurance of physical contact with the sense of freedom she also needed. A combination impossible, or so she felt, with a human being. She adapted it from the kind of squeeze chute used to restrain cattle, on farms, on the way to slaughter. She would get into this machine for, say, twenty minutes and not only would she feel calm, she would feel love and empathy for the world at large. 'I guess others get this through relation with other people,' she says. But the machine has something 'other people' do not: switches and dials. She can switch it off. Hers is a way of experiencing touch where she feels utterly in control.

Few expressions of autistic paradox can be quite as esoteric as this, and yet Temple Grandin has parlayed her 'hug machine' into a successful career. Not only has she designed machines for human use, for herself and similarly needy others, but she has become one of the world's foremost designers of squeeze chutes for cattle.

Her starting point, nevertheless, has been to help herself and those similarly afflicted with autism; and there are very good reasons, she says, why her therapy should have taken this particular form.

Animal research, she points out, supports the crucial importance of touch. Research on pigs shows they will become quiet and inactive by stroking. Tactile stimulation raises endorphin levels in chicks. Monkey studies, in particular, have shown the positive benefits of touch and its associated socialization. If baby monkeys are raised alone, they will develop autistic behaviours, and neurochemical abnormalities can be detected in their blood. But if they are reintroduced to other monkeys, the renewed social stimulation can reverse the process.

In particular, points out Temple Grandin, 'S. J. Suomi at the University of Wisconsin found that isolated autistic monkeys can sometimes be rehabilitated by younger "therapist" monkeys. An active juvenile monkey will repeatedly touch the isolated monkey and force it to interact.'

Young monkeys are much better at this, apparently, than adults.

Nevertheless, as ever in this tale, all roads lead back to one ultimate question: can the undoubted emotional benefits that the Mohawk boys give their charges, whether through touch, play or just plain empathy, help the autistic children in any long-term ways?

Mohawk's evidence, powerful though it may be, is entirely anecdotal. No scientific studies have been done on 'Mohawk therapy'. But very little such work has been done anywhere else, either; not least because few things are less quantifiable than the hopelessly subjective world of emotional relationships. Such reports as do exist tend to lack independent verification and that crucial characteristic of proper experiment, appropriate controls. Martha Welch describes remarkable results from her holding therapy (see above) and E. Royds (see chapter six) records the mute children who spoke in the secure environment of horseback riding, but neither found a way of comparing those who benefited from their therapy with those who lacked it. Yet how do you do this, in the diaphanous world of feelings? One monkey study compared the reactions of a baby monkey 'raised' by an imitation monkey made of wire with another whose imitation mother was made of fur as well. Unsurprisingly, the baby with the furry mother developed far more happily. But how do you reproduce this kind of thing with human beings? As Ronnie Laing put it, commenting on a comparable problem in psychiatry: 'The really decisive moments . . . as every patient who has ever experienced them knows, are unpredictable, unique, unforgettable, always unrepeatable and often indescribable.' And you can't, realistically, experiment on people like apes.

Whatever the research results of 'emotional therapy', organizations exist, worldwide, that believe in the long term therapeutic power of relationships. Perhaps the best known of these is the Son-Rise Program (also referred to as the Options Institute) based in Sheffield, Massachusetts. Son-Rise originated back in 1975 with the response of founders Barry and Samahria Kaufman to the problems of their own son, Raun.

Raun was diagnosed at eighteen months as irreversibly autistic, with an IQ below 30. Faced with the experts' despair, Barry and Samahria decided to try a little DIY. They created their own intensive, home-based therapy programme for Raun, which lasted three and a half years. It seems it succeeded. Raun has now grown up to become bright, gregarious, and has a degree in biomedical ethics.

Since then, hundreds of families from all over the world have been taking the intensive one or two week Son-Rise programmes which the Kaufmans have since developed. Among the many success stories, one is familiar to TV viewers in the UK, as it was the subject of a BBC TV documentary. The subject was the British Broadrick family and their son Jordan, who has autism. The Broadricks spent two weeks in the USA, then set up a home-based programme in the UK. Their son's improvement was remarkable.

Most interesting about the Son-Rise Program, in a Mohawk context, is its insistence on meeting autistic children on their own ground – entering their world – and helping them by an extraordinarily exhaustive programme of one-to-one, concentrated attention; so exhaustive, indeed, it requires a fully fledged team of volunteers.

With Jordan, says the Son-Rise Program, 'Son-Rise facilitators crawled on the floor . . . held food in front of their faces to encourage eye contact, and expressed enthusiastic appreciation for every response Jordan made. They observed his eating habits, his self-help skills, his areas of highest motivation, and his game-playing attention span, praising and participating at every turn. With their playful energy, they drew Jordan into games of hide-and-seek, chase, and splashing in a sink full of water. They joined him in imaginative games which they constructed around books, a small plastic slide, a puzzle and a fire engine. They offered him hugs and squeezes and rides on their backs.'

And such activities are an all-day affair. When the Broadricks returned to England, Son-Rise devised a schedule for the Broadricks, and their volunteers, that stretched from six in the morning to eleven at night.

Such rigour is more American than British, but the parallels with Mohawk are plain. 'We do not judge the children,' says Samahria Kaufman, 'we endeavour to help . . . instead of pushing them to conform to our priorities, we try to enter and understand their world.'

And, like Mohawk, their interest in mechanical improvements is limited.

'Mastering a wide variety of practical and useful life skills is one desirable outcome of the Son-Rise program, but such behavioural goals are considered much less important than the long-range impact of igniting a child's desire to relate to those who live with him and to participate in the world around him.'

Above all, and always, the primacy of relationship.

The Son-Rise Program quotes hundreds of testimonials to the treatment's success; yet here, too, no proper scientific tests have been made. (They wish they had been, say Son-Rise; the problem, apparently, is such studies' high cost.) What there has been is a string of evaluative visits by professionals in the field; and their verdicts have on the whole been highly favourable. John Richer, for instance, has been to their Massachusetts HQ and declares: 'The power of the Option (Son-Rise) approach lies in its love for people, the non-judgemental attitude, the need for people to find their own solutions.' While Rita Jordan, senior lecturer in education at the University of Birmingham, who also visited the Institute, described its service as 'very professional', its training methods as 'exemplary' and further declared: 'Educational theory often pays lip service to a child centred approach; this is one that actually practises it.'

And yet Rita Jordan, too, points out that 'there is no systematic recording of progress after leaving the Institute and no organised follow-up of cases'.

Yet if the impact of love, play, and trust on autistic children remains hard to measure, that is not to say it does not exist. The Scottish legal verdict of 'Not Proven' exists for a reason: it reminds us of the simple fact that not being able to prove something means just that and no more. Some of the most important things in life – virtually all the important things in life – are utterly unsustainable by quantitative data and yet may remain, nevertheless, the most crucial things of all. How am I to prove, quantitatively, that I love my wife?

To say that certain things are unprovable is fair. To say that they therefore do not exist is foolish. There continue to be questions, always, which can legitimately be asked.

A good example are those raised by a story of Maria Montessori's, that paragon of inspired childhood observation. As she put it, in her *Secret Of Childhood* (1936):

> I once found myself involved in a pathological case. I was not called in directly as doctor, but I was a witness to all

that happened. A family had just arrived from a very long journey, and one of the children was too small to stand the strain – or rather, that was the opinion of all concerned. Its mother, however, said that on the journey everything had gone smoothly. They had spent their nights at very good hotels, where everything had been prepared for them, with food and a proper cradle for the baby. They were now staying in a comfortable furnished flat; there was no cradle, but the baby slept in a big bed with its mother.

Its illness had begun by restlessness at night and digestive trouble. At night it had to be walked up and down, for its screams were thought to come from bowel pains. Specialists had been consulted, and one had prescribed modern foods with a high vitamin content, which were prepared with scrupulous care. Sunbaths, fresh air treatment, and all the most modern physical methods had failed to give any relief. The baby was growing worse and the nights were despairing vigils for the whole family. Finally convulsions set in. The baby, when in bed, writhed in alarming spasms. These convulsions began to occur two or three times a day. The baby was still too small to speak, so the greatest aid in knowing its trouble was wanting. It was decided to call a consultation with one of the most famous specialists in nervous diseases of children. It was then that I intervened. The child seemed healthy, and, from what its parents said, had been healthy and quiet the whole journey. The cause of its symptoms might therefore be psychological – one of the enigmas of infancy.

Then, I had a sudden intuition. The baby was in the big bed, in a fit of agitation. I took two armchairs and set them one in front of the other, so that they made a kind of little bed, walled in by the arms like a cradle; in it I put blankets and sheets, and, without speaking, I dragged it to the side of the bed. The baby looked at it, stopped crying, rolled over and over till it reached the edge of the bed, and let

> itself drop into the improvised cradle, saying 'Ulla, ulla, ulla!' (from culla, Italian for cradle). And immediately, it went to sleep. The symptoms of illness never recurred. It had been protesting, in its way, against a horrible disorder – that of doing away with its bed and putting it in a big bed made for grown-ups.
>
> Evidently the baby was sensible to the contact of a small bed, enveloping its body, and giving support to all its members, while the big bed gave it no such shelter. The result was a disorder in its inner orientation, and this disorder was the cause of the painful conflict, which had brought it into the hands of so many doctors.

No one, surely, who is familiar with autistic children can avoid the maverick thought: was this child, in any sense, autistic? Or might she have become so, without Maria Montessori's intervention? Did Maria Montessori 'cure' her?

We will never know.

However you rate Mohawk's healing power, the attraction of the place for its autistic visitors is palpable, and very easy to understand. Rather more of a mystery, however, must be Mohawk's attractiveness to the scouts – certainly those aspects of Mohawk life which seem so demanding.

And yet this, perhaps, is less strange than it might seem. Certainly the notion that children enjoy, even need serious work, has had plenty of advocates among those who liked to theorize, notably Maria Montessori.

Arguably, indeed, this was her most revolutionary idea of all. Forget, she argued, the prettified, ghettoized, nineteenth-century idea of childhood; forget, even, the 'importance' of play. (There is a stern streak to Maria Montessori.) 'It is certain,' she writes, 'that the child's aptitude for work represents a vital instinct, for without work his personality cannot organise itself, and deviates from the normal lines of his construction. MAN BUILDS HIMSELF THROUGH WORKING' (her capitals). So the role of the adult, and especially the teacher, is above all to facilitate this innate process, and not get in nature's way by separating the child from his educational 'birthright'.

What is this birthright? That the child should find his own way to adulthood by making his own experiments. Such experiments can take distinctly prosaic forms. A child will naturally wish to clean, to cook, to build, to do all the things, in fact, they see adults doing around them; just as they will equally naturally wish to draw, to write, to read. 'Every passing minute is precious to him, representing the passage from a slightly inferior state of being to a higher one.'

And as for work like that of the boys at Mohawk, it is equally natural, argued Maria Montessori, for children to want to help and succour others:

> There is no counting the number of cases of child heroism when children have saved or tried to save the lives of their playfellows. I will quote only the case of a fire in an institution in California, in which one wing was reserved for blind children. The bodies of normal children were found, who, though living on another part of the building, had run to lead the blind ones to safety. In child organisations like the boy scouts, or in bodies of mobilised childhood like the Balilla, every day brings some example of heroism.

And the Montessori revolution, as it soon came to be called, introduced yet other ideas about children which also mirror Mohawk. She believed, like Mohawk, that expectation was crucial and that children could, say, handle kitchen knives with perfect safety if they felt trusted; that adults should, wherever possible, let children work without adult interference; that children were, in adults' absence, perfectly capable of running classes on their own.

And if Maria Montessori broke the mould others swiftly followed. Soon Bertrand Russell, John Dewey and the American educator Homer Lane, who worked in England, advanced similar ideas. At the bottom of it all was a new respect for the child, and this, in turn, was based on a new idea of what childhood meant. For centuries children had been seen as embodiments of original sin, innately fallen creatures who could only be hauled upwards towards something approaching civilization by means of didacticism, discipline, and, very often, cruel punishment. But the new thinking was almost precisely opposite. For here, rather, the starting point was the Romantic idea that childhood was if anything a higher state, a special, Wordsworthian sensibility from which, as we grow older, we decline.

And such thinking links naturally with another critical plank of the new educational theory: the notion that children should be given the maximum possible autonomy and self-control. After all, if children are naturally good, with an inborn need to learn and to do serious work, then there is every reason to give them their head, so they can carry on and do just such sensible things.

And here, too, Maria Montessori blazed the trail. For though in some ways her ideas were undeniably prescriptive (the famous, carefully-designed Montessori educational aids, for instance), in others she had a sense of freedom comparable to Skip's and utterly different, beyond any doubt, to the nineteenth-century norm. For in a way, like Skip, she believed that adults should be 'seen and not heard'. Yes, adults should provide the schoolhouse, lay out the equipment, devise learning sequences, even. Yet while they will inevitably be prominent in the opening stages of the learning process, they should, she argues, steadily retreat, while the children advance. So that eventually, ideally, the teacher should have disappeared into the shadows; effectively an onlooker, while the class works away independently. Skip says adults should be seen and not heard. Maria Montessori quotes (like the good

Catholic she is) the words St John said of the growing Messiah: 'He shall increase and I shall decrease.'

Maria Montessori, nevertheless, is arguing that adults, however low profile, should remain in ultimate control. Others have gone much further towards the Mohawk ideal that the children themselves should organize their own lives. Homer Lane, for instance, believed in child self-government. Between 1913 and 1918 he ran the 'Little Commonwealth' in Dorset. This took children aged between a few months and nineteen; all those over thirteen were there because they had been categorized as delinquent. Nevertheless, all rules and regulations were made by the children themselves. The fifty-strong community even had its own 'law' court, where disputed points were decided by majority vote.

The more widely known A. S. Neill, who was much influenced by Homer Lane, instituted a comparable system at his famous boarding school, Summerhill. This is probably the place most people have in mind when they think of pupils' 'self-government'. At Summerhill, too, the pupils made and enforced the school 'laws', in this case via regular general meetings. Here, too, the pupils were given maximum autonomy and freedom – most notably, and to some notoriously, in their freedom to go, or not to go, to lessons.

Yet mechanical devices of this kind, while important in their way, are surely less vital than the spirit that informs them. Both Lane and Neill were masters of child psychology. Lane told a typical story. One day a delinquent boy was handed over to him by the courts. He gave the boy a pound and told him to find his own way down to the Little Commonwealth in Dorset. What he *didn't* do, he stressed, was tell the boy 'I trust you to take the train', for if he had, Lane argued, 'he probably would have spent the money, for my saying so would have shown him that I didn't trust him at all'. Yet again, the power of expectation: the boy went down to Dorset without a murmur.

A. S. Neill told another story, of a similar flavour. One day, he says, he caught one of his boys thieving. He felt, as do many professional psychologists, that this was a plea, however perverse, for love. Instead of punishing him he gave him money. The boy never stole again; and from then on that was Neill's regular treatment for theft and, he says, it never failed.

While the new educational reformers shared much in spirit, they could differ sharply in detail. Maria Montessori and A. S. Neill, for instance, disagreed on the importance of play. While Maria Montessori believed play (especially fantasy play) was a distraction from the child's high-serious purpose of growing up, A. S. Neill thought play (especially fantasy play) was crucial. He went further, indeed, than many educational progressives. He believed play was less a means to an educational end, more an end in itself. Life should be pleasurable; play was a pleasure; so play, clearly, was its own justification.

So far, so Mohawk. Yet Neill was also highly suspicious of the kind of 'good works', whether DIY building or autistic care, which are also, of course, central to Mohawk. Whenever you found boys doing them, he said, you would also find some charismatic adult, cheering and enthusing the boys into doing things they would naturally leave well alone. Remove the adult, went his argument, and exit the work.

Well, you don't have to look very far at Mohawk for such a 'charismatic adult' but it is hard to believe that the scouts' care programme would collapse if Skip disappeared. There are just too many times and places, usually half a dozen a day, when the boys themselves show their own, profound, self-motivated dedication. And there is a further point, which Neill doesn't address; that curious, but vital, question of where work stops and play begins. Central to the whole Mohawk ethos is the way the scouts regard the autistic children as friends. Are the autistic children, then, workmates or playmates? Is looking after them fun, or a chore? If both, perhaps there's less difference between Skip and Neill than at first seems.

And yet, while different educationists stress different aspects of this twentieth-century revolution, there has, nevertheless, been a remarkable consensus on certain key values: trust; autonomy; spontaneity; the primacy of the emotions over the intellect (crucial to Homer Lane and, as we have seen, to Skip); decompartmentalization – a suspicion that things go better without formal divisions of subject matter; comradeship before hierarchy; and, above all, and in all things, love and friendship before compulsion. Not only do the same values reoccur again and again, but they are palpably interdependent and mutually reinforcing. And, slowly, as the twentieth century moved on, they spread into the educational mainstream; so that by the early sixties primary education, in particular, was unrecognizable compared with what had been on offer a mere generation before. But then the same values had flooded, to a remarkable extent, through society at large, notably in the new popularization of child psychology, especially by one Dr Benjamin Spock.

There is a natural synchronicity, in fact, to the date when Skip launched his troop: the mid-sixties. True, he was as innocent back then of overt childcare theory as he is today, and a lot of Mohawk's values sprang straight from the East End. Nevertheless, we are all children of our times.

And times change. Skip's scout troop went independent in 1969. Before that it had been part of the Baden Powell association. So the story of its growth has been that of the last thirty years of the twentieth century, which is also the story of the grand conservative reaction, in childcare as in everything else.

By the mid-seventies, the first tremors of uncertainty appeared as James Callaghan initiated the educational 'Great Debate'. By the eighties, a Conservative government was trying to reimpose, by law, the old traditionalism and formality. Quite why this should have been is a question for the economist, or even the psychologist, quite as much as for the educationist. All that can be said for sure is that a social zeitgeist of confidence was replaced by one of apprehension, even fear; and this affected childcare as it affected everything else.

The new instinct was, above all, for control. Teachers had to teach a prescribed curriculum; there was a surge in numerical measurement; league tables appeared; there was a rediscovery of the benefits of traditional 'chalk-and-talk'. Logical arguments were duly deployed to explain all this, yet one could not but note that it emerged, somehow, as part of a wider social mood, of which little was logic-based.

One striking statistic expresses this new, restrictive world as well as any. A report by the Policy Studies Institute found that in 1971 80 per cent of 7- and 8-year-old children were allowed to go to school on their own. By 1990 this figure had dropped to 9 per cent. Of course, well-founded fears of traffic had a lot to do with it; but so did less well-founded fears of child molestation, which had much more to do with the ever-escalating social psychology of threat. The results, however, were plain. Any time up to 1970 the journey to and from school, haphazard and slow, had been one of many de facto freedoms built into a child's day. Today, like many comparable freedoms – for instance, the old-time tendency of kids with bikes to disappear, in the school holidays, for a whole day – it is virtually dead.

Instead, increasingly, parents feel they have to pack their children's diaries themselves. Writing in *The Sunday Telegraph*, in February 2000, Ysenda Maxtone Graham described the advent, on kitchen noticeboards, of the gridded timetable, produced each month on the family computer: 'February 2000. Lots of grey shading, black blocking, and, in the 3.30–5 pm slot at the bottom: "Mon, H swimming. Tue, H and J piano. Wed, H Kumon maths, J gym. Thurs, H judo. Fri, Paula to collect: H and J tennis. Sat, H riding . . ."'

As she points out, the overscheduling of children began in America and is now spreading around the world; and while it purports to be for children's benefit *New York Magazine* has apparently identified 'a new breed of ambitious mothers who have given up financial careers and now off-load their frustrated ambitions onto their children'.

Worse, argues Ysenda Maxtone Graham: 'The truth is that parents use planned activity as a way of avoiding the chore of having to be spontaneous with their children, or having to enter into their make-believe world', and she wonders about the long-term effects on the kids. 'How can a child develop an idiosyncratic sense of humour, or become a bookworm, or a poet, or a passionate geologist if days consist of a succession of regulated activities? The system produces all-rounders; and what the world badly needs is eccentrics and geniuses.'

In such an environment the freedom Mohawk keeps alive is more crucial than ever. For as the explorer Jean Liedloff points out, comparing the extraordinary self-reliance of the Amazon jungle hunter-gatherer tribes she lived among for seven years with the equally extraordinary timidity of the average, protected young Westerner: 'Americans are perhaps the most carefully protected children in history as regards external safeguards and are therefore the least EXPECTED to know how to look after themselves.'

Once more the crucial role of expectation; and Liedloff was writing in the seventies. Things are far worse now. As Liedloff points out, not only can such over-protection mean, paradoxically, more accidents for children, but it leads to accidents, in the adult life of Westerners, that could equally be avoided. There is a strong theory among UK road safety experts that our current tendency to ferry children around in cars is the cause of the bulge in road casualties around the late teens. When the children do finally hit the streets on their own they have more accidents because they have never learned how to look after themselves.

Liedloff quotes the instance of a Midwestern American city where a blizzard stopped traffic, which included fire engines, for several days. The local fire chief got on TV to warn locals that they would have to look after any fires themselves. Magically, from forty-odd fires a day the average plummeted to four until the streets were cleared, when the figure went back to normal. 'Apprised of the change in placement of responsibility,' comments Liedloff, the locals 'unconsciously cut the figure by ninety per cent'.

Mohawk, as we have seen, takes a different view. It loads responsibility on to the child, whether it is responsibility for self-regulation, for self-building, or, of course, for looking after some of the most difficult and accident-prone children to be found. And it acts out so many of the other, naturally linked values mentioned earlier as well: trust, spontaneity, playfulness, humour. So far, indeed, so acceptable; especially when put in this kind of formal, abstract language.

Having said this, it is equally plain that Mohawk takes 'spontaneity', say, to lengths which most comparable organizations would regard as excessive, or even dangerous. And yet it is at the very least arguable that it is at just these moments, when Camp Mohawk parts company with the mainstream of professional care, that it is most valuable of all.

Take that most striking aspect of its operations, time management, or rather lack of it. We have seen how often a Mohawk project can get delayed, altered or just plain cancelled according to the changing mood, or even whim, of the moment. Now one can easily sympathize with the advent of a new-broom Mohawk administrator who might feel all this is highly amusing, charming even, but how could one argue that it is in any sense serious? Where's the virtue, for heaven's sake, in unpunctuality?

Curiously enough, the new broom and the old guard would have agreed on one thing: that time management matters, and is worth arguing about. And in this they would agree with a range of cultural historians, notably the Americans Lewis Mumford, who felt the advent of the clock was the seminal moment in

Western history, and E. T. Hall, who felt that that the North American 'schedule', in particular, was the single most important thing about Western life. For not only is the schedule, i.e. the elaborate, detailed, blocked-in appointment system (see children's version, above) the most gridiron system of control, it is also the expression of a quite remarkable optimism.

When we prearrange that at nine o'clock on Saturday we will work, at twelve o'clock we will socialize, and at two o'clock we will play golf, we are premising our behaviour on the act of faith that we will feel like doing exactly those things at just those times. What happens if we don't want to? Why, of course, being good Westerners we will go ahead and do what has been blocked in anyway. At two o'clock, in fact, we will play golf and enjoy it, if it kills us.

The difference with the Mohawk way, the practical expression of true spontaneity, is that it turns time management from a science into an art. Things are done when they feel right; if they don't feel right they are not done at all. Above all, the decision as to what constitutes right or wrong is taken intuitively, by hunch, by acute, if half subconscious, observation and by a sense of how all parties concerned feel. Like the teenager planning his first kiss with his girlfriend there is no grid, chart or concept that can teach you this. It is a matter of pure intuitive subjective art, just as it is for the violinist who must decide when to start, speed up, slow down or finish a phrase.

When, as happened that afternoon in late August, John Lee first arranged, then cancelled, then rearranged that most memorable of walks – the one where he helped the autistic child solve his crisis at the paths – he was responding to the ebb and flow of feeling among those who were intending to take part. If he'd gone at the wrong moment (in this case the wrong moment would have been earlier, but it could just as well have been later) the walk might never have been such a success.

So it is with Mohawk's other seeming eccentricities, like its horror of maps, or its associated horror of weather forecasts.

(Even when planning a whole day outside, the Mohawk leadership adamantly shuts its ears to the Met Office predictions.) For these, too, are about something far more serious than at first seems, and are, like Mohawk's philosophy of time, evident attempts to defend themselves against something felt, instinctively, to be profoundly threatening. What is that something? It is, I think, the same fear which makes people dislike all forms of mechanism: a sense that what is gained in efficiency, albeit narrowly defined (the quantity, if not the quality, of things made or done), is lost in freshness, originality and relish. In the end, in fact, it is the faith that spontaneity is life where mechanism is death.

But then this, too, is a fight much larger than Mohawk and has, of course, been fought in every society that ever had an industrial revolution, from the India described by E. M. Forster, to the Spain described by George Orwell in the thirties, to the USSR which so alarmed American diplomats (socially) as late as the sixties. For despite their country's Stalinist heavy industry, despite their Sputnik, Muscovites still retained, apparently, that pre-industrialist tendency to drop in unannounced which is so noticeable in classic Russian novels. Why did they do it, wondered the Americans – their beloved schedules shot to shreds – when they could so easily have picked up the phone? There were phones, after all, and unlike Cairo, they actually worked. The answer, surely, was that at a very deep level the Russians didn't want to ring up and plan; even if it meant quite regularly going over to a friend's and finding they were out. They wanted life unplanned, unpredictable and spontaneous.

Mohawk's instincts in this regard are plain. A year with Mohawk is its own evidence. Yet time management is just one of Mohawk's 'eccentricities'. There are many others. We have already noted Mohawk's love of humour and seen how a theoretician like Nikolaas Tinbergen approves. Yet Mohawk's humour shades, too, into something which many people might find ... well, somehow, less appropriate, above all in a place which some might see as a kind of care home.

Jokes are one thing, telling funny stories another, but what about clownish behaviour? What about Dave, say, when he starts behaving foolishly, like that time he shot off from France to England? In what sense is that kind of eccentricity therapeutic? Come to that, what about the rows? Shouldn't care workers have a bit more self-control? And then there's the drinking! Should care workers be drinking at all, let alone getting utterly legless? What part does alcohol play in a sensible care regime?

To which the answer is simple: Mohawk is not a 'sensible care regime'. It is something far more valuable. It is a group of friends. That is the whole point. For all its indefatigable courage, patience and devotion, for all the considerable amounts of organization that do, in fact, take place, it remains, at bottom, a genuine community, in a word, a family. That Beckton front room . . .

Instead of the controlled, charted, 'targeted' 'delivery' of care, it is a collection of people who are together because they like each other. Instead of an 'advanced' organization that is sufficiently Californian to see that humour and playfulness are good for people, and which will therefore try to inject it, say, in the Saturday slot, between two and four, it is a bunch of friends who make each other laugh – quite as much by what they do as what they say, and by what they are as what they do. Instead of a balanced sensible, sober group of people who never have a row, or a party, above all a spontaneous one, because they fear it would undermine their glacial altruism, it is a crowd of friends who argue and make up and then start rowing again, who are happy to get drunk sometimes for the fun and pleasure of it, just as they take pleasure – pleasure – in looking after autistic kids.

Indeed, consider Mohawk for a moment as if it really were a family, with the adults as parents. Which family would *you* rather be in? One where the parents were always impeccably behaved, utterly sober, incapable of fun? Or one where the grown-ups enjoyed themselves? And if you were weak, vulnerable or unhappy, who would be likely to treat you best, those who enjoy themselves or the self-denying?

'As a rule,' wrote W. H. Auden, 'it was the pleasure haters who became unjust.'

It is at this stage, when the arguments about Mohawk stray into the foothills of philosophy, that one realizes the wider significance of an organization like Mohawk, its place in the world.

For Mohawk is nothing if not a microcosm. Its faults and virtues, the very wars, indeed, being fought within it, between the old, instinctive ways and the looming world of flow charts, grids and diagrams, are themselves a miniature version of a titanic battle being fought out globally. Whether modern life itself is in any way 'autistic', or 'causes' autism (depending on what exactly is meant by autism), one can see what Nikolaas Tinbergen meant when he said 'our entire society has moved into efficiency-consciousness and competitiveness' and talked of the 'genuine psychosocial pollution which is only part of the overall process of disadaptation to which our civilisation is subjecting us'. The life we are increasingly choosing may not 'cause' autism but it surely *does* cause (and is caused by – here, if ever, is the original vicious circle) something that looks, to the lay observer, very like it: our increasing wariness of genuine relationship, our crisis of trust.

When Julie Burchill, that tortured, turbulent journalistic embodiment of the spirit of the age, went a grudge too far and actually suggested the redundancy of friendship (not marriage, sexual fidelity, gender roles but friendship – that was meant to be the shock) she was, like any dutiful observer, merely expressing the remarkable timidity of the times, to which a raft of terror advertising and *Weakest Link*-style game shows pay witness. Autism may not be 'caused' by modern life but yuppiedom, which surely contains, as a world-view, no shortage of 'autistic streaks', most certainly is.

Which is why, as we saw at the beginning of this tale, autism has so notably caught the popular imagination. So that it is as an antithesis to such a fervid, fearful, inward-looking world view that Mohawk's values matter most. Against fear it offers confidence; against timidity, courage; against tight-fisted, anal selfishness, flooding generosity; against the brittle, abstract, strangulated spirit of late capitalism, it offers the immediate, tactile, sensual pleasures of real life.

For in the end, the argument – like all arguments, really – comes down to human nature. Anatole Kaletsky of *The Times* says: 'capitalism is natural, because unlike communism, it faithfully reflects human nature . . . The true essence of capitalism lies in the dominant role it accords to markets, competition and greed.' The reality is the precise opposite: selfishness and greed are the unrealities of life. The Thousand-Year Reich lasted just a dozen years, while systems like the Catholic Church, based, however tenuously, on courage and love, survive the centuries. Or as John Ruskin put it: 'Government and co-operation in all things the laws of life; anarchy and competition the laws of death.'

Mohawk knows what soldiers tell us in their memoirs, time and again, with the authority of those who have seen men at their most desperate: that human nature is, at bottom, good; that the human spirit is indomitable; that generosity, as in any happy family, is a kind of inspired selfishness, for while to get is good, to give is the deeper joy.

Camp Mohawk is a living testimony to such truths.

ELEVEN

The last fortnight of camp passed by in relative calm. When Jeremy and Edward left, the autistic children who came after were easier to manage. Indeed, poor Tariq Aziz, who stayed right up to the final day, was the last child who was in any way exceptional.

The familiar themes of the camp rumbled on. The running gender/cultural wars, in which the women, with decreasing hope, tried to impose some order on the place, continued. One morning, assigned to breakfast duty, I found all necessary ingredients had magically disappeared. In best male style, I panicked. It was the logical Diana who appeared from nowhere, calmed everything down, and sorted things out. Later, however, in the kitchen again, she tried to impose a different kind of order on Troy Northcote and Fred Robinson. That led to the worst row Diana ever got involved in. They reduced her to tears. Meanwhile, the lovely Carrie-Ann had the opposite problem. The boys were getting over their initial shyness and were steadily escalating the only way they knew of relating to her, physical horseplay. One afternoon the kids took the jostling and 'wrestling' with her to such lengths she almost had to be rescued; at the last moment, fortunately, they simmered down.

Yet Sheila, who represented the third face of the triadic view the boys seemed to have of femininity – bossy-boots, girl-friend and, in Sheila's case, earth-mother – found herself fulfilling a familiar role with Matt Polesden. Bernard Naisbitt had had to go home early. The same evening I asked Matt if he would miss Bernard. Not really, said Matt; well, maybe just a bit. Next morning he appeared at Sheila's surgery complaining about his finger. And for the life of her, Sheila couldn't find anything wrong.

The endless, mildly mysterious building programme continued. Now Skip took to sitting on top of the flat-roofed sheds at a height of ten feet, the better to direct the ongoing work. This throne-like exaltation made him look more than ever like Henry VIII. Occasionally he would descend and drive a machine across the camp. Ian Pool continued to look out for my interests. As usual, he gave me thunderous slaps across the back. To his friendly, periodic theft of my notebooks was now added a programme of sudden, unprovoked neck massages, when he would spot me sitting down, steal up behind me, and start suddenly plunging his thumbs deep into my neck, ploughing the neck muscles till I cried out for reprieve.

But if in some ways the place carried on as usual, in others there was a slight, then gradually escalating, sense of change. Cards began appearing on the canteen wall from grateful parents; already, the summer camp was becoming part of the past. Boys talked more and more about their families. They were missing them. Even Dave Hamblin started speculating about what he might do when the camp was finished. He'd go mushrooming, he announced one day, that's what he'd do! And just like that time back in the spring, with the boys, he started on yet another rhapsody about his favourite vegetable. Remarkably, he talked for two hours. Did we realize this was the time of year when mushrooms came up? Did we know that they actually grew – from first peeping out of the ground to fully-fledged stalks – in just three days? Had he ever told us this before? No word of a lie, but they developed so fast he'd once seen a mushroom actually growing before his very eyes, why, he'd even seen little bits of dirt fall off it as it grew . . .

And there was a stealing change in our environment, too. The grand calm of the summer, whose apogee had been that afternoon of John's walk, had gradually begun to fray around the edges. First stray tufts, then full-blown blasts of wind arrived; then fractious, scurrying little showers. A sense of stability and peace was replaced by a mood of change. The more the wind ruffled the trees, the more you noticed the silver in the leaves, as if the trees themselves were ageing with the year.

Perhaps this climactic doublethink affected our moods. Certainly Mohawk's ever-volatile mood-swings seemed more volatile than ever as that August faded into September. I remember one evening when Skip was sitting with Sheila out on the terrace, around six o'clock. The sun was dropping down on the fields below; the sky was flawless; the atmosphere serene. Inspired, it seemed to me, by the benevolent mood, Skip started telling one of his 'miracle' stories. Some years back a businessman had got wind of the camp, thought he might help out financially, and came to visit. He was impressed by what he saw, but, as a good businessman, he wanted specifics – cash flow, costing, the works. Skip said, certainly, by all means, but pointed out that it would be a nonsense really, there were too many variables. What he could do was make a pretty good estimate of what would solve the current crisis. Based on experience it was £16,500. What was more, said Skip, whether the businessman felt able to help or not, he was certain he would get the money. He just knew. It had always come in the past. Why should now be any different? The businessman took another look round and left. He made no offer, but, as he got into his car, he simply said: 'I have never come across faith like this in all my life.' The next day Skip got a letter. Inside was a cheque for £16,500.

As Skip finished the story we were joined by John. He was

sorry to butt in, he said, but he felt Skip had been overharsh with one of the scouts earlier that day. He'd been wrong, yes, but he hadn't deserved the bawling-out he'd got. In particular, he said, he didn't think Skip should have made him run down the hill to the front gate, and back up again.

Skip went ballistic. Absolute nonsense, he said. If anything, he should have been harsher still. The kid concerned was a disaster area, a waste of space. He didn't deserve to be in the troop! In fact, they'd do a lot better to get clean rid of him, and any other kids like him come to that, they should clear all the rubbish out once and for all . . .

And then moments later someone made a joke, someone else gave him a cup of tea and lo! he'd palpably forgotten what he was so het up about, he was back in a good mood. Then something else disturbed him and he got in a state; then something else pleased him again and he calmed down.

We were all a bit like that, as the camp came to an end. The psychologists say it is normal when people are just about to part. Their security threatened, they become erratic. Up and down, harsh and mild, looking forward and back, sad, happy, schizophrenic.

Nevertheless, one final, triumphant twist had occurred in the Dave/Sheila saga. Three weeks of tortuous self-questioning by Dave, in which most of the camp had been co-opted at one time or another as listener, had been resolved. His brother had given him his fare to Australia – and Dave was going. For three months. More wonderful still, Skip had advanced him several thousands of pounds of back 'pay' for all his volunteer work over the years, which Dave was taking to Australia as spending money.

Well, this was what the boys said. In fact, on closer examination, this wasn't what was happening at all. The truth was that Sheila had advanced Dave his fare, while his brother had given him a further £500 for expenses. But the other, more exotic version was another instance of the power of the scouts' imaginations, the fairy-tale quality of their minds. Seeing both Skip and Dave as parents, the thousands-of-pounds gift was how they wished to believe their parents treated each other. In fact, Skip didn't owe Dave a penny, not legally anyway. Nevertheless, the scouts' fiction had its own truth. As fairy tales go, there was a beautiful generosity to it.

There were other surprises, too. One day I saw Tim Fenton padding uncertainly across the camp with his customary uncertain, hang-dog air. John Lee called his name. Tim froze, one foot stretched forward, like a cat. His face flashed alarm. 'What have I done now?' he said. 'Calm down mate,' said John, grinning. 'I just wanted to tell you how superbly well we all think you've done on this camp. Skip, Dave, Sheila – everyone's noticed it. No one but you could have done what you did with Tariq. You're a pain in the backside,' said John, perhaps a little bluntly, 'but you've done brilliant.' If Tim looked alarmed before, he now looked positively startled. All this was new. How was he supposed to adjust, just like that, to all this praise and success, after years of blame? Nevertheless, he wriggled with delight.

Finally, inevitably, we reached the last day. The whole long, fervid year, which had began way back before Christmas 1999, was over. The last of the autistic children and parents had left. The troop was finally left alone to face itself.

Pegasus stood out on the drive, primed and ready to take the kids back to Beckton. Michael had come down for the day to do the drive. In the canteen, a series of little ceremonies were held. Clare had just received the report from social services and she read bits out. It was a stunner, the best the camp had ever had. It was above all the attitude of the scouts themselves, apparently, their selflessness and devotion, which had impressed the inspectors.

Then John Lee, to frantic cheers, gave out some prizes. Ian Pool and Tom Pollard, unsurprisingly, came first equal as best scouts of all; and then – a gasper – Tim Fenton got the award for 'Best Average Scout' and had to adjust, yet again, to the problems of success. Then all the women got flowers. Then Sheila got up and made a farewell speech, and burst into tears. Then Dave thanked Diana, on everyone's behalf, and now Diana burst into tears, but for good reasons this time, unlike that row with the boys in the canteen. Even Rod and I were given bottles of wine, and as I sat down Ian Pool pounced on me for one last final pummelling neck massage. It was quite terrifying, the most violent of the lot, like three rounds with a grizzly bear. I felt garrotted.

Soon, parents began to arrive – most of the boys were going home in Pegasus but some were being taken home by car – and, as if picked off by snipers, boys started to vanish. But the key moment came when Dave and Sheila left. They had somewhere to go that evening and drove off together. The boys lined the drive as they left, disappearing, to cheers, into the setting sun. It was for all the world like the departure of the bride and groom at a wedding, which was appropriate enough, after all.

When they'd gone – again, rather like a wedding – there was a sudden sense of anticlimax. Suddenly it became urgent to finally finish the camp off. The boys disappeared into the tents to get their gear, and reappeared dressed specially for the journey. Many wore jewellery: Joe Beckford was in a T-shirt and matching blue slacks, plus gold ring; Rob was in khaki, with three rings, and a gold cross round his neck. They'd clearly dressed to impress their mums and dads.

Not that this stopped them passing the time as usual as the bus was loaded up. Cheerily they punched, wrestled and rolled around. Some got on each other's shoulders and had a chariot race. Gradually they swarmed and jostled on to the bus, still swapping blows. Pete Pollard was last, throwing two left jabs and one final drop kick as he vanished through the door. Michael revved up the engine, slipped the coach into gear and, with a last re-echoing shriek, the boys were gone.

The sudden quiet was frightening. The few remaining adults felt small and irrelevant. As the coach vanished down the drive it was as if the heart of the camp was dropping away, shooting down between the long green arms of the meadows.

Yet the forest and hills remained. They stood there as they had stood all summer, and as they would for all those future summers to come. Calm, grave in the waning evening light. Parental.

BIBLIOGRAPHY

Aldington, Richard; *Portrait of a Genius . . .But*; William Heinemann Ltd, 1950

Baron-Cohen, Simon and Bolton, Patrick; *Autism: The Facts*; Oxford University Press, 1993

Bettelheim, Bruno; *The Empty Fortress*; The Free Press, Macmillan Publishing Co. Inc., 1972

Carlton, Stella; *The Other Side of Autism*; The Self-Publishing Association Ltd, 1993

Claridge, Gordon; *Sounds From The Bell Jar – Ten Psychotic Authors*; Macmillan, 1990

Frith, Uta; *Autism, Explaining the Enigma*; Basil Blackwell, 1989

Grandin, Temple and Scariano, Margaret M.; *Emergence Labelled Autistic*; Arena Press, 1986

Happé, Francesca; *Autism – An Introduction to Psychological Theory*; UCL Press, 1994

Huxley, Aldous; *The Doors of Perception*; Chatto and Windus, 1954

Kaufman, Barry Neil; *Son-Rise, The Miracle Continues*; H. J. Kramer Inc., 1994

Liedloff, Jean; *The Continuum Concept*; Duckworth, 1975

Luria, Alexander; *The Mind of a Mnemonist*; Basic Books, 1968

Montessori, Maria; *The Secret of Childhood*; Longmans, Green and Co., 1936

Montessori, Maria; *Education For a New World*; Kalakshetra, 1948

Montessori, Maria; *The Montessori Method*; Schoken Books, 1965

Neil, A. S.; *The New Summerhill*; Penguin Books, 1992

Park, Clara Claiborne; *The Siege*; Colin Smythe Limited, 1968

Richer, John and Coates, Sheila; *Autism – The Search for Coherence*; Jessica Kingsley, 2001

Sacks, Oliver; *An Anthropologist on Mars*; Picador, 1995

Sacks, Oliver; *The Man Who Mistook His Wife For a Hat*; Picador, 1986

Selfe, Lorna; *Nadia, A Case of Extraordinary Drawing Ability in an Autistic Child*; Academic Press, 1977

Stehli, Annabel; *The Sound of a Miracle – A Child's Triumph Over Autism*; Doubleday, 1991

Tinbergen, Niko; *Autistic Children, New Hope For A Cure*; The Tinbergen Trust, 1993

Welch, Martha G.; *Holding Time*; Simon & Schuster Inc., 1989

Williams, Donna; *Nobody Nowhere*; Doubleday, 1992

Williams, Donna; *Autism – An Inside Out Approach*; Jessica Kingsley, 1996

Williams, Donna; *Autism and Sensing*; Jessica Kingsley, 1998

Wiltshire, Stephen; *Cities*; J. M. Dent, 1989

Wiltshire, Stephen; *Drawings*; J. M. Dent, 1987

Wing, Lorna; *The Autistic Spectrum*; Constable, 1996